DOWNTOWN MARDI GRAS

DOWNTOWN

Mardi Gras

NEW CARNIVAL PRACTICES IN POST-KATRINA NEW ORLEANS

Leslie A. Wade, Robin Roberts,
and Frank de Caro

UNIVERSITY PRESS OF MISSISSIPPI / JACKSON

Publication of this book has been generously supported by the
Fulbright College of Arts and Sciences and the Department of Theatre
and Department of English at the University of Arkansas.

The University Press of Mississippi is the scholarly publishing agency of
the Mississippi Institutions of Higher Learning: Alcorn State University,
Delta State University, Jackson State University, Mississippi State University,
Mississippi University for Women, Mississippi Valley State University,
University of Mississippi, and University of Southern Mississippi.

www.upress.state.ms.us

Designed by Peter D. Halverson

The University Press of Mississippi is a member of
the Association of University Presses.

First printing 2019
∞

Library of Congress Cataloging-in-Publication Data

Names: Wade, Leslie A., author. | Roberts, Robin, 1957– author. | De Caro, F.
A., 1943– author.
Title: Downtown Mardi Gras : new carnival practices in post-Katrina New
Orleans / Leslie A. Wade, Robin Roberts, and Frank de Caro.
Description: Jackson : University Press of Mississippi, [2019] | Includes
bibliographical references and index. |
Identifiers: LCCN 2018058795 (print) | LCCN 2018061545 (ebook) | ISBN
9781496823793 (epub single) | ISBN 9781496823809 (epub institutional) |
ISBN 9781496823816 (pdf single) | ISBN 9781496823823 (pdf institutional)
| ISBN 9781496823786 (hardcover : alk. paper) | ISBN 9781496823847 (pbk. :
alk. paper)
Subjects: LCSH: Carnival—Louisiana—New Orleans—History. | Hurricane
Katrina, 2005—Social aspects—Louisiana—New Orleans. | Community
life—Louisiana—New Orleans—History—21st century. | New Orleans
(La.)—Social life and customs—21st century.
Classification: LCC GT4211.N4 (ebook) | LCC GT4211.N4 W34 2019 (print) | DDC
976.3/35—dc23
LC record available at https://lccn.loc.gov/2018058795

British Library Cataloging-in-Publication Data available

To our grandchildren, Amelia, Evangeline, and Isaac Pierce, and Grace and Josephine Collins, in the fervent hope that Downtown Mardi Gras will continue and provide them with joy.

Leslie A. Wade and Robin Roberts

CONTENTS

ACKNOWLEDGMENTS

We gratefully acknowledge the assistance of Michael Riha, Chair of the Department of Theatre, Dorothy Stephens, Chair of the Department of English, Todd Shields, Dean of the Fulbright College of Arts and Sciences (University of Arkansas), for their support that enabled the photographs in this book to appear in color. Some pages from chapters 1 and 4 first appeared as "Emerging New Orleans Mardi Gras Traditions: The St. Joan of Arc Parade and the Red Beans Krewe, 2010," in *Louisiana Folklore Miscellany* 20 (2010): 1–29; and a portion of chapter 2 appeared in "Women Artists Recycling the Skull: New Bone Gang Traditions in Post-Katrina New Orleans," in *Western Folklore* 71.4 (2015): 30–57. An interview with Dianne Honoré appeared in a special issue on Visions of Black Women in American Culture in the *Journal of American Culture* 42.1 (March 2019). At the University Press of Mississippi, Katie Keene and Mary Heath provided invaluable and efficient support, and Craig Gill's encouragement was critical. Colleagues at LSU, Carolyn Ware and Angeletta Gourdine, read versions of Roberts's chapters and provided helpful insights. At the University of Arkansas, Yajaira Padilla, Susan Marren, and Lissette Lopez Szwydky-Davis read and strengthened chapter 3. Will Rigby improved the book through careful copyediting, Valerie Jones, editor, provided efficient and professional management of the manuscript, and Kristin Kirkpatrick created our index. The two anonymous readers of the manuscript offered encouragement and helpful feedback. We want to acknowledge Rosan Augusta Jordan, Joseph Ross, Geoff Clayton, Michael Reese, Laurie Kelly, and Bernard Lavoie, who have been a part of our Mardi Gras experiences over the years. And of course, our greatest debt is to the many interview subjects who graciously offered their time and insights to the completion of this book. We are so grateful for their expansion of Mardi Gras practices, which we have enjoyed as participants and as audience members.

DOWNTOWN MARDI GRAS

Downtown Mardi Gras

Leslie A. Wade

Mardi Gras 2006 / 2017

Following the devastation of Hurricane Katrina, a destruction in scale never experienced by an American city, New Orleans faced innumerable challenges heading into the year 2006: how to rebuild homes, businesses, and infrastructure; how to facilitate the return of thousands of residents scattered across the country; how to address the stark racial and economic divides the storm exposed to a global media audience; how to bring to the city a daily working order with open schools, basic mail delivery, and operating public transit? Amidst such an array of truly daunting issues, the citizens of New Orleans faced another difficult, highly emotional, and often polarizing concern: Should Mardi Gras go on? Should the city go forward with the signature event that for decades had signified New Orleans and its distinctive culture to people around the world?

Heading into 2006, the city still was missing nearly half of its population (Plyer "Facts for Features"). Damaged or destroyed properties dominated many swathes of the city. Police and fire departments struggled with depleted ranks. Many argued against the celebration of Carnival in the initial aftermath of the Katrina disaster, citing the inadequacies of public services, the continuing diaspora of citizens, the expenditures (both public and private) demanded by the event in the face of so much need. Chief among concerns was the appropriateness of festivity, of Carnival revelry so soon after the city had undergone such trauma. For many the idea of celebration seemed unthinkable given the physical and emotional losses of the populace who had witnessed the rising waters engulf their homes and bring the city to its knees.

Whether Mardi Gras 2006 would occur or not proved a matter of considerable public and private debate. Mayor Ray Nagin initially sided with cancellation but decided on going through with the event. Discussion within the Zulu Social Aid and Pleasure Club was vigorous, often heated. A former Zulu king threatened legal action to halt the group's participation, though its current officers argued passionately for proceeding, for honoring the parade's traditional neighborhoods, for being "on the streets at full strength" (Laborde 102). Proponents of going on with the holiday did not seek to minimize the suffering brought by Katrina and the failure of the levees; rather, they argued that honoring Carnival would prove a tribute to the people of New Orleans, affirming the life of the city in face of demoralizing and often degrading experiences. Local writer Chris Rose, whose *Times-Picayune* columns provided inspiration and comfort during this time, wrote in unambiguous terms: "We need to send a message, that we are still New Orleans. We are the soul of America. We embody the triumph of the human spirit. Hell. We ARE Mardi Gras" (1 *Dead in Attic* 144). In this light, Mardi Gras offered the opportunity to demonstrate survival, to uphold the city's unique way of life, and to collectively embody an unbroken spirit, one tested by epochal suffering and loss.

The city brought a stirring commitment and a profound sense of pride to this first post-Katrina Carnival. The season of 2006 was a diminished one, though Carnival did go on. Krewe du Vieux, the satirical walking group known for its pointed and often salacious humor, helped kick off Carnival with its trek through the Marigny and French Quarter, sporting costumes and floats utilizing blue tarp as a prominent material, exhibiting signs and placards that excoriated FEMA and federal inattention—suggesting a return to France: "Buy Us Back, Chirac!" The krewe (the local term for a Carnival organization) was embraced with fervor and elicited strong response from the crowds, a communal expression born in part by frustration, in part by defiance.

All orders of celebrants pitched in to make Mardi Gras happen. The Rex organization worked on a short timeline to have its floats ready to roll. The Rex Den, which housed the krewe's floats, costumes, and artifacts, took water and experienced considerable damage—wooden wagon wheels had to be shipped to Texas for repair (Hales 151). Though the route was shortened, the parade went on and was enjoyed by revelers up and down St. Charles Avenue. Reports estimated a crowd of 350,000, which was well below the usual million-plus figure (Capper). Though the crowds were smaller, the city did manage to stage its most famous celebration. Rex hailed the mayor before Gallier Hall; Zulu rolled with painted coconuts; Bourbon Street hosted its contest of drag costumes in all its expected dazzle and imagination.

While many displaced residents ventured to the city to share in the celebration, many were unable to do so. The city experienced a kind of shadowed Carnival, informed by competing and often conflicting emotions, of joy and anguish, of hope and frustration. Those on the streets experienced an exuberant commitment to the day at hand, and a concomitant awareness of loss. Local writer Ian McNulty expressed the anxious anticipation of this day, fearing random violence or some wayward mishap, suggesting that an appropriate "group prayer" might be: "Please, God, let us just do this right and not be humiliated yet again in the eyes of the world. Let people see how unique and wonderful this place really is" (*A Season of Night* 148).

At the end of the day, many experienced a kind of joy and a relief. Mardi Gras had happened, summoning recent sorrows, recalling past pleasures, enacting a full-throated celebration. Those in attendance experienced an exhaustion, a profound communal catharsis, rooted in suffering and loss, and an attendant uplift, a rare jubilation. In the words of McNulty, "In that winter after Katrina, at the tail end of that dark and terrible season of night, New Orleans ... needed believers and it needed Mardi Gras" (*A Season of Night* 139). The first post-Katrina Mardi Gras marked a significant turning point; the city had managed to return to a kind of regularity, to honor its most noted civic holiday, and, while so much work remained to be done, New Orleans had accomplished one gesture of recovery, and its cherished way of life could move ahead.

It would be interesting to know the number of revelers on Mardi Gras Day, February 26, 2017, who had been present for the emotional Mardi Gras of 2006, as this later Mardi Gras seemed a very relaxed affair, upbeat and effusive, devoid of the gripping and often anguished emotions that marked Carnival eleven years prior. After several years of cold or rainy conditions (2014 saw drizzle and a high temperature of thirty-eight degrees), Mardi Gras 2017 experienced a glorious sunny day. The city saw swelling crowds, with numbers rivaling those of Carnivals before the disaster. The traditional krewes paraded down St. Charles (the breakdown of a float delayed the proceedings, which for many locals signaled normalcy). The Society of St. Anne meandered its way from Marigny to the foot of Canal Street. The Mardi Gras Indians (African American groups who wear enormous, beautifully beaded costumes that often take a year to create) danced under the overpass on Claiborne Avenue. The North Side Skull and Bones

Gang prowled the streets of Treme attended by the Black Storyville Baby Dolls. The Bourbon Street Awards, a spectacular event recognized as "the most famous drag-queen contest in America" ("Mardi Gras Bourbon"), celebrated its fifty-third anniversary with stunning designs on display and spirited audience interactions. The crowds basked in the warmth of the day, enjoying a Carnival far removed from any blue tarp, FEMA invective, and traumatic Katrina memories.

In the interim between the first Carnival following Katrina and the 2017 celebration, New Orleans worked to further recover and gain a new kind of normalcy, as New Orleans saw its profile among American cities rise in notable and unexpected ways. A 2013 *Atlantic* article noted this upturn in the city's fortunes: "In the last five years, the city has won an astounding number of city awards, but many of them are a variation on the 'most improved player' theme. In 2011, the *Wall Street Journal* named it the most improved metro. *Forbes* has dubbed it the Number-1 metro for IT job growth. . . . Just last week, the Brookings Metropolitan Policy program named it the number one recovery city in the country" (Thompson). A New Year's editorial in the local *Times-Picayune* trumpeted these welcome trends as worthy of celebration, highlighting the new optimism of the city, citing as testament a visiting columnist's characterization of the recovery as "a magnificent comeback by a truly great American city" ("Wrapping up a good year"). New Orleans was identified as "one of the world's top 10 cities" by *Travel and Leisure*; and *Good* magazine ranked New Orleans as seventh on the list of the "50 Most Inspiring Cities in the World," a distinction enjoyed by no other city in the United States (Bronston vii).

Given the widespread devastation of Katrina and the fears that New Orleans had entered an ineluctable death spiral, the city's recovery has in many ways been quite remarkable. However, the dynamics of recovery have not brought the realization of all hopes; its benefits have not been equally distributed. The narrative of a phoenix-like ascent is a partial one. National attention on the storm's tenth anniversary brought focus to the city's gains but also its challenges. Prominent headlines read "Rebirth and Resentment" (Roig-Franzia) and "Uneven Recovery and Unending Divisions" (Dart). In the post-Katrina era, the city has continued to deal with perennial problems with infrastructure, education, the justice system, racial and economic equity, crime, and homelessness. Many problems have been exacerbated in the recovery process, related to affordable housing, wage fairness, and the displacement of longtime African American residents, many recognized as culture-bearers, from their neighborhood homes.

Mardi Gras has experienced repeated challenges over the decades, from threatened federal censure over Reconstruction politics to suspensions due to pestilence, weather, and wars, to police strikes, to legal challenges over segregationist membership practices—though the celebration has persisted. On one level, Mardi Gras certainly serves as a potent icon of the city for the outside world, conveying associations of the city's flair for celebration, performative exuberance, and *laissez-faire* regard for a mainstream American ethos—"New Orleans knows how to party," a perception that feeds the city's tourism engine and brings in millions of visitors each year.

Mardi Gras also speaks powerfully to the world of New Orleans itself, as the holiday functions as a touchstone, organizing relationships and rivalries between its citizens. For locals Mardi Gras stands as a key constituent of identity and belonging. As Carolyn Kolb writes, Mardi Gras exists as "an intrinsic part of every Orleanian's inner calendar" and that "for those who are away from the city in the first quarter of the year, life seems unbalanced" (73). Mardi Gras functions as the city's principal synecdoche; yet, the holiday can also serve as a barometer or indicator of fluctuating civic tensions, as Carnival has remained fluid and changeable, sensitive to the altering complexions of the city—its demographics, politics, economics, and social organization. Minka Stoyanova, a native New Orleanian and participant in two of the parades discussed in this book, Chewbacchus and Red Beans, explains that she has lived in other cities but that none approach New Orleans and its Mardi Gras in making "public space a living, organic environment where dialogue and exchange occurs" (interview with Roberts, July 5, 2018). (While "Mardi Gras" actually denotes the climactic day Fat Tuesday, it is commonly used interchangeably with "Carnival," the holiday season.)

A recent *Times-Picayune* column concerning Carnival 2017 observed the proliferation of new organizations and their rise in visibility, citing such parading groups as 'tit Rəx, the Krewe de Jeanne d'Arc, and the Intergalactic Krewe of Chewbacchus. Highlighting the rich energy and pageantry these groups are bringing to Carnival, Doug MacCash asked: "Is there a downtown Mardi Gras . . . a 21st-century Mardi Gras with a different meaning?" ("The first downtown"). This book is in effect an answer to this question, and, yes, post-Katrina New Orleans has witnessed a new order of celebration, evidenced in the proliferation of do-it-yourself walking krewes that add novel energy and fresh numbers to the Mardi Gras experience. ("Walking krewes" are also spoken of as "walking clubs," "marching groups" or "marching clubs"; "dance groups" could also come under this umbrella.)

While the all-female Krewe of Nyx participates in this post-Katrina surge in new Carnival activities, following the Uptown route and old-line protocols, most of these new groups are Downtown walking krewes, oriented to the eye-to-eye pedestrian experience of the street. They are egalitarian in outlook, often whimsical or satirical in expression, and many of their members never experienced Carnival participation prior to Katrina. This remarkable number of new enterprises highlights the affirmative energies of New Orleans and underscores how Mardi Gras has been reinvigorated and refashioned. Traditional themes and protocols are here given new dimension, demonstrating new modes of reinvention, effecting new bonds of civic belonging. These street performances, however, also reflect the tensions of recovery and new dynamics at play in the city. As urban sociologist Alan Blum reminds us, claims of civic identity can both unify and disunite: "the aura of uniformity ... must collide with its diversity in practice" (71). These performances thus may effectively function as snapshots of post-Katrina Carnival, revealing what holds firm in the city, and what gives over to flux and change (and the debates that inevitably ensue).

This book examines seven emergent walking krewes that now stand as regular components of post-Katrina Carnival. This type of street performance might well be regarded as the most distinctive and notable feature of our current phase of Mardi Gras history. *Downtown Mardi Gras* explores the Uptown/Downtown dimensions of Carnival, as the new walking krewes express an egalitarian ethos that often stands at odds with or parodies traditional Uptown Mardi Gras. It looks at membership dynamics and demographics; many of these krewes consciously attempt to widen membership and have accommodated many recent transplants. In this respect, the book follows a template that focuses on prevalent and often contestatory concerns—that is, how these new krewes: 1) draw from traditional practices while introducing novelty; 2) exhibit and speak to dynamics of race and gender; 3) represent differing economic levels and degrees of professionalism; 4) function to assimilate transplants and address the resentment of natives; 5) embody negotiations of urban space, including neighborhood rivalries for status and resources; 6) manifest or invoke different visions of Carnival and different visions of the city; and 7) operate under a shared umbrella of civic identity, one that bestows belonging or status as a New Orleanian.

The seven krewes examined in this book cumulatively represent both the variance and shared dimensions of the Downtown parading community. They enjoy different degrees of visibility and cachet; they represent different neighborhoods and different performing styles. Yet they all derive from and convey Downtown energies and outlooks. While these groups are among the most vibrant and colorful of the Carnival scene, their inclusion in this study does not necessarily rank them ahead of others in the wide expanse of street performances that has come to invigorate Mardi Gras.

One book could not do justice to the wondrous array of groups that continue to enrich the streets of Carnival; dozens of walking groups and dance organizations merit scholarly attention. One could trace the acceleration of participation from the pre-Katrina days of the Rolling Elvi, the Bearded Oysters, and the Camel Toe Lady Steppers, to the post-Katrina aftermath, which has seen an explosion of activity—from the 610 Stompers to the multitude of women's krewes (see chapter 2). The emergence of new groups representing the city's Latinx population invites further attention, evident in the efforts of Amigos de los Amigos and Ritmeaux Krewe, as does the participation of the city's LGBTQ community, seen in the glam/drag aesthetic of the Krewe of Robyn (much gay and lesbian street performance occurs in the Southern Decadence and Pride parades).

The approach of this book is both scholarly and personal. The orientation of analysis draws upon folklore studies, on the notion that populist performances and folkloric expressions merit close academic attention; it takes up the "folklorist's job"—to "document" such practices and their contexts, to "unravel their organizations and meanings" (Oring xvii). To this end, the authors utilize perceptions of Barbara Kirshenblatt-Gimblett on the framing of local performance. The work of Frank de Caro, who conducted groundbreaking research on post-Katrina Carnival and helped inspire this study, plays a prominent role for its focus on the resituation of folkloric practices, how traditional events can be reinterpreted, refashioned, and reinvented, serving new historical moments and cultural needs.

In this vein our book draws upon notions of repetition and reiteration at the core of performance studies, noting Richard Schechner's seminal notion of performance as "restored behavior," or "twice-behaved behavior" (84), a repeated event susceptible to change over time. It is this same dynamic that informs Joseph Roach's monumental work *Cities of the Dead*, and it is perhaps fitting that this current study of New Orleans culture hearkens back to Roach's influential effort, which gives such insightful attention to Zulu and the Mardi Gras Indians (both are African American Carnival groups with unique and fascinating traditions). *Downtown Mardi Gras* honors Roach's work, as it employs one of his key concepts, "surrogation" (1), that is, the process by which performative acts work as substitutes, filling in gaps that open up in times of social turbulence. Certainly, the effects of Katrina brought rents and tears to the city's physical and cultural landscape, opening new gaps and spaces. This book in effect investigates the surrogations—specifically the Downtown marching krewes—that have emerged in this open civic space, how these new instantiations work to recast the traditions of Mardi Gras, to set themselves in relation to past practices (and the citizens who performed them), and to advance new performance styles and new civic identities.

Our analysis will take an interdisciplinary approach, also utilizing Mardi Gras histories, studies in race and ethnicity, sociology, feminist inquiry, and urban geography. Such a methodology intends to extend context, to investigate and illuminate new Carnival krewes as a specific performance phenomenon that both works within and represents wider cultural dynamics.

The book is also personal and ethnographic in orientation. In addition to supplementing published research with ephemeral documentation, material that works to "capture the moment" of different points in the city's recovery, this book draws heavily from numerous interviews that, we hope, have given participants and practitioners of these walking krewes the opportunities to articulate their histories, their aims, and their contributions to Carnival culture and the city. Finally, the book also issues from a sense of the authors' lived experience, as we three have resided in New Orleans through Katrina and the recovery period; we have also experienced these walking krewes as both close observers and participants. We acknowledge that our perceptions are particular, viewed through the lenses of our individual experiences and backgrounds. We hope that what is personal might not appear presumptive, but that our distinct, individual expressions might elicit a nod of assent, some flash of communal recognition.

A scholarly interest informs our willingness to engage in this topic—we have all published in different areas of local culture in recent years. The endeavor is also inspired by an unabashed affinity for New Orleans. Andrei Codrescu is accurate in his assessment that "no one loves their city like New Orleanians love their city" (266)—though such affection allows no easy dismissal of civic shortcomings. New Orleans has indeed rebounded from a near-death blow, and it continues to prove home to arguably the country's richest cultural life and most distinctive civic personality. In this regard, our investigation of recent Mardi Gras practices offers up new Carnival expressions as a testament to the resilience of the city. We wish to promote awareness of these krewes, drawing attention to their leaders and participants; in so doing we hope to highlight the creativity that permeates post-Katrina culture and street life. We celebrate this new aspect of Mardi Gras and regard it as a prime indicator of New Orleans's continuing status as one of the world's most inspiring places.

Destruction and Defiance

One of the slogans encouraging New Orleanians following Katrina was the ubiquitous "Rebuild, Restore, Renew." And citizens brought an amazing determination and doggedness in their efforts to restore the city. They endured a gauntlet of challenges: negotiating the labyrinthine red tape of insurance claims, engaging with suppliers and contractors, abiding temporary housing in ammonia-ridden FEMA trailers. For some residents, life returned to a recognizable normal much sooner than for others, especially for those in the areas that did not sustain flooding, known variously as the "sliver by the river" and the "isle of denial." One central question concerning the recovery has involved the varied and sometimes inequitable gains made in the years following Katrina, and it is certain that restoration came much easier to some than to others.

New Orleanians have long been famous for their fierce affection for their city, often expressed in hyperbole, such as the claim of R&B legend Ernie K-Doe: "I'm not sure but I'm almost positive that all music came from New Orleans" (qtd. in Irrera). Such exaggeration speaks to the special regard New Orleanians have for their home. The vast destruction brought by Katrina flooding wrought extreme physical damage upon the city, a material devastation that ushered untold grieving; however, citizens saw Katrina beyond its physical threat, as a force of destruction that jeopardized a way of life and a set of rare and beautiful cultural practices. In *New Orleans, Mon Amour*, Andrei Codrescu describes this habitus as "a *style* of living and a modus vivendi that couldn't be mistaken for anything else" (266). In *Why People Live in New Orleans* Christine Allen Ewy endeavors to explain the city's allure, contending that the "culture could not be recreated or transported elsewhere" (2). The city's near-death experience activated a profound affection and regard for the rituals of New Orleans life. Following Katrina, the local penchant for extolling the city's difference only grew more prominent. Noted photojournalist Leon Morris gave voice to this sentiment: "It is very difficult to describe to someone who hasn't spent time in New Orleans just how intoxicating this city can be. There is nowhere else like it on Earth" (12).

Current member of the Amazons walking krewe Lynette Johnson, a native New Orleanian who had moved away from the city, recounts seeing TV images of a flooded New Orleans and immediately packing her bags, knowing she had to return to help her city (interview with Robin Roberts, August 17, 2017). Johnson's attitude and actions were shared by thousands who made the rebuilding of New Orleans a personal quest. Famed trumpeter Wynton Marsalis gave expression to this yearning for regaining a threatened way of life: "We want our city. And we don't want it to come back like no Disneyland for adults. . . . Just give us a chance to collect ourselves" (qtd. in Rutledge, *Do You Know*, frontispiece).

Inspiring the rebuilding movement was the city's vaunted lifestyle. David Rutledge underscores this point, emphasizing that locals were restoring "not just a city, not just houses," but "a culture" ("Preface" 9). Prominent New Orleans geographer Richard Campanella notes how cherished icons served to stir allegiance to the city, to spur return and recovery. All kinds of channels—editorials, public service ads, commercials, radio conversation, etc.—circulated endearing images of the city, acting to lift spirits and instill a sense of perseverance. Revered symbols included beignets, streetcars, live oaks, the bells of St. Louis Cathedral, and, importantly, Mardi Gras. Campanella writes: "Other American cities might have been hard-pressed to draw upon such a deep reservoir of cherished symbols to unify and motivate their scattered citizens. In its darkest hour, New Orleans discovered its most precious asset—itself" (*Geographies of New Orleans* 405).

Each citizen experiencing a homecoming can point to countless moments that stirred strong feelings for New Orleans, many personal and idiosyncratic, others public and large-scale. The first post-Katrina Jazz Fest was hailed as an achievement for the city. Headliner Bruce Springsteen gave an emotional two and half hour set, including "O Mary, Don't You Weep No More" and "My City of Ruins," a performance he later described as "one of the most meaningful of my work life" (qtd. in Pope). The event welcomed hometown favorite performers and was described by producer Quint Davis as one of the most extraordinary experiences in his thirty-seven years of Jazz Fest. Award-winning artist Terrence Blanchard voiced his happiness in being onstage in New Orleans: "I don't' know about y'all, but I'm sure damn tired of people asking me is New Orleans coming back . . . I tell 'em, I tell 'em all the time, Goddamn right we're coming back . . . I came home, I had a fried oyster and like to cried. I said damn that's good!" (qtd. in Rutledge, *Do You Know* 45).

Many other instances large and small bolstered the city during this period, including the reopening of Dooky Chase's restaurant, the start-up of the streetcar lines, etc. The international art project known as Project 1 brought internationally acclaimed artists to the city and situated art displays across New Orleans in over thirty different exhibits. In January 2006 the neighborhood of Treme saw its first second-line parade since the storm. ("Second-line" can have multiple meanings designating musical rhythm and dance steps; it primarily designates a "massive parade organized by African American benevolent societies in New Orleans inner-city neighborhoods" [Regis and Walton 411].)

Scores of individuals, still displaced by Katrina, traveled back to New Orleans to celebrate this event. Organized by Tamara Jackson and Michelle Longino, the parade was "meant to stake a claim to the city's historically black neighborhoods on behalf of their former residents" (Hirsch). Over three hundred social aid and pleasure club members were in attendance, accompanied by three brass bands. Father Jerome LeDoux stepped out from St. Augustine's Catholic Church to bless the group. The parade drew a massive crowd and was thought by some to be the largest ever second-line (Hirsch). Though regrettably the end of the event was marked by gunfire, this second-line served as a passionate defining moment for the city's recovery, providing hope for the return of displaced residents and the continuance of the second-line tradition.

Another of the most celebrated moments in the post-Katrina years was the Saints' return to the Superdome, where the New Orleans team, inspired by Steve Gleason's blocked punt, enjoyed a victory over the rival "dirty birds" of Atlanta. Spectators also saw a spectacular musical entertainment by Green Day and U2, supported by Trombone Shorty, New Birth, and Rebirth Brass bands, featuring the song that would become a local anthem, "The Saints Are Coming." Bono injected the song with these original lyrics: "Living like birds in the magnolia trees / Child on a rooftop, mother on her knees / Her sign reads 'Please, I am an American . . .'" (Stokes). This event allowed the city collectively to thump its chest before a national TV audience, one of the largest viewership for any NFL game. This reverie spurred by the team would reach its culmination in the Saints' unlikely and inspiring run to the 2010 Super Bowl championship.

For the occasion of the fifth anniversary of Katrina, Mario Tama wrote that the "hard work of making the world again" was mostly left to the residents themselves, who have "porch by porch, block by block, built their lives anew" (8). This context of destruction and defiance is crucial to understanding the history of post-Katrina Carnival, as—like other civic conduits such as sports, music, art, and grass-roots organizing—Carnival served to channel this fierce and determined civic energy. Samuel Kinser writes that experiences "of disaster are often times of heightened festive abandon" (99), and in the years following the storm, New Orleans celebrated Carnival with a recalibrated enthusiasm and fervor.

It has famously been said that Mardi Gras is the greatest free show on earth, a comment that focuses on the visitor and touristic aspect of the event. While those in Downtown Mardi Gras may find themselves photographed and cheered on by outsiders, the parades are not designed for touristic consumption. A significant aspect of this performance lies in the fact that they are enacted on behalf of locals, directed to other citizens, as an expression of solidarity, presented before friends, relatives, neighbors, and fellow New Orleanians. David Gilmore observes that "ritual brings people together physically and expresses in powerful symbolic terms common goals and shared values" (27). Downtown Mardi Gras confirms this perception, as the parades have drawn participants into close proximity, conveying a kind of insider knowledge and commitment. These performances are colorful, exuberant enactments that physically declare: we are claiming our streets, we are coming back, we will not be washed away.

Informing Tensions: Uptown/Downtown, Throne/Street

A number of Carnival practices enjoy status as iconic or quintessential and have come over the years to function as a kind of shorthand for Mardi Gras, such as the Lundi Gras riverfront meeting of Rex and Zulu (high-profile, high-status white and African American krewes respectively), the super-floats of Endymion (a newer parade with floats many times the size of traditional ones), the decorated shoes of Muses (a highly popular all-women's parade, launched in 2000), the flashing of breasts for beads on Bourbon Street. And in truth there are as many versions of Mardi Gras as there are revelers, as citizens and visitors can experience the event in distinctly different and highly enjoyable ways. For some, watching parades with family on the neutral ground (or median) of St. Charles, a prominent Uptown boulevard, epitomizes Mardi Gras. For others, the highlight of the day might be the appearance of the North Side Skull and Bones Gang (the current-day enactment of a long-standing African American masking practice) from the doorway of the Backstreet Cultural Museum. And for others the height of experience might come on the back of a flatbed truck, tossing beads to thinning crowds late in the day, in the do-it-yourself family floats that follow the conclusion of Rex. Mardi Gras engenders a multifocal, multisensory effect, and much of its power draws from its inexhaustible capacity. Each experience works in mosaic fashion to assemble a collective representation of Carnival, and this book does not intend to minimize the range of activities or undervalue the passion that is brought to each by its various practitioners.

Downtown Mardi Gras chooses to give emphasis to one rich, potent vein of Carnival experience, one that has emerged in a highly visible way in the last number of years: the walking krewes localized in the city's Downtown neighborhoods of the French Quarter, Treme, Marigny, and Bywater. These krewes largely operate outside of the attention of national media who come to New Orleans for Mardi Gras. They exist without the often-hyped tourist promotions for the city during Carnival. They perform as foils to the super krewes and thronging crowds. What emerges as defining features of these groups includes their do-it-yourself inventiveness, an emphasis on homemade and hand-crafted accoutrement, relationships often built on neighborhood ties, and a strong assertion of small-group, personalized creative expressions. They function as a counter-Carnival to the Mardi Gras touted in promotion and publicity, the *Girls Gone Wild* Carnival, what the nation sees as an "uninhibited, frenzied festival ... the great American blowout bash" (Flake book jacket). Claudia "Mardi Claw" Gherke, leader of the all-women Skinz n Bonez, challenges this widespread perception, claiming "Mardi Gras is NOT what people think it is" (e-mail to Wade, September 11, 2017). Skinz n Bonez offers an alternative—the small-scale, home-grown experience that prizes creativity and neighborhood affiliation.

Location plays a central role in understanding these new krewes and their countervailing outlooks. In this respect the geography of performance acts in an informing and determining factor, as this Carnival phenomenon draws from the spaces, energies, and identities that operate in the Downtown area. In his study of performance spaces in urban contexts, Marvin Carlson underscores how different locations or zones in a city have signified different meanings and usages, informing how "audiences [have] viewed and interacted" with performance (10). This perception illuminates the contrastive practices of Uptown and Downtown, how each carries its own styles and significations. A geographical marker that has long informed New Orleans's self-understanding and neighborhood relations is that of the Canal Street divide, the boundary that distinguishes Downtown and Uptown New Orleans (this designation has at different times come under revision; some today use "downriver" to reference areas such as Bywater). Importantly, this line of demarcation has worked to organize two distinct modes of Carnival performance.

Historically, Downtown (downriver of Canal) has signified the older areas of the city, chiefly the French Quarter, home to a French aristocracy that was "royalist, colonialist, hierarchical, status conscious Catholic" (de Caro and Ireland 38). This area housed the Cabildo, the seat of city governance, and St. Louis Cathedral, one of the earliest Catholic churches in the United States. The populace followed French tradition in business and in culture (opera proved a much-prized civic treasure). Downtown also includes the African American neighborhood of Treme, the area lakeside of the French Quarter, which hosted a significant population of free people of color. Treme had its own commercial life and schools and cultivated an array of vibrant cultural activities.

In the course of the nineteenth century this Downtown area experienced continuous diminishment, with the decline of city's Creole power base; Treme suffered legal and political discriminations that heightened racial separations and subordination. The Downtown area fell in both its economic and social standing. In the early twentieth century the French Quarter was considered by many as a virtual slum devoid of any remarkable historical significance. Downtown proved a magnet for newly arrived immigrants, especially Italians, whose presence led to the moniker "little Sicily." In the 1920s an emergent bohemian population took residence in the Quarter; writers such as William Faulkner and Sherwood Anderson praised the quaint architectural beauty of the neighborhoods and its Latin sensibility. The memoir *Uptown/Downtown* conveys the amicable dialogue between two women who grew up in these respective areas before World War II. Elsie the Downtowner cedes Uptown its "class, desirability" (Martinez and Le Cogorne 1); however, she prioritizes Downtown for its "rich variety of peoples and cultures," for its distinctiveness of feel and atmosphere, what she recommends as "character" (Martinez and Le Cogorne 16). Current Downtown resident Thomasine Bartlett confirms this perception, strongly affirming Downtown, its cultural life, its integrated aspect, and its status as "the first New Orleans" (interview with Roberts, July 5, 2018).

During the twentieth century, especially following World War II, the French Quarter emerged as the visitor and entertainment hub of the city. It gained historical landmark status and housed art galleries, boutique shops, and fine restaurants, becoming the heart of the city's tourism industry. Richard Campanella has traced the development of Bourbon Street and its rise to prominence (assuming the illicit performance energies of the city's famous prostitution district Storyville). The street also drew recognition (with Preservation Hall) as the center of jazz, the music form that arose from the brothels, bars, and street corners of Treme. Campanella elucidates how in recent decades the vortices of charisma have migrated across the Downtown area, to the bars of lower Decatur, to the music clubs of Frenchmen, and more recently to the alternative nightspots, eateries, and galleries of St. Claude. He in fact cites Marigny, Bywater, and Treme as emergent neighborhood magnets, attracting "hyperhip creative types and cultural envelope pushers" (Campanella, *Bourbon Street* 290), generating the cachet of a Downtown scene.

Uptown New Orleans reflects a different history and thus a contrastive sense of identity and outlook. Its origin comes with Louisiana's sale to the United States in 1803 and the subsequent incursion of Americans, who brought to New Orleans their attitudes, customs, and investment capital. In ensuing decades, the financial and political might of the city gravitated to the upriver side of Canal Street, home of the city's burgeoning American population. Grandiose civic institutions, such as Gallier Hall and the St. Charles Theatre, found home Uptown. The great wealth of the antebellum city led to the mansion-lined thoroughfare of St. Charles Avenue, which became the symbol of American affluence and prestige. Anglo city leaders formed exclusive sanctuaries such as the Boston and Pickwick Clubs. Following the Civil War, Uptown political leaders embraced a pro-Confederate sentiment—their clubs serving as "bastions for Confederate ideology" (Grams 196). Well into the twentieth century, this area cultivated a genteel air and sense of white class privilege. In *Uptown/Downtown* Margaret the Uptowner confesses to being "only vaguely aware of downtown's existence"; she writes: "To the typical uptowner New Orleans *was* uptown" (11).

A broad-brush survey of Uptown may fail to acknowledge the working-class Irish Channel and African American blocks (and its Mardi Gras Indian heritage) that exist in quiltlike fashion across the area; yet, Uptown retains its image of waspish privilege, with private schools and neighborhood security patrols. Conversely, Downtown houses a more eclectic population and its own offbeat vibe. Ryan Ballard of the Intergalactic Krewe of Chewbacchus favors this sector above the "beautiful, clean" Uptown, characterizing the former as "rougher, scrappier, more wild and free" (interview with Wade, October 2, 2017). This cultural/geographical demarcation remains active in the city, continuing to energize different identities and allegiances. The rivalry is often friendly and humorous, as seen in New Orleans's Southern Repertory Theatre's running soap opera *Debauchery*, which mines conflict and comedy from the domestic relations between an "uptown family and its downtown mother" ("Stage"). Other times the tension can become more consequential, such as how different neighborhoods receive funding and attention—the French Quarter was recently granted exclusionary protection from Airbnb activities, while the Uptown Garden District, despite heavy lobbying by its residents, was denied this status.

The Uptown/Downtown divide not only informs two distinct sensibilities; it accounts for two very different enactments of Carnival culture. The origins of Mardi Gras in the city trace back to the Creole aristocracy, who wished to emulate French practices. Carnival celebration included street reveling but gave greater emphasis to masked balls, as markers of status and wealth. One historical account has estimated that by 1837 "upwards of one thousand balls" took place each year (Guren and Ugan 37).

It was, however, the Uptown Americans who inaugurated what we today consider traditional Mardi Gras protocols. Eager to replicate and enjoy Carnival practices in the mode of the French, Uptown leaders initiated their own Mardi Gras (drawing from the Cowbellians of Mobile) and founded the Mystic Krewe of Comus, the city's first Carnival krewe (for the history of New Orleans Carnival, see Laborde; Costello; Schindler; Huber; Guren and Ugan; Young; Leathem; Kinser). A strong narrative line of Carnival history holds that the Anglo-Protestants saved Carnival by introducing a novel procession of floats and tableaux, which defused the unwanted rowdyism of the streets. This practice thus became the template for other krewes that would follow in the nineteenth century, such as Rex and Momus. The members of these secretive groups represented the white, Protestant business and civic leaders of Uptown New Orleans, who used Carnival processions to manifest their status and to assert a social and moral superiority. An early invitation to a Comus ball captures the emblematic and ideological aspects of this enterprise, showcasing a "gavel for law and order" along with "the winged wand of the God of Commerce" (Salaun).

Uptown has emerged over the decades as home to the traditional, iconic Carnival parades that proceed along St. Charles Avenue, the nineteenth-century "hub of economic and social life in the New Orleans" (Laborde 34). On this route the royalty stop for a toast at Gallier Hall, and then proceed to the tourist throngs along Canal. These organizations honor long-standing protocols, such as that of each Duke of Rex wearing a purple, gold, and green ducal medallion (Hales 48). Their membership is exclusive and costly, sometimes willed to relatives (Tallant 13). While much effort and pageantry go into the parades themselves, the more venerable aspect of Carnival for these krewes is the masked ball, "the epitome of the elaborate caste system on which New Orleans society has thrived" (Guren and Ugan 64). Uptown Carnival plays out a spectacle of faux royalty, of jeweled luminous ostentation, one that Rosary O'Neil engagingly conveys in *New Orleans Carnival Krewes*, a work drawn from her own experience as a Carnival debutante.

Though these parades formerly traveled through Downtown New Orleans, city codes in 1973 prohibited their passage in the French Quarter due to crowd concerns. That noted, Downtown has regularly hosted a different order of Carnival experience, one that is unruly, exuberant, and dispersive. Many individual establishments and small social groupings orchestrate their own Mardi Gras celebrations. The Krewe of Dirty Dotty, for instance once held festivities in a laundromat on North Rampart (Osborne and Laborde 142). The dominant practice of Downtown is simple meandering, strolling through the jammed streets, taking in the range of extravagant costuming, partaking of the riotous and intoxicated celebration.

Referencing the street suggests another defining tension between Uptown and Downtown Carnival, one involving an aesthetic trope of performance, that is, the assertion (or omission) of an embodied verticality of presentation. One may consider this contrast in terms of competing points of focus—between the throne and the street. Tony Giordano has published an appealing book of photographs documenting the imaginatively decorated ladders, "the perfect observation tower[s]" (108), that are often employed on the St. Charles and Canal parade routes to facilitate the catching of throws and the viewing of royalty. Reflecting a similar aim, many pay for bleacher seats along St. Charles Avenue in order to enhance sight lines (and to be raised above others on the street).

The Uptown parades are in fact predicated on a principle of elevation. The royalty and court of the krewe proceed above the masses on floats so that they are literally always looking down upon the crowds; the protocol hearkens back to the early parades of Comus and Rex that enchanted the masses with "instructive and uplifting spectacles" (Leathem 2). The floats are interspersed with marching bands and walking krewes that serve as points of contrast to those atop the floats. Onlookers at street level effectively offer adulation to the royal court, the "beautifully dressed aristocrats, physically raised above the multitude" (de Caro and Ireland 30). Attention

and abeyance before the implicit lines of demarcation are effectively pa-
trolled by the dukes on horseback, who ride between the floats in colorful feathered and jeweled costumes, whose faces remain hidden behind
masks, creating an ominous sense of threat and remove. The entourage
is illuminated by the walking flambeaux, historically working-class African Americans who bear torches and who dance for tips as they pass—a
striking visual conceit for the racial/class hierarchy of traditional Uptown
Carnival.

In her influential work *The Archive and the Repertoire*, Diana Taylor
highlights the difference between authorized, sanctioned performance
that is written into histories (the archive) and the more ephemeral and
often overlooked performances of the street (the repertoire). The difference between the two involves their distinct relation to social status,
cultural power, and civic authority. The former is hegemonic, the latter
evanescent and resistant. In this light, the Mardi Gras practice of the
original krewes, well established through decades of continuous performance, documented in the journalism of various periods and explained
in numerous histories, may be considered a kind of archival performance,
one establishing the fundamental template of Carnival protocol; Rex,
for example, operates within the realm of the archive. By contrast, an
anarchic, boundary-defying energy has always counterpointed the more
formalized Carnival activities, conveyed in the performances of the street.
Taylor would identify this ephemeral enactment as a performance of the
repertoire, "a nonarchival system of transfer" between participants (*The
Archive* xvii)—exemplified in the early morning meandering trek of the
North Side Skull and Bones Gang on Fat Tuesday, who follow no posted
schedule or parade route.

Taylor's analysis proves helpful in highlighting the unruly, uncontained
aspect of street performance, as street celebration serves as the defining
element of Downtown Mardi Gras performance. A 1912 newspaper article
drew attention to the fluid and unbridled aspect of street revels: "By far
the most interesting feature of Mardi Gras [opposed to the activities of the
traditional krewes] is the parading of promiscuous maskers. . . . Singly or
in groups these merrymakers affect almost every grotesque and fanciful
character imaginable, and their antics provide the real fun of the culminat-
ing day of the Carnival" (qtd. in Schindler 111). Carnival energy has long
operated at the level of the street, as a force that can mock or simply ignore
the status hierarchies of conventional krewes. Mikhail Bakhtin, the noted
scholar of the carnivalesque, writes of the peoples' carnival that expresses

this unruly, anti-authoritarian aspect, where satire and hybridity are given free reign, where the powerful and privileged are decentered. The streets of New Orleans have allowed at different times participation for those who otherwise would not gain visibility; during Carnival women and African Americans (and gays and lesbians) have often presented themselves in defiant, celebratory display, taking on "temporarily assumed identities to cross lines of class, gender, and race" (Leathem iii).

New Mardi Gras practices embody and affirm the contention that Carnival "is not an activity commanded from above" but is rather "the sum of thousands of separate activities" (*Throw Me* 34). Recent Mardi Gras has witnessed the proliferation of disparate, do-it-yourself enterprises, which, according to one observer, have multiplied post-Katrina "like mushrooms after a spring rain" ("31 marvelous"). These enterprises follow in the steps of the notable Jefferson City Buzzards, the city's first walking krewe, that undertook its inaugural march in 1889. They also draw inspiration from and the Society of St. Anne (1969) and Krewe du Vieux (1987), fixtures of the Downtown scene. In this respect, the streets of New Orleans have long offered an open stage for revelry, costuming, and invention. Beyond the example of the aforementioned groups, one can corroborate the multi-fractured, perambulatory aspect of Carnival by simply walking through the Quarter any time on Mardi Gras day and encountering pirates, drag-queen nuns, moss swamp monsters, French maids, Mexican wrestlers, gorillas, vampires, honey bees, satyrs, etc.—what one might consider "endless improvisations of a rough cultural democracy" (Berry 324).

Lyle Saxon's fictional account of a Mardi Gras day in *Fabulous New Orleans* stands as one of the most famous evocations of Carnival, as his characters celebrate both Uptown and Downtown, effectively carrying readers "back and forth over the line" (Kinser 141). This illustration points us toward the different "vortices of behavior" (Roach 28) operating today in the Uptown/Downtown polarity. Uptown signifies the traditional protocols and pageantry of the long-established krewes, representing affluence and lineage; Downtown invokes adult Mardi Gras—drag contests, nudity, the public display of sensuality and non-heteronormative sexuality. It also signifies the perambulatory experience of middle and working-class revelers, in often whimsical and creative costume, taking to the streets in rather improvisatory fashion, celebrating their friendships and neighborhoods, exercising their right to participate in public display. If Uptown Carnival evokes images of the King of Rex toasting the mayor, two elites eye to eye above the crowd, the Downtown marching krewes stir images of members walking shoulder to shoulder, in an undisciplined regiment, insouciant and exuberant, mixing in and out with other revelers on the streets.

This study endorses the observation of Louise McKinney, that "the streets are the best places to see the face, or faces of this city" (24). Beyond the eclectic names of New Orleans thoroughfares—Music, Desire, Benefit, Humanity, Hope, etc. (Asher 15)—its streets serve as significant sites of expression and encounter. Streets also serve as a kind of laboratory, giving "rise to new forms and modes of perceiving the world and relating to it" (Dikec 3). The street can be a site of aggression and violence, as is all too frequently the case in New Orleans; it can also be a place of alliance and affiliation, of new discoveries. Perhaps like no other city, New Orleans presents and defines itself through its street culture. Invoking the "homemade processions" meandering the Downtown streets on a Mardi Gras morning, Ian McNulty finds "magic in the spontaneous glee and bonhomie" of these efforts; he continues, "the unscripted theatre of the costumed street—that's what MG means to the locals who embrace it" (*A Season of Night* 137). *Downtown Mardi Gras* shares this valuation of homemade Carnival and its ebullient energy. Such performative expressions can serve as an effective window to grass-roots, communal organization; they also act as powerful incarnations of the spirit of regeneration that has imbued and enlivened post-Katrina New Orleans.

Chapter Overviews

In chapter 1, Robin Roberts and Frank de Caro document the history of the Joan of Arc parade, a women's enterprise that celebrates the birthday of the famous saint, which happens to fall on January 6, Twelfth Night, the traditional commencement of the Carnival season. The parade runs through the French Quarter, concluding at the gilded Joan of Arc statue on Decatur Street ("Joanie on a pony"). The chapter looks at the feminist aspect of the group, which celebrates this female icon, a woman who spoke truth to power and actively fought against it. The parade also is significant for drawing on European history in a way that underscores the French heritage of the city. The Joan of Arc parade has established itself as one of the two key krewes that launch the city forward into Carnival season; in this respect they stand with and distinct from the Phunny Phorty Phellows, a group that began in the 1880s and plays a contributing role in the disposition and outlook of traditional Uptown Carnival.

Chapter 2, by Leslie A. Wade, highlights a new invocation of the skull and bones tradition—the Downtown women's group Skinz n Bonez, who recast elements of a traditionally African American, all-male practice in their performance of female solidarity. The chapter surveys the bone gang history, focusing on the lineage and enactments of the North Side Skull and Bone Gang, the inheritor of this practice. The chapter then examines the emergence of the all-female group, chiefly white in membership, and how it has advanced its own style and identity. The interplay of the groups highlights often vexing issues of post-Katrina culture, including matters of cultural hybridity, the propriety of established traditions, and the degree to which such iterations act as a kind of appropriation or as a form of dialogism.

Chapter 3, by Robin Roberts, focuses on a parade that through its name and practice presents an inversion of traditional Mardi Gras's emphasis on excess. The 'tit Rəx parade offers an ironic twist on the gigantic, expensive, and traditional krewe and parade, Rex, whose king is THE King of Carnival, and whose parade runs the traditional Uptown route. Using interviews and images, this chapter analyzes 'tit Rəx through representative participants and floats. 'tit Rəx provides an example of how parades can be read as resisting and revising traditional Carnival. Like the other new parades, 'tit Rəx raises issues of gender and class. 'tit Rəx also accords with Errol Laborde's observation that "downtowns are inherently adult" (55), as this Downtown parade is salacious in aspect. While 'tit Rəx floats are tiny, evoking schoolchildren's Mardi Gras floats made from shoeboxes, they are political and often sexually explicit.

Chapter 4, by Roberts and de Caro, focuses on a new parade, a new surrogation, that has assumed an empty spot in the Carnival calendar, Lundi Gras, the Monday before Fat Tuesday. This chapter explores the Krewe of Red Beans and the ways that this new parade draws on New Orleans culture, from its signature red beans and rice dish, to the Mardi Gras Indians' costumes, to the second-line tradition. Like the other new Downtown parades, Red Beans fosters artistic expression (and competition); displays whimsical and political humor based on local culture; and valorizes the domestic (a common meal and food stuff), and thus the feminine. And like the other new Mardi Gras parades, the krewe wrestles with an evolving New Orleans and the role transplants play in precipitating change. In addition, like the 'tit Rəx organization, the krewe has had to deal with rapid expansion due to increasing membership interest.

Chapter 5, by Wade, features the fastest growing of the new Downtown Mardi Gras organizations, the Intergalactic Krewe of Chewbacchus. New

Orleans culture is not conventionally associated with science fiction or futurism; however, this krewe has tapped a rich and vibrant vein, blending conventional Carnival with science fiction fandom—the mashup of Bacchus and Chewbacca from *Star Wars*. This chapter examines the egalitarian impulse of Chewbacchus, which clearly situates itself in opposition to traditional Uptown krewes. The chapter also investigates its relation to the Downtown neighborhood of Bywater and how the color and energy of the enterprise both reflect and contribute to the gentrification of the area. Finally, the chapter speculates on the krewe's fantastical expressions and implicit utopianism, how its carnivalesque, otherworldly aspect might alter or affect actual social realities.

Chapter 6, by Roberts, concludes the book's exploration of new Downtown Mardi Gras with an analysis of two inclusive, exuberant krewes, the Amazons Social Aid and Benevolent Society and the Black Storyville Baby Dolls. The Amazons is a group of breast cancer survivors, both natives and transplants, who provide support to other survivors while celebrating life through costuming and parading. Wearing breastplates and brandishing swords, the group commandeers a militaristic posture that exudes strength and power. While the group's main focus is social aid and support, the members use Mardi Gras parades to make a public statement of women's empowerment. Founded by New Orleans native Dianne Honoré, an African American Creole woman, the group draws on the mythological Amazons and their example of female strength. The Black Storyville Baby Dolls, also founded by Honoré, draw directly on the African American tradition of Baby Dolls, the historical practice of adult women dressing as young girls, in beautiful outfits made of satin, dancing in the streets, and acting tough (smoking cigars). Both groups exemplify the use of Carnival as an opportunity to resist gender norms. The social tensions of native/transplant, male/female, black/white, rich/poor all play a part in these new Downtown organizations, reflecting the current life of the city. What makes the groups unique is their emphasis on African American women; at the same time, they welcome other ethnicities and incorporate men in associative satellite groups.

Significance and Value

While New Orleans received unprecedented media attention in the disaster of Katrina and its immediate aftermath, the city and its recovery have proven a story less widely circulated. And though Mardi Gras continues to engender fascination both nationally and internationally, little scholarly attention has focused on post-Katrina Carnival (recent books on Mardi Gras—see Laborde, O'Neal, and Costello—give only passing mention to the organizations presented in this volume; Aurélie Godet examines post-Katrina parading in an insightful article that focuses on funeral second-lines, Mardi Gras Indians, and the Krewe of Eris). As the only extended analysis of the Downtown Carnival phenomenon, this study offers unique documentation and assessment of these new krewes, how they have given play to new alliances, identities, and imaginations—chiefly expressive of a Downtown, egalitarian street theatre.

This book welcomes a popular audience, readers who wish to learn about new Carnival activities and how Mardi Gras continues to evolve. This study also invites scholarly readers interested in an interdisciplinary approach to Mardi Gras; it follows Diana Taylor's belief that "a community's 'intangible' practices [or performances] serve vital aesthetic, epistemic, and social functions" ("Performance and intangible" 91). In this light, Downtown Carnival offers its performance as a lens into the crucible of post-Katrina New Orleans, providing illumination of energies and anxieties affecting the city in this period. It also gives recognition and value to the distinctive, shared kind of "knowing" experienced by those participating in the parades and by those standing on the curbside cheering.

In a fundamental way, this book attempts to evoke and capture one manifestation of the fascinating and imaginative performative life of New Orleans. A local handbook, *New Orleans: The Underground Guide*, affirms that the city's "artistic communities are still as unique and vibrant, and conjure up as many important new creations as ever" (Welch 1), and indeed this resurgent vibrancy merits acclaim and advocacy. We invite readers who value grass-roots enterprises and collective art endeavors. We hope to engage those who share affection for New Orleans's rich and unique culture, for those moments of New Orleans experience that come unexpectedly and astonishingly, of marvelous and wildly theatrical incarnations that can appear almost at any time, around any street corner.

Downtown Carnival demonstrates the transformative aspect of street presentation and thus connects to wider dynamics of mass public display, a subject of considerable scholarly attention in recent years, given the impact of public protests in instances such as Occupy Wall Street and the Arab Spring. The authors of *Taking the Square* emphasize that "active democracy requires physical space for its performance"; the site of the street assumes privileged importance—it is "where the public sphere *happens*" (Rovisco and Ong 3).

This contention illuminates a principal significance of these new Carnival performances. While giving vent to festive energy, these practices act as a kind of symbolic assertion of civic will. At times these parades are overtly political and partisan in messaging. More often their embodied expressions, as a claiming of the streets, extend a broader impulse, one that advocates democratic, participatory involvement. These parades have physicalized hope and offered bodily defense of a wounded, often maligned city. Defend New Orleans.

This study ultimately sides with those scholars who view carnival (the generic practice) in terms of empowerment, that ludic expression can alter social givens. Craig Colton's post-Katrina recognition, that amid "the devastation, there . . . emerged countless examples of hope-driven creativity" (61), relates to the profoundly purposeful and restorative aspect of these new Mardi Gras practices. Such hope-inspired efforts have on many levels worked to repair the rents and ruptures suffered by the city, and have helped usher forth new realities.

No gesture can replace lost lives, no performance can fully claim restoration of memory. Viewed as surrogations, new instances of Downtown Mardi Gras have stepped forward in these vacancies, presenting new possibilities, precluding others. Ed Blakely, the short-lived recovery czar after Katrina, often drew ridicule for his boastful claim that the city would be seeing "cranes in the sky," especially in light of the city's slow start at recovery. New Downtown Mardi Gras krewes have given vent to festive exuberance; they may more fundamentally stand as investments of labor, drawing together a phalanx of believers working together to build anew. Anyone looking to certify the energy and evidence of recovery in New Orleans could today look at the city's skyline, with its signs of remodeling and new construction; better advice would be to cast an eye lower, to the Downtown streets of New Orleans and its parades of motley revelers, who in feathers, beads, horns, face paint, and glitter, repair and reimagine the life of the city through the labor of play.

CHAPTER 1

The St. Joan of Arc Parade, Gender, and Pride of Place

Robin Roberts and Frank de Caro

It seems appropriate to open this book about new parades by beginning with the first new parade of the Carnival season, Joan of Arc. Participants refer to the parade variously as the Joan of Arc parade; while its official name is Krewe de Jeanne d'Arc, the sponsoring organization is the St. Joan Project. Like the participants and parade-goers, this chapters uses the names interchangeably. In addition to its role in opening Carnival, Krewe de Jeanne d'Arc provides the opportunity to examine the history of walking krewes. As this book will show, Amanda Helm's view that "if it's a living tradition, you need a new guard, new participants" is key to Mardi Gras (interview with Roberts, October 24, 2017). She claims, with justification, that the Joan of Arc parade "has been instrumental in reviving the Twelfth Night tradition" (interview with Roberts).

Central to the krewe's development is the leadership and vision not only of its founder, Amy Kirk-Duvoisin, but also the other two key organizers, Amanda Helm and Antoinette de Alteriis. Each has brought a different emphasis to the group, from Kirk-Duvoisin's emphasis on cultural connections to France, Helm's emphasis on spirituality, and de Alteriis's pride in the inclusion of young women. Drawing on interviews with all three, as well as a few other participants in this parade, this chapter examines the features that make Krewe de Jeanne d'Arc successful, focusing on elements of the procession, their throws, and the parade's impact on participants.

In addition to the parade's defining features, this chapter also explores the impact of gender on new Downtown parades. Perhaps not surprisingly, given their eponymous heroine, Joan of Arc, the organizers of her parade are primarily women. Their view of art and craft defines the parade, as does their gendered world view, which includes teaching and bringing others into their collaborative vision of the organization and the parade. The parade implicitly and explicitly challenges male dominance of Mardi Gras in general and the beginning of Carnival on January 6, specifically. While membership is racially integrated, the parade is dominated by white members. The group's celebration of a medieval European saint undoubtedly attracts and reinforces this aspect of the krewe. Its use of humor also is part of its success; it is perhaps a bit unexpected, for example, that one of their throws is commemorative matchbooks, in an event that honors a saint martyred by immolation (other throws include wooden sticks with cotton at the end, a traditional fire-starter).

Jeanne d'Arc

St. Joan of Arc is a very intriguing figure, revered in France as someone who performed the nearly impossible task of rallying that country to defeat the English who threatened the very existence of the French kingdom in the fifteenth century (although sometimes she has been specifically associated with conservative political causes). She is both religious and secular in her importance and can be seen as a spiritual presence and national symbol, as a powerful female figure and an embodiment of youthful energy, as well as someone who, in the eyes of many, received divine guidance and fulfilled a divinely ordained destiny. She accomplished amazing things in a very short time during a rather short life, while her execution/murder by being burned at the stake provided a dramatic if grisly end to her life, at a remarkably early age and in the context of betrayal and the machinations of evil enemies. She has been the subject of several literary works, including the play by George Bernard Shaw, *Saint Joan*. Amy Kirk-Duvoisin, long a fan of this remarkable woman, seized upon Carnival's opportunities for performance to allow the creation of many versions of Joan through a Mardi Gras parade. Krewe de Jeanne d'Arc is one of a series of Carnival innovations in walking groups over the past century.

Historical Walking Clubs and Parades

Given the carnivalesque nature of Carnival and its associated spirits of satire, disorder, and license to behave in unorthodox ways, there have always been possibilities for creating alternative structures of participation in Mardi Gras. In addition to individual masking and informal group partying and celebration, there have been developments of other new parading traditions, notably walking clubs like the Jefferson City Buzzards and Pete Fountain's Half-Fast Walking Club, to note only two of the best known (Howard; Lind). Both of these groups proceed on Mardi Gras Day itself, generally following the main Uptown parade route but in only semi-organized fashion, which might at times be taken by some observers for casual if costumed strolling. The Buzzards were founded in 1890 and Fountain's group marked its fiftieth anniversary in 2010, but more recently there have been occasional new groups parading. The Downtown Krewe du Vieux parade, established in 1987, for example, processes at night, is made up of smaller, self-contained groups, includes a number of small bands, uses mules or marchers themselves to pull homemade floats, and emphasizes, like several other organizations, satirical themes. Some regard it as having revived and as maintaining the forms and spirit of nineteenth-century Carnival.

Krewe du Vieux's ribald attitude and popularity led to, for example, a new walking parade appearing immediately after it. In 2009 the Krewedelusion was founded by actor Harry Shearer, who organized a small parade that followed Krewe du Vieux on a route through the Marigny neighborhood and then the French Quarter (Reid). Krewedelusion makes its allegiance to parading history explicit in its mission statement: "By establishing a Foundation, appointing a Benevolent Ruler and embracing the forms and traditions of New Orleans' Satirical Parading Krewes, our mission is to save the Universe, beginning at its center, New Orleans" (http://www.facebook. com/KreweDelusion). Harry Shearer, a part-time resident of New Orleans, is an engaged citizen, appearing at City Council meetings and Planning Commission meetings, and his creation of a new parading group is, like that of the founders of other new parades, an important and effective form of activism.

Transplants and the Creation of New Parades

One significant factor in Downtown Mardi Gras is the key role of transplants, people who were not raised in New Orleans but who, after moving here, have become actively involved in creating new Carnival traditions. Transplants have an important role to play in new Downtown Mardi Gras, as evidenced by the example of Matt and Jennifer Johnson, who also became part of another, even newer January 6 parade. Matt and Jennifer moved here more recently but—like Ann Witucki and Dawn Sprague (who appear in chapter 6) and Devin De Wulf, founder of the Red Beans krewe (see chapter 4)—have always felt drawn to New Orleans and its culture. In 2008 they bought a small condo in the city; in 2010 they moved to Baton Rouge, and in 2014 they relocated to New Orleans permanently. Like many newcomers, they felt drawn to move to New Orleans after the levee failures, the disaster having made it clear to them how much they valued the city's culture, especially its music. Their first Mardi Gras experience came in 2009, after they had put down roots in the form of their first property here. Invited to attend parades by a New Orleans neighbor, they began to participate in a parade in Baton Rouge. Now they both ride in a New Orleans Uptown parade, King Arthur (from a connection made at their church, St. Mark's United Methodist Church, located in the French Quarter) and a new Downtown krewe, the Not-So-Secret Society of the Elysian Fields Mardi Gras krewe, also known as "La Société pas si secrète des Champs-Élysées." Like the Joan of Arc parade, the SdCE (their acronym) celebrates the city's French heritage.

Like the Joan of Arc parade, the Not-So-Secret Society marches on January 6 to commemorate the beginning of Carnival. Like the Phunny Phorty Phellows, this streetcar krewe rides public transport, in a privately hired streetcar. But while the Phunny Phorty Phellows run Uptown, this new group rides the recently opened Rampart Street streetcar. Founded by David Roe, a longtime New Orleans resident and avid Renaissance Fair member, the krewe shares with other new parades openness to Mardi Gras Downtown and an egalitarian openness to members. The costs are low ($50 fee for returning members, $100 for new), and the krewe is open to both men and women. The Johnsons' connection started, as many social activities do, with an encounter in a local bar, in this case, Buffa's, a bar known for its music and food, located on Esplanade Avenue, at the boundary of the French Quarter. The Johnsons consider it their local bar, and Matt Johnson began playing trumpet with a band, Some Like It Hot, that performs there every Sunday—now he plays with them regularly in other venues.

Like other new krewes, the Not-So-Secret Society engages in philanthropy, for example, collecting and providing aid to Houston residents after Hurricane Harvey. Two of the krewe's members actually live in Houston. Not only transplants but also non-residents are welcome in some new Downtown krewes (see the other chapters for examples). The Johnsons'

Matt and Jennifer Johnson, La Société pas si secrète des Champs-Élysées. Photo by Robin Roberts.

understanding of the significance of Carnival is relevant to the discussion of St. Joan of Arc Parade. Matt Johnson comments, "Many people don't understand the religious aspect [of Carnival]. It fills in a gap in the church calendar; it fills a void" (interview with Roberts and Wade). Both Matt and Jennifer Johnson demonstrate the social justice commitment found in many of the new Downtown Mardi Gras krewe members: both serve on the St. Mark's United Methodist Church board, Matt is the chair of Staff-Parish Relations, and Jennifer is the Finance Leader and Lay Leader. Matt explains the misconceptions he notices about Downtown Mardi Gras. "People don't understand that Mardi Gras happens throughout the city ... neighborhoods take their own twist [on Mardi Gras]. Chewbacchus [discussed in chapter 5] is very different from the Not-So-Secret streetcar parade" (interview). Jennifer Johnson notes that "people attending Chew-bacchus would never have thought to cross Esplanade" (Avenue, which divides the French Quarter and the Marigny). Both see the importance of transplants, and are also aware of the delicate nature of their participation as white transplants to the city. They note that even Downtown krewes still tend to be mostly white, and Matt Johnson further explains, "I am careful with my words ... I am careful to say 'I live here now and I try to be a part of here'" (interview).

Krewe de Jeanne d'Arc offers a model of the transformation that can be effected by transplants looking to find a way to belong and to contribute to New Orleans. Excluded from most Uptown parading groups by their gender, and from all by the cost and exclusivity, Kirk-Duvoisin, Amanda Helm, and Antoinette de Alteriis drew on the model of walking parades in the French Quarter to reinvent this tradition in a more inclusive fashion. The parade was founded by Kirk-Duvoisin, who in her role as marketing director for the French Market Corporation in the French Quarter, had a job that reflected her interest in promotion and the city's French heritage. Her enthusiasm led to her creating a parade, where she could not just market but foster artistic celebration of St. Joan.

The Founder's Francophone Vision

The parade is an end-result of Amy Kirk-Duvoisin's thinking about and organizing around the historical/legendary Jeanne d'Arc, Catholic saint, icon of French identity, and indeed a figure embodying a variety of symbolic possibilities. A native of Ohio, Kirk-Duvoisin came to New Orleans in 2004, a year before the hurricane Katrina and the disastrous levee failures. Raised a Catholic, she became particularly aware of and interested in Joan at the age of nineteen (the same age Joan was when she was executed by the English).

The idea of a parade appealed to her background in the theater (she is a playwright who has worked in other capacities in the theater world as well), as a parade involves public performance. Additionally, she felt that New Orleanians, although very open to new ideas and possibilities, liked the new to be tied into the old and familiar; connecting the parade and Joan to Mardi Gras brought something new but placed it firmly in the context of already well-established tradition. Plus, although private celebration of Carnival might begin on January 6 (there is, for example, the old-line Twelfth Night Revelers organization and their ball), there was little in the way of public activity to mark the occasion other than the availability of king cakes (the circular coffee cake–like pastry that traditionally is available on January 6) and the Uptown street car ride of the Phunny Phorty Phellows.

In a series of factors, Kirk-Duvoisin realized the wealth of possibilities for public performance, artistic creation, and celebration of St. Joan. The French heritage of New Orleans, the Orléans/New Orleans connection, the local Catholicism, the St. Joan statue, the January 6 date, even the local popularity of king cake, the ritual food of Mardi Gras that may involve a playful coronation as part of its consumption (Joan was importuned by her visions to save the king of France, and she did in effect bring about the coronation of Charles VII as king), all tied in with New Orleans and Carnival, whose principal form of expression is the parade. In this material, Kirk-Duvoisin saw its rich potential for a Mardi Gras krewe and parade. However, those locals to whom she broached the Joan festival idea were not sufficiently enthusiastic or supportive for her to create such an event. Then she noticed that January 6, the Feast of the Epiphany, sometimes has been considered Joan's birthday (in the early fifteenth century peasant births were not recorded, and Joan herself was not even certain of the *year* of her birth—probably 1412—but one historical document indicates January 6 and some biographers have accepted this as at least a possibility), although her feast day is in May. Hoping to gather like-minded people, and to inspire others to participate, Kirk-Duvoisin turned to social media. Her invitation to participate via this medium is characteristic both of Downtown Mardi Gras and its use of online resources to recruit members.

Kirk-Duvoisin recalls that, as she began working on the first parade, she found New Orleans to be a place in which personal connections are particularly important and in which those connections sometimes seem particularly fortuitous. Reading Kirk-Duvoisin's posting in a Nola.com Mardi Gras forum that she needed an equestrian Joan of Arc, someone who wrote in mentioned a neighbor, Caye Mitchell, who already rode as one of the Lady Godivas, a group of women who ride on horses costumed as the legendary Godiva in the Muses parade (as Lady Godiva was famous for riding naked, perhaps costumed is not entirely the right word, but the parading Godivas wear scuba suits that have been airbrushed to suggest naked bodies—and also keep the riders warm on chilly nights—and have other regalia).

Mitchell agreed to be the first Joan (with her fiancé, who owned a knight costume, portraying the Bastard of Orléans—that is, the illegitimate brother of the Duc d'Orléans and the commander of the royal forces at Orléans

Amy Kirk-Duvoisin, Founder and Flaming Heretic. Photo by Kim Welsh. Permission of Krewe de Jeanne d'Arc.

who became a key comrade of Joan during the famous siege) for the first St. Joan parade in 2009, and the growing organization of the parade attracted other people to be involved. In fact, the first parade (which was compromised by bad, rainy weather) included multiple Joans representing different aspects of Joan of Arc: the warrior Joan in armor on horseback (Mitchell), a peasant Joan (Corinne Bachaud, a McGehee School student), the imprisoned Joan (Australia James, a New Orleans Center for the Creative Arts student who had played Joan in a production of Shaw's *St. Joan* and who recited an appropriate monologue from the play), and a sainted Joan (Kelley Faucheux), also on horseback and attired in gold like the gilded Joan statue. In 2010 Kirk-Duvoisin herself donned a heretic's hat (the historical Joan wore such a hat after her condemnation and its inscription is known) to portray the Joan accused of (and, indeed, burned at the stake for) heresy. That the founder chose to portray this version of Joan points to the reclamation of her as a heroine as well as the importance of various aspects of the feminine that the different portrayals of Joan evoke. There is also attention to education with the essay and monologue, with their emphasis on promoting images of strong women for girls. Jeanne d'Arc holds many costume workshops, an annual St. Joan day conference, filled with presentations and history, and a celebration of the saint's Feast Day, in addition to other social events.

The parade's feminist emphasis on strong women and education is allied with the emphasis on connections and culture of France. Kirk-Duvoisin's husband, a New Orleans native of French descent (she was originally Amy Kirk), urged her from an early point to get local schools involved (schoolgirls in France are much involved in the annual May 8 parade, which celebrates VE Day but includes a Joan connection and is indeed celebrated on the day the Siege of Orléans was lifted), and the group's Joans have tended to be high school students. In fact, the St. Joan Project group has instituted a 250-word essay written by students as a means of selecting Joans. Although originally there was interest in selecting Joans from girls who spoke French and had other interests in French culture, the essay asks students to write about how they see themselves as being like Joan of Arc. They still should be students of French and able to speak some French, and the St. Joan group considers New Orleans's historical connection to France and French culture to be something of importance to the parade and to the St. Joan organization. (The French consulate in New Orleans initially took a wait-and-see attitude toward the St. Joan group and its activities, but has since warmed to the idea; a newsletter published by the French Embassy in Washington has profiled the parade, as has the magazine *France-Amérique*.) Amy Kirk-Duvoisin, then, has seen her dream of cultural celebration and stronger ties between Orléans and New Orleans realized. Despite or perhaps because of its openness to a wide range of participants, its emphasis on do-it-yourself artistic production, and its link to the city's French heritage, Krewe de Jeanne d'Arc has grown and prospered.

Claiming Space for Jeanne d'Arc

Having a parade on January 6 fit St. Joan's putative birthday, but that date was already claimed by an all-male Carnival group. Part of Downtown Mardi Gras is its insistence that there should always be room for new celebrations, but growth can lead to competition for space and attention. Based on the liturgical calendar, the Carnival season begins on January 6. Traditionally, the all-male Phunny Phorty Phellows mark the opening of Mardi Gras season, parading in the Uptown section of New Orleans. This revival of the nineteenth-century group began in 1982, riding the St. Charles streetcar and holding a countdown to the beginning of Carnival. Like the other krewes discussed in this book, the Phunny Phorty Phellows group looks to historical Carnival for its roots; an all-male group with this name marched after Rex on Mardi Gras Day, beginning and ending in the late nineteenth century (http://www.phunnyphortyphellows.com/history/). Since 2009, the Phunny Phorty Phellows have had a competitor for their first-day of Carnival celebration in the Krewe de Jeanne d'Arc. These two organizations reflect a geographical and cultural divide in the city; as noted in the introduction, New Orleans's Uptown/Downtown split has been significant throughout the city's history

The gender binary implied in each parade's name is significant. The Phunny Phorty Phellows mask, celebrate with inebriation, and revel in their tie to traditional, male-dominated Mardi Gras. Historically, male-dominated Mardi Gras exhibited its dismissive attitude toward women not just through its subordination of women's participation but also through the themes of floats. In 1880, for example, Momus, an elite Uptown parade, used the figure of Joan of Arc to oppose women's rights. Karen Leathem explains its significance for Francophone New Orleans, "Betrayed by a jealous general, tried by the English and sentenced and burned to death for wearing trousers—a warning to all strong-minded women who favor the bloomer costume" (81). The following year, the Phunny Phorty Phellows explicitly criticized women with their parade theme: "Ye Women Fair: Eccentricities of the Fair Sex." Leathem explains that its attack on women was recognized by the public; she cites another newspaper, the *Daily Picayune*, which described the parade as "a travesty of the Women's Rights' Doctrine" (82).

In contrast, the Joan of Arc organization exemplifies the openness typical of new Downtown Mardi Gras in particular: the parade celebrates images of strong women, not only Joan of Arc but also other female figures including nuns and Amazons, is open to various sub-krewes, and features women and men as members. The Krewe of Jeanne d'Arc's decision to parade on January 6 "displeased some onlookers by causing an older organization [the Phunny Phorty Phellows] to give up its exclusive claim to the Jan. 6 starting date of the Carnival Season," according to Doug MacCash, who covers Mardi Gras for the *Times-Picayune*/nola.com (MacCash, "The first downtown"). And now there is a third contender, another streetcar parade that takes place on the Rampart Street line. But this group, the Not-So-Secret Society of the Elysian Fields, is careful not to conflict with the Phunny Phorty Phellows, deliberately starting a half hour later than they do, and thus ceding them rights to "first parade."

Gender politics rear its head when I ask Helm about the Phunny Phorty Phellows, and she is quick to point out that the group is only a recent twentieth-century revival of the nineteenth-century group. In addition, Helm tells a story of an ancestor of hers, a woman who traveled to New Orleans for Mardi Gras in the late nineteenth century. The family retains a letter she wrote from New Orleans, where she describes the Phunny Phorty Phellows as parading on Mardi Gras day, thus proving, says Helm, that the Phellows' claim to be the first parade of the season is suspect. Helm's father sent her the letter pointing out, with some acidity, that Joan of Arc deserved the credit for being first. Helm notes that despite their parade being much larger than Phunny Phorty Phellows, the newspaper always lists the Joan of Arc parade second. While the krewe is open to men and women, Helm admits that "we are a female-dominated krewe" (interview). This gender conflict, then, is not resolved—unless you consider that, with the much larger crowds and impact, Krewe de Jeanne d'Arc has their victory over the Phunny Phorty Phellows.

Parading as Art

While Kirk-Duvoisin founded the parade, like many founders she has involved others in important roles in the krewe. These three women share a common vision, grounded in the figure of St. Joan, medieval costuming and handmade throws, and French culture. Yet how each woman fulfills her duties in the krewe has shaped and guided its development. These other leaders have put their stamp on the organization. Krewe de Jeanne d'Arc, like other Downtown Mardi Gras groups, prides itself on its unique and handcrafted throws. Much of the artwork and graphics are produced by a member of "the A-Team," Amanda Helm, another transplant who also serves as the group's membership coordinator. She sees her role as encouraging others to follow her artistic endeavors in creating original, handmade throws. Her aesthetic sensibility is echoed throughout the krewe, and Helm actively teaches others how to create special, handcrafted items. A business marketing professor at Xavier University, Helm explains, "I got the job at Xavier so that I could move here" (interview with Roberts, October 25, 2017). Her story reveals the ways that New Orleans calls to people and provides them with creative outlets for their talents, in her case specifically through a Downtown Mardi Gras krewe.

Thanks to Helm's insistence and willingness to teach others the necessary skills, the krewe's throws reveal an emphasis on craft and handiwork. Candles, specially decorated with a tag noting the parade as well as a cardboard guard to protect against the drip of hot wax, were passed out and matches were used to light many of these white tapers, although keeping them lit while parading or even in the slightly breezy night proved difficult. The intent was to hand out 598 candles to celebrate the saint's 598th birthday so that attendees could participate in a sort of roving birthday cake. Kirk-Duvoisin sees both the distribution of matches and a performance by fire dancers (the performance was eliminated after the 2016 parade) before the parade as referencing Joan's execution by burning. Instead of these features being sacrilegious or inappropriately macabre, Kirk-Duvoisin sees the inclusion of these allusions to Joan's dying as "taking control" of this fact. The audience has relished the creation of a special St. Joan matchbook, which changes from time to time, and the matchbook is a much sought-after Carnival "throw." The walkers provide the "throws" expected of a Carnival parade (here mostly handed out rather than tossed) to people along the route. The parade's items include miniature images made by a New Orleans nun of St. Catherine of Alexandria, who was one of the supernatural voices heard by Joan of Arc. Another unique throw is ceramic butterflies, referencing the story that Joan's actual banner was followed by white butterflies; the St. Joan Project wants throws to reflect Joan's story, the times in which she lived, or her Catholic or French associations.

The throws are all handmade, harking back to traditional Mardi Gras. The creation of these throws is taken very seriously, with the krewe holding several workshops during the year to teach techniques and share ideas. This attention to detail is part of the founder's vision: Amy Kirk-Duvoisin has said that "she first saw the procession as performance art" (MacCash, "The New Mardi Gras"). As MacCash says, "the handmade throws lovingly

Amanda Helm. Photo by Kim Welsh. Permission of Krewe de Jeanne d'Arc.

passed out by most of the New Orleans Mardi Gras parades are works of art" ("The New Mardi Gras"). The handcrafted nature and themes of these throws reflect the parade's emphasis on an intimate performance and the participant's commitment to small crafts, traditionally feminine activities. By making these throws desirable and handing them to individuals in the crowd, the krewe emphasizes personal interaction and small-scale artistic production. These features result in a unique and sometimes spiritual experience of parading, appropriate for the parade's namesake.

Helm explains, "I love the organic nature of the parade . . . there is a magical connection, a personal connection as you hand someone a handmade throw" (interview with Roberts). She finds a creative outlet in creating graphic designs and unique throws, and sees the contact between parade and parade-watcher as art itself: "it's an exhilarating short-term fleeting moment of art" (interview). In addition, Helm values seeing the artistic growth and development of new members, as they move from buying the handmade throws from the krewe in their first year, to producing original and beautiful throws as they gain confidence in their own vision and crafting abilities. As membership director and in her leadership role, Helm guides new members and encourages them, teaching members how to use Microsoft Publisher, helping them identify open-source medieval manuscript images. Helm designs the krewe's collectible playing cards and designed a new logo for the group's tenth anniversary. The logo, which includes Joan of Arc's actual coat of arms, was revised to acknowledge the group's emphasis: the crown is tilted to represent the krewe's whimsical take on Joan's story, including matchbook throws, "Joanie on the Pony" references to the statue in the French Quarter. Helm also added four teardrops to the design, to represent the rain that marked the first parade. In addition, each member receives a certificate with a unique border copied from actual medieval manuscripts. She adapts the image, cleaning it up and adding color, as she does also for an annual photobook that features members' costumes and their unique handcrafted throws. Helm also maintains the krewe's website.

Helm sees the parade itself as an art form. Her church team from Wisconsin found the 2009 parade very disorganized, and attributed this aspect to it being the parade's first year. But as Helm explains, "then it dawned on me—this is it—it's organic. This is the art form. The leader doesn't know. She has no control, who shows up, how they are interpreting the focus on Joan of Arc. There is so much room for individual expression . . . it was kind of crazy but beautiful" (interview). Helm defines her decision to move to the city as being shaped by this magical experience of the parade.

St. Joan as a Symbol of Female Strength and Spirituality

From her first experience as audience member, Helm has maintained her focus on the spiritual aspects of the parade. The specifics of a strong female saint are also important to Helm, who relishes the promotion of this female icon. While not Catholic, Helm appreciates the spiritual aspect of the parade. The prayer cards she designs always contain a prayer written by a krewe member, and the messages are inspirational. The group sees Joan of Arc as a woman who worked to make change happen, and who had the courage to make a difference. The members of the Krewe of Jeanne d'Arc see a parallel in their commitment to the city of New Orleans, its recovery, and their organization's impact on Twelfth Night celebrations.

The St. Joan Project has taken care to point out that the group is secular in nature; it has maintained a certain distance from religious adherents of Joan, but has inevitably attracted people interested in St. Joan for religious reasons, whether the very devout (in a city with many serious Catholic practitioners and conservative strands of Catholicism) or people who may no longer attend church but who retain certain psychological ties to Catholicism such as a devotion to saints. One of the several Joans told Frank de Caro that she considered it "an honor" to have portrayed the saint.

Amanda Helm's experience is typical of many transplants who find the city has an irresistible spiritual pull. After a magical night in the city while she was visiting during college, Helm made it a point to visit New Orleans at least once a year. Horrified by the disaster that threatened the city she loved in 2005, Helm felt called to help the city. Helm describes the experience as a conversion, where "a passing interest" in the city "became an obsession" (interview). She joined numerous church volunteer groups that traveled to the city for rebuilding projects; one year, she came on four such trips. While here in 2008, she saw Kirk-Duvoisin's announcement of the first St. Joan Parade for January 6, 2009. By this time a leader of the church group trip, she persuaded half of her members to join her in participating in the parade. Despite bad rain and cold weather, she found the experience of a walking parade spiritually powerful, and she has participated in every parade. While she is not Catholic, Helm finds the experience of the parade very powerful and spiritual. Her sub-group is the Voices of Joan Battalion, and she plays the character of the Archangel Michael, one of the three saints through whom Joan heard God speaking. Helm remarks that she was "a little envious that St. Joan heard God's voices so clearly, and that she knew what God wanted" (interview).

Another Leader's View: Family and Structure
in the St. Joan Parade

Antoinette de Alteriis, the third member of the "A-Team" that runs the Joan of Arc organization, similarly lauds her group's impact on Carnival. As costume director, she has a critical role in maintaining the parade's unique medieval look. Her organizational skills are essential to the parade's success, and to the krewe's outreach missions. The organization has a crowd spotter, who takes photographs and extrapolates the number on the streets to view the parade. For 2017, according to this count, there were over 27,000 people in the Quarter for the parade. De Alteriis points out that the Joan of Arc parade evokes solemnity and majesty, in contrast to other Mardi Gras groups. She describes the crowd reaction thus: "when they see the tableaux, they're in awe" (interview with Roberts, October 24, 2017).

De Alteriis also notes that in addition to growing through new members every year, the group has also formalized its structure, now having a board of directors and a coordinator of volunteers, Dottie Watson. She attributes the growth to the krewe's low membership fee (as little as $100, $50 for non-parading members), and their efforts to raise money through the sale of throws and a Café Press site where they sell merchandise. In addition, the organization is run frugally because the work is done by volunteers. Other features that de Alteriis feels make Joan of Arc unique include, as she states with pride, "we are the only krewe who costumes our security in historic, on-theme outfits" (interview). (While the Chewbacchus parade has costumed security, the Redshirts, the members buy their own shirts.) Attired in medieval garb as the Knights of Orleans, the security workers relish being so much a part of the scene. The group's creative and thrifty artisan work includes taking car sun shields and turning them into knight's armor, a very economical and clever adaptation.

While Kirk-Duvoisin and Helm moved here after Katrina, de Alteriis moved here in June 2005, just before the levee failures in August of that year. She had moved here to run the Ripley's Believe It or Not attraction. Like her home, the Ripley's building was damaged, and it closed for good in 2007. Despite this tumultuous beginning, de Alteriis loves New Orleans, describing it as "having the benefits of a big city with the feel of community of a small one" (interview). Her dedication to the Joan of Arc parade is made possible by the other members of the "A-Team," who she describes as having a sisterly relationship of love and support. De Alteriis knew

Antoinette de Alteriis. Photo by Kim Welsh. Permission of Krewe de Jeanne d'Arc.

Kirk-Duvoisin after Katrina, and they live near each other in Metairie, a suburb of New Orleans. "We all respect each other and Amy's [Kirk-Duvoisin] vision" (interview). Her description of the organization's leaders (who include parade marshal Rafael Monzon and the manager of horses and riders, Caye Mitchell), in familial terms, is echoed in de Alteriis's description of the group overall.

To de Alteriis, the family aspects of the parade are important in terms of its commitment to community and also to continuity. De Alteriis stresses that her parade is "family-friendly" (interview), and it is unusual in that it allows children over the age of six to march. She describes a child who participated in the first parade, dressed as a sheep, who now, ten years later, is costuming as a shepherd, herding other child-sheep. Similarly, she recounts with pride the involvement of Kristen Palmer, a New Orleans councilwoman, who participated in the parade because of her sister, an artist who belongs to the krewe, and her mother, who brought the king cakes the first year the group paraded.

In addition to allowing children to participate in costume, the krewe also holds events directed at children. At least twice a year, Mitchell, who manages therapy horses and supplies the horses for the parade, holds an event called "Joanie's Ponies," where local children are invited to ride horses for free. This service for locals is greatly appreciated by residents, but de Alteriis also points to the impact the krewe has on tourism. Their fan page is visited by many out-of-towners, and she says that her friends in the hospitality industry see the impact of the parade on hotel rooms and restaurants. Many come for the parade and stay the weekend, despite having to work around the hefty prices charged for the Sugar Bowl weekend, usually held just before Joan of Arc's January 6 running date. In addition to the parade and the children's events, the organization also presents a scholarly symposium on Joan of Arc and related medieval topics, and honors Joan by laying a wreath at her French Quarter statue for her saint's day. The spiritual aspects of the parade are important to de Alteriis, who is Catholic, but she emphasizes the organization's openness to all faiths, explaining that they have "Wiccans, Protestants, Baptists, and many other faiths" (interview). In addition to the emphasis on spirituality and ceremony, the procession also stresses a historical vision.

Historical Accuracy

The group has been concerned with retaining historical accuracy and retaining Joan's historical interest. For example, bagpipers really did precede Joan at Orléans in 1429, Scotsmen who had joined the French to fight against their mutual enemy, the English. More recently a krewe member has created a cannon; cannons, fairly new at the time of the historical Joan, played a significant role in Joan's actual strategy. For the first parade costumes were improvised, with people drawing material and inspiration from various sources (including the New Orleans familiarity with costuming techniques and the tendency for New Orleanians to own costumes and parts of costumes), but the group has run costume workshops and additional effort was made for the second parade (although of course those costuming are inevitably limited by available materials).

As with other facets of the parade, the group has stressed historical authenticity in costuming, although achieving the "spirit" of medieval costume is important (and the costumes of Joan's many peasant followers were relatively simple). People involved in the Society for Creative Anachronism, who have considerable interest in reproducing medieval-style costumes, have begun to show an interest in the parade, and the organization has attracted people who enjoy dressing for Renaissance fairs and similar occasions. De Alteriis, one of the group's leaders, has been and maintains active participation in Renaissance fairs. Artist members are often active in creating costumes. A few costumes are owned by the krewe, although costumes are mostly the responsibility of individual members. That costuming is left up to individuals addresses an important feature of new Downtown Mardi Gras: it is both affordable and requires the artistry and skill of its participants. That all items are handmade reinforces the vision of St. Joan's time-period, pre–mass production, but the throws also endorse the value of small artistic work or craft, traditionally associated with women.

Throws and Their Significance

The range of perspectives and world views appears in the variety of the artifacts handed out by the parade marchers. Their investment in these items is significant, for they have spent many hours devising and creating the throws. The artistic, handmade throws contrast with Uptown throws made in China, of plastic, and selected by committee rather than the individuals in the krewes. Jeanne d'Arc throws evoke aspects of St. Joan, some with humor and some with high seriousness. One of the most common throws is matchbooks featuring the krewe's logo in gold on a black background, "Krewe de Jeanne d'Arc." The matchbooks are identified by year, and have slightly different covers. 2017 matchbooks, for example, depict an image of Joan in flames, with words forming a square border around the image: Saint/Joan of Arc/ Flaming Heretic/1412–1431. The dark humor comes from the krewe's distribution of matches to honor a saint who was martyred by fire. A "Happy Birthday, Joan!" card recognizes the symbolism of January 6, with copy on the other side that extols Joan of Arc's virtues: "we continue to celebrate you and your inner fire, fierceness, holiness, and goodness. . . . We admire your tenacity and hope to emulate this as we continue to revive and ignite our City's creativity and blessed uniqueness." Like a prayer card, the throw reminds us of Joan of Arc's spiritual qualities, but also links her to New Orleans's rebirth after Katrina and connects Carnival paradings with lofty and significant city goals. "Please continue to stand by us with your sword of fearlessness and your golden light of faith, and help guide us in our battles, from hurricanes to hopelessness," the invocation implores. Part humorous and part serious, playing cards featuring the historical personages with whom Joan interacted are also prized throws. These cards could be used in a card game, but they also provide historical information. When you turn them over, each card contains a specific, highly detailed account of the figure's history. Some are famous, like "The Bastard of Orleans," but other are less well known, such as "La Hire," one of Joan's compatriots.

Very somberly, women and men dressed as medieval religious figures hand out sprigs of real rosemary, for remembrance. In keeping with Mardi Gras tradition, there are also doubloons, but befitting the medieval period, these are wooden coins. Decorated with the year, there are also unique coins with the king's or queen's name upon them, coins that proclaim "Joanie on the Pony," and other incarnations of the saint. Scrolls of various kinds are handed to the crowds, usually with a historical or moral statement on them. One throw from 2016 was a hand-carved wheel, with a ribbon and a calligraphy quotation from Joan of Arc: "Be Strong." Many different types of handmade necklaces are created as throws; some of the necklaces include images of Joan's face on a silver chain, others a highly detailed sword on a braided leather rope. Rarest of all, and most prized, are full-size decorated swords. The throws, then, represent the participants' desire to share historical information and bestow gifts. They educate the crowd about St. Joan and her milieu, and have both humor and spiritual aspects. In their celebration of female strength, the throws and the parade create a feminist message, appropriating St. Joan for our times.

The Parade's Growth and Changes: An Overview

Some aspects of the parade's route and logistics have changed since its inception. In 2010 the parade began at the statue of Sieur de Bienville, the French Canadian founder of New Orleans, located in a tiny park between Decatur and North Peters Streets. The Bienville portrayer was eliminated in the 2016 parade, as the parade no longer begins at the Bienville statue; the starting point has been moved to a position further down North Peters Street, to allow for more needed lining-up space. The performance of fire dancers was likewise eliminated after the 2016 parade, largely because the group could no longer afford to give them the space needed, though also both eliminating an expense and increasing the safety of the parade and parade-goers, who have increased in numbers. (The krewe itself has grown larger; between 2012 and 2016 it grew from 50 to 117 paying members, with growth of all classes of members [not all pay dues; for example, there are now around 79 foot soldiers who volunteer to provide security and do not pay] from 66 to 289; for the 2016 parade the size of the crowd was estimated as being around 25,000.) Instead of fire dancers, artist Annie Lousteau, a St. Joan krewe member, created what Kirk-Duvoisin has called "colorful flamelike batons" which will be used by a local dance troupe, the Organ Grinders, as a sort of replacement for the actual fire dancers. The parade proceeded up Conti Street, then right along Chartres Street, across the cathedral end of Jackson Square, further along Chartres, finally turning right down St. Philip Street to the gilded equestrian statue of "Jeanne d'Arc, Maid of Orleans, 1412–1431," situated on the edge of the French Market between the again diverging lanes of Decatur and North Peters Streets. As one participant put it in regard to the 2010 parade, this was *not* "a big, raucous Mardi Gras parade," and she appreciated its low-keyed-ness and being able, at the end of the parade, to share with strangers the king cakes she had brought.

The 2016 Parade: A Specific Illustration

The 2016 parade, with music provided by bagpipers as well as a New Orleans–style brass band, made three "stops," once at the Historic New Orleans Collection at 400 Chartres Street, to be toasted by the consul general of France, once at St. Louis Cathedral, where the Very Rev. Philip Landry blessed Joan's sword, and finally at Washington Artillery Park, near the Joan of Arc statue and the Mississippi River. Caye Mitchell rode again as Warrior Joan in 2016, and a young woman, Margaux Schexsnider, the student contest winner, also rode on horseback as the principal Joan, with Martha Pinney as Joan the shepherdess (with life-size pull-toy wooden sheep), Mary Langston on a horse tricycle as Joan the Leader, Rebecca Sell wearing a "flaming" dress as Joan the Heretic, Holly Connor as "ghost" Joan fighting to clear her name, and portrayers of St. Joan with her angels and Joan on trial. Those who walked in the parade were dressed in "medieval" costume and a few pulled a medieval-style cart (made by Delgado College students and now kept in storage for future use).

The French consul general Gregor Trumel appeared high above the parading group on the balcony of the Historic New Orleans's Chartres Street facility to offer a ritual toast to St. Joan. He spoke in French, echoing Kirk-Duvoisin's idea that if there had been no Joan there would have been no Orléans and if no Orléans there could have been no New Orleans. Below, a participant dressed as an executioner kept the crowds back and participants called out "Vive la France." Though the French have been a bit slow in warming to the Joan parade, perhaps particularly by conservative political groups because of the use of St. Joan, Consul General Trumel has been exceptionally supportive of the parade. His wife was a medieval studies major and the couple were married in Chinon, where the historical Joan first encountered the Dauphin who was to become (thanks to her) King Charles VII. The second stop involved the blessing of the sword. This part of the ceremony was created when Monsignor Kern, rector of St. Louis Cathedral, took an interest in the parade, which passes by the very doors of his church. When Kern passed away, the Very Rev. Philip Landry, the current rector, agreed to continue the ritual of sword blessing.

Finally, the parade streamed along Decatur Street, in a sense covering territory it had already covered (though on parallel Chartres Street) until it reached the Washington Artillery Park, where steps lead up to an overlook (the view is of Jackson Square in one direction, of a parking area and the approach to the Mississippi across railroad tracks in the other). Here the parade's knights cleared a pathway up the steps for the king, who represented Charles VII, the historic king of France "saved" by Joan, who was duly crowned. The pathway was marked by the Amazons, who made two lines with upheld swords and shields, through which the king and queen mounted the stairs. Then the crowning of the krewe's king and the ingestion of king cake took place. Because the parade supposedly celebrated Joan's birthday, the crowds sang the traditional happy birthday song to her. A large faux cake with illuminated, battery-powered birthday candles, sat at the base of the steps. (King cake is the New Orleans food most associated with Carnival and only made and eaten during the season, a custom that has changed in recent years, however, especially as cakes of the same type have been made for various occasions.) Whereas in 2010 king cake was provided by the group, in 2016 attendees were urged (emphasis added): "*Bring your own king cake* to eat your first king cake along with the king and Joan." The inability to feed the crowd provides an index to the parade's success, as it is now included in *Arthur Hardy's Mardi Gras Guide*, and despite the inclement weather in 2016 and 2017, there were large crowds all along the route.

Examining this experience from the viewpoint of one of its "Joans" helps explain its meaning to its participants.

A Krewe Member's View: Why She Parades

Mary Langston has been featured as one of the Joans in the parade since 2010. While she had been active in Mardi Gras krewes before the disaster, Mary Langston also felt the pull of Downtown Mardi Gras, and greatly increased her participation in Carnival after the disaster. She explains, "After Katrina, I realized that we can't let the culture of New Orleans die. It wasn't dying, but there was less interest. I had never gone to see Mardi Gras Downtown before. After the evacuation experience, I realized that the culture here really is different and worth preserving" (interview with Roberts, September 11, 2017). She elaborates the importance of Mardi Gras by explaining that, until she rode in the Muses Parade the first Mardi Gras after Katrina in 2006, she didn't feel that she was truly back in the city. The experience was very emotional (as I can attest, having also ridden in that parade), with tears being shed by float-riders and parade-goers both. Parade-goers shouted "Thank you for parading! We love you," and those cries were reflected back as riders shouted "Thank you for coming to the parade! We love you" (interview with Roberts).

Langston felt herself drawn to the new grassroots organizations that developed after the disaster; she read about them in the local newspaper, researched them online, and invited herself to the krewes. For Jeanne d'Arc, she located Amy Kirk-Duvoisin's e-mail, and sent a note explaining she enjoyed creating costumes, and could she join? An enthusiastic response led to her participation. She describes the krewe's leaders as very open and inclusive. The parade, she says, "is constantly evolving. If there is a way to include someone or something, they do it" (interview).

As other members often do, Langston used her creativity to add to the parade's motifs and impact. At first, Langston considered riding a live horse, as some participants do, but she felt the cost was prohibitive. While joining the krewe wasn't expensive, renting a horse, a groom to lead it, and someone to clean up the horse droppings seemed too much to spend. So, she turned to an artist friend, Jacob Martin, who led a workshop for Langston and others to create papier mache horse and other animal heads. Langston's vision of herself on a horse materialized, but with a horse's body mounted on a large tricycle. In addition to its uniqueness and beauty (it is a white horse), Langston also has a ride she can use and reuse, not only in the Jeanne d'Arc parade but also in other parades.

Like Helm and de Alteriis, Langston identifies an uplifting, mystical aspect to the parade. She enjoys the historical aspects and the educational

Mary Langston on her pony. Photo by Kim Welsh. Permission of Krewe de Jeanne d'Arc.

mission of the krewe, but nothing compares, she insists, to the experience of marching in the French Quarter by torchlight. Langston is not Catholic, and she does identify a tension between the members who revere St. Joan as a Catholic saint, and who wish to emphasize her sacred and spiritual aspects, and those members who see her as a figure of female empowerment, and who are also drawn to parody and possibly bad-taste jokes about flames. Yet Langston says that this disagreement is not acrimonious, and that the krewe has enough events and participation that all feel included. A core feature is the educational aspect of the krewe: as Langston describes it, "you are constantly learning what medieval people wore, drank, and about historical personages" (interview). Langston still parades with Muses, and keeps up her activities with her float members, but she acknowledges, "I like the small walking parades better. It's a smaller, more creative, less of a financial burden" than uptown parades (interview). Even more important to her, is the context, where she feels "more connection to audience because you are all at the street level" (interview). In a vivid evocation of the Jeanne d'Arc's unique parading style, Langston describes the powerful emotions she feels "when walking through Jackson Square, by the cathedral by torchlight, and hearing the cathedral bells. For just a moment, it feels like a medieval square. That was magic, to be able to capture that sense, that feeling, for a moment of time" (interview).

In addition to their own krewe members, Jeanne d'Arc also encourages other women's marching groups to parade with them, including the drumming krewe, Skinz n Bonez, (discussed in chapter 2), and the Amazons Benevolent Society, a marching group of breast cancer survivors and supporters (discussed in chapter 6). De Alteriis points to the participation of these groups as an example of the krewe's commitment to women's strength and empowerment. The Amazons belong, de Alteriis explains, because of the Joan of Arc project's "focus on history and focus on strong women" (interview).

Though the St. Joan Project was inaugurated as part of Carnival, Kirk-Duvoisin, Helm, de Alteriis, and others clearly see it as extending beyond Mardi Gras. Like other new Downtown krewes, and indeed Uptown organizations, the Joan of Arc krewe holds activities year-round. In this fashion, it increases group solidarity, provides other occasions for its well-made costumes to be used, and keeps its presence felt in the city. In 2010 they produced a fête or salon several days before the parade, primarily a conference at which panelists explored different aspects of the St. Joan phenomenon, along with a costume-making workshop; the salon (a seventh was recently held at Loyola University, whose Department of Medieval Studies has been a sponsor) and costume workshops have continued. And on February 6, before the debut in the Super Bowl of New Orleans's beloved Saints football team, the group was part of a pep rally for the team in and around the French Market (for which Kirk-Duvoisin happened to be the director of marketing). Blair Davis, 2010's armored Joan, reappeared in costume to lead a procession of Saints supporters to the Joan of Arc statue, and later in the day members of the Joan of Arc organization came to present offerings to the saint at the statue asking for her intercession ("intercep-tion") for the team.

Other parading opportunities include appropriate French holidays; in 2009 they took part in Bastille Day celebrations at the French Market. In May 2010 they joined with the Louisiana Renaissance Fair for a music and costume party at Deutsches Haus (including Renaissance dance and medieval costume–making workshops). On St. Joan's feast day that same month, they planned a jazz funeral and prayers asking for her intercession for the hurricane season and summer, shifting the prayer to account for the Gulf of Mexico oil disaster and joining the protest against the oil company BP after their own ceremony. The St. Joan Project has now held three Feast Day parties at the Beauregard-Keyes House in the French Quarter, near the May 30 date of St. Joan's feast day, and the Alliance Français, the organ-ization devoted to the promotion and teaching of the French language in New Orleans, has offered a special class to Project members. According to a recent communication particularly directed to new members, plans called for a walk to the St. Joan statue after the Feast Day party to call attention to its regilding and repair. And some members of the krewe were part of the cast of a video which aimed to call attention to the creation of a mural depicting French Quarter life. Clearly members are interested in a broader view of Joan (and French culture and New Orleans), not just Joan as the focus for a Mardi Gras parade (though Amanda Helm, the membership director, has represented St. Joan in the Red Beans krewe's parade on Lundi Gras, an interesting example of cross-krewe participation). This crossover is also typical of Carnival participation, as succeeding chapters will show. As mentioned earlier, Mary Langston, who played Joan the Leader, also has marched with the Amazons, Red Beans, and also is a member of Muses, the Uptown all-female krewe.

Conclusion

The Joan of Arc parade shares several features with other new Downtown Mardi Gras groups. The krewe is historically based, with a strong connec-tion through French association and culture in the city. The famous gilded statue of Joan of Arc, located in Downtown New Orleans on Decatur Street, offers an iconic image of their patron. The city's strong Catholic heritage also comes into play with this new parade, and the group uses the historic New Orleans Collection and the French Consulate as part of their parade activities. While the parade is not a revival of a preceding group, like the Phunny Phorty Phellows or the Black Storyville Baby Dolls discussed in the final chapter, the Joan of Arc organization does reinstate the practice of a French Quarter parade, a historical tradition lost when traditional parades grew too large for French Quarter streets. In addition, the group fits in with another Mardi Gras development since 2000 that increased after Katrina: parades that feature strong female role models. Finally, the three key leaders, Kirk-Duvoisin, Helm, and de Alteriis are all transplants, not from New Orleans but very aware and appreciative of its culture and traditions, a pattern in common with other new Carnival groups. Coming here because they love the city, and shut out from its elite traditional parades, newcomers have adapted and expanded New Orleans Mardi Gras by adding new parades.

Like the other parades examined in this book, Joan of Arc reveals the central role of newcomers in developing Downtown Mardi Gras parades. The group's focus on a powerful female saint, its female leadership, and its emphasis on inclusion, crafts, and humor are features that make it representative of Downtown Mardi Gras. This parade, like all the others discussed in the book, emphasized accessibility, including inexpensive dues. A commitment to marching rather than riding in floats in this and other new Downtown parades enables closer contact between participants and parade-goers. The Krewe of St. Joan emphasizes individual artistic creation, not only of costumes but also of their throws. In this way, new Downtown Mardi Gras draws on a historical New Orleans style of parading, but also with a more contemporary emphasis on creativity, artistry, quirkiness, humor, and inclusiveness.

Yet as the parade celebrates Joan of Arc and the beginning of Carnival, the parade also reveals the tensions in civic performance. The contestation over who has the honor of opening the Carnival season, the gender conflict between The Phunny Phorty Phellows and Joan of Arc, and the romanticization inherent in celebrating a female medieval martyr evokes other themes. The association of St. Joan with a season of frivolity and excess offers an instance of reclamation of Mardi Gras's religious roots.

At the same time, it allows those who wish to celebrate the city's European heritage to revel in their explicit connection to France, a tie strengthened recently when members of the krewe traveled to that country to march in a parade there. According to one Joan portrayer this activity "is not just about a Mardi Gras parade but honoring a sister city and Joan" (interview with Frank de Caro, spring 2010). In its inaugural trip to the

Krewe de Jeanne d'Arc in France: Joan Fox, Antoinette de Alteriis (back row), Amy Kirk-Duvoisin, Amanda Helm (Archangel Michael), Linda Seabright, Martha Pinney (Joan with crown on 2nd row), Carol Lynch (New Orleans Sister City Liaison), Lil Pinney. Permission of Krewe de Jeanne d'Arc.

sister city of Orléans, France, to participate in the Fete de Jeanne d'Arc, the organization has made literal its celebration of New Orleans's ties to France. Antoinette de Alteriis embodied this exchange through her costumes, wearing a French costume loaned by the Orléans Fete in the 2017 New Orleans Jeanne d'Arc parade, and in 2018 wearing her local costume to the parade in France. Achieving international collaboration and honoring the city's French roots is but one measure of this krewe's considerable success. In adding a strong female presence to Carnival in its first parade, in celebrating and championing handmade throws (and by implication, women's traditional handiwork), and including spirituality as an explicit aspect of Carnival, Krewe Jeanne d'Arc has set an ambitious template for other Downtown Mardi Gras krewes to follow.

CHAPTER 2

Skeletons Rising in Skinz n Bonez

Leslie A. Wade

The street dance of skull and bones holds particular emblematic significance for New Orleans, given the city's death-rebirth narrative in the post-Katrina era—bones rising, relics from the past, rattling in the present. The current-day practices of this fascinating tradition of African American men and boys dressing in skeleton costume reflect the vitality of Downtown Mardi Gras, demonstrating the spirit and longevity of this Carnival ritual and the emergence of new, reimagined manifestations. Current skull and bone street performances showcase the interplay of past and present; they also demonstrate the city's fluctuating sense of self, as dense interweavings of identities and outlooks, complex and often ironic, find play in these early-morning Mardi Gras performances. In *All on a Mardi Gras Day: Episodes in the History of New Orleans Carnival*, Reid Mitchell casts the history of Carnival as a chronicle of contestations, with different groups and interests competing at different times for pride of place and authority—between Creole and American, American and immigrant, etc. (3). This chapter places similar emphasis on Carnival's contestatory energies (not necessarily adversarial) and examines how the practices of the skull and bone gangs, continued by generations of the city's African American residents, have enjoyed revitalization in present-day black Carnival, and how the practices have travelled into new locations and contexts, informing the recent emergence of the all-female krewe Skinz n Bonez.

Highlighting an African American folkloric practice that may date back two hundred years, this analysis draws upon the work of Richard Schechner and his famous understanding of ritualistic performance as a "twice-behaved behavior" or "restored behavior" (84). As Schechner points out, patterns are repeated and reenacted, effecting group cohesion and continuance; each iteration, however, allows for variance, for alteration, dependent upon the contingent needs and participants of any given moment. Schechner's basic insight finds rich development in Joseph Roach's acclaimed *Cities of the Dead*, which gives attention to New Orleans culture and the racial dynamics of Carnival. Roach popularized the concept of "surrogation" (1) to illuminate cultural changes and contestatory energies, how, in effect, new performance practices step into gaps created in times of social turbulence and work to recast these practices, often with new political or cultural intent and consequence. Attention to the New Orleans skull and bone tradition demonstrates fascinating instances of such reiterations, as this African American folkloric practice has been resuscitated and recast, contributing to the emergent energy and variant expressions of the Downtown Mardi Gras panoply.

Given the crucial role that the celebration and showcasing of the city's cultural traditions have played in the city's recovery, this analysis of skull and bone performance highlights the passion and determination of those who have carried this Mardi Gras tradition forward; it also emphasizes the migratory dynamic of the practice. This chapter begins with an introduction to the traditions of the North Side Skull and Bones Gang, then documents its recent reinvigoration under the leadership of Bruce "Sunpie" Barnes; it proceeds to an in-depth investigation of a new surrogation of bone-gang performance, the Skinz n Bonez, a feminist enterprise led by Claudia "Mardi Claw" Gehrke. This group of women march in the streets on Mardi Gras drumming and dancing, displayed in skeletal iconography, affirming their passion for New Orleans and its culture while asserting gender solidarity. The chapter gives focus to the origin, leadership, protocols, attitudes, and evolution of this new krewe, then concludes with an examination of North Side and Skinz n Bonez in relation, how these current surrogations of the bone-gang tradition invoke wider contestations of post-Katrina times, often fraught with unease and heated debate, involving issues of racial interplay, rivalry and alliance, affirmation and appropriation. This inquiry raises questions of cross-racial encounter, how relations of engagement might offer new recognitions and new affiliations, and how Downtown Mardi Gras might foster Carnival practices that open new possibilities for a re-envisioned city.

North Side: The Guardians

Understanding of New Orleans performance rituals must begin with a recognition of the city's creolized culture and its deep African American roots. Keith Spera reminds us that New Orleans has often been described as "the northernmost point of the Caribbean" (2), and the city has famously been recognized as a hemispheric point of convergence, where European, American, and African influences have through centuries intermixed and contested, producing a unique cultural amalgam. While not always given due significance in historical accounts of the city, New Orleans's African American legacy has been profound, contributing in a formative fashion to the city's physical, social, spiritual, and artistic life. The African American populace has generated and enriched the celebrations of Mardi Gras. Reid Mitchell cites records from the early 1800s documenting African American Mardi Gras performances, reporting "King of the Wake" at the head of the "great Congo-dance" (7). Roger D. Abrahams et al. view such early performances in light of a "plantation context," as gestures of resistance and life enhancement where "history could be replayed, ancestral styles and subjects reinforced, and new power roles developed that proved incredibly long-lived after emancipation" (6).

The performance of the skull and bones gang is one particular strand in the rich tradition of African American Carnival. The origin of the practice cannot be pinpointed, though it is commonly assumed that the iconography and enactments may have come to New Orleans via the Haitian immigration of the early 1800s (Royce Osborn, interview with Wade, August 7, 2012). Maya Deren's documentary film *Divine Horsemen* shows the imagery of skull and bones in dance rituals of Haiti (Deren), and Royce Osborn has identified elements of Haitian attribution in the costumes of New Orleans Mardi Gras practitioners. Louisiana State University anthropologist Helen A. Regis observes that skeleton costumes are common in Carnival celebrations throughout Africa, the Caribbean, and Latin America (for instance, in the Carnival of Santiago de Cuba). Regis writes that the masquerade practice "honors the dead, comforts the bereaved," and provides connection "to those who came before" ("Skeleton" 180). She also notes how the masquerade can serve as a social equalizer, able to express "bawdy truths and poke fun at the pretensions of the powerful and the hypocrisy of the pieties of the day" (Regis, "Skeleton" 180). In this light the skull and bones masquerade has operated both as a critique of the powerful and a purveyor of community, honoring the dead while drawing awareness to the politics of the present and the promises of the future.

While other African American Mardi Gras practices have gained considerable attention and analysis—such as those of Zulu and the Mardi Gras Indians—the skull and bones gangs have largely gone under the radar of both journalistic and scholarly attention. A scant number of newspaper articles documented the practice in the last decades of the twentieth century. It was the work of documentary filmmaker Royce Osborn that brought the skull and bone gang ritual into wider visibility, as his PBS film *All on a Mardi Gras Day* did much to disclose the practices of black Carnival to a broader audience (Osborn 2003). Significant interest in African American culture has followed in the wake of the Katrina disaster, and the gang tradition has increased its public and scholarly profile (see Costello; Laborde; O'Neill; Welch; Wehmeyer).

The skull and bones practice stands as a captivating yet enigmatic display of Carnival culture. Steeped in the folkways of African American New Orleans, the bone gangs follow a simple yet compelling mode of performance: wandering the neighborhood at dawn of Mardi Day, a small group of men and younger boys meanders the streets, making noise, rattling doors, shaking windows, and frightening onlookers. Dressed in homespun skeleton costumes with papier mache skull headdresses, the revelers wear butcher-aprons sporting such phrases as: "The Worms Go In, The Worms Go Out," "You Next," and "If You Don't Live Right, The Bone Man Is Coming for Ya" ("New Orleans Original Skull and Bones Gang—North Side Skeletons"). The figures are invited into homes to scare children. The skeletons energize the morning, with movements both playful and threatening, casting a surreal and macabre presence, serving as a somber contrast to the license and color of Carnival, cautioning that death is always near.

The North Side Skull and Bones Gang survives as the inheritor and guardian of this deep tradition, which continues to animate Downtown Mardi Gras with intrigue and delight. This bone gang developed out of New Orleans's Treme neighborhood, one of the country's oldest African American districts (its position north of the French Quarter informs the name of the gang). Bruce "Sunpie" Barnes, current chief of North Side, claims that the practice enjoys a near 200-year continuity; he himself has heard anecdotes of skeletons marching in the 1930s (interview with Wade, September 21, 2012). Longtime leader Arthur Regis became chief in the 1940s. Chief Al Morris assumed the mantle in the 1970s; however, the bone gang through the following decades experienced significant diminishment,

North Side Skull and Bones Gang on Mardi Gras Morning. Photo by David Grunfeld. Permission of the *Times-Picayune*/NOLA Media Group.

viewed as something of a relic, unable to draw the interest of new practitioners. Osborn recounts one Mardi Gras where he and Chief Al were the only two skeletons on the streets (Osborn interview). By the time of Katrina, North Side was nearing extinction (Swenson and Etheridge 39).

The lifeblood of the North Side gang issues from its Downtown home in Treme, whose shifting fortunes have intimately affected the gang's history and continuance. Recognized as the "oldest black neighborhood in America" (Rivlin 65), Treme in the nineteenth century became the home of a thriving African American population (including many free people of color), with prosperous businesses, the country's first black newspaper, and vibrantly diverse cultural activity—the origins of jazz are attributed to the slave performances of its Congo Square. Home to famous jazz clarinetist Sidney Bechet and Homer Plessy (of *Plessy v. Ferguson* fame), Treme commands respect as "the epicenter of the city's—and even the nation's—early black culture, spiritual, social, civic, and political life" (Thomas 21).

Treme has continued as a vital incubator of African American performance, though by the time of Katrina the neighborhood was facing many challenges. City planners had dealt a literal and figural blow in the 1960s when an interstate was built along the Claiborne Avenue corridor, Treme's symbolic center. Michael E. Crutcher Jr. notes that Treme was never monolithic, economically or racially, but that the neighborhood had come to house significant pockets of poverty, with "low educational attainment, low-wage occupations, unemployment, violent crime, and drugs" (11).

In 2014 Treme's iconic Circle Food Store, once inundated with flood-waters, reopened with much celebration. However, manager Dwayne Boudreaux noted a shift in the grocery's customer base, with higher numbers of Latinos, international visitors, and affluent whites. He reported: "We now have an imported cheese section that I really couldn't sell before Katrina" (qtd. in Allman, "The New . . . Part 2").

Changes at the Circle Food Store speak to emblematic shifts affecting Treme and the city's African American community at large. A year after the storm, 70 percent of those displaced were African Americans (Klinedinst 66). While there has been an increase in return migration, the city has lost over a hundred thousand black residents (Thomas 23). Working-class black citizens, many employed in the service industries, have felt a widening economic divide. The city has seen its low-income residents increasingly pushed to cheap rental units on its outskirts, leaving New Orleans "wealthier at its core and poorer at its edges" (Morris, "Freret's" 8).

During these years New Orleans witnessed an inrush of entrepreneurially minded newcomers. Treme has drawn many of these transplants, as a preferred residential area (Campanella, "Gentrification"), due to its proximity to the Quarter, architectural beauty, and rich heritage. Home sale prices have climbed more than 40 percent in ten years (Roig-Franzia, "Rebirth" 36). There are now two hundred more white households in Treme than pre-Katrina (Burdeau). This increase in affluent residents—both black and white—have caused tensions to flare over the vaunted performance life of the neighborhood, with attempts to limit music clubs and second-line parades. Longtime residents worry about the changes and whether the neighborhood can retain its soul.

Hurricane Katrina and its subsequent flooding opened both literal and figural spaces within the Treme landscape, what Joseph Roach would call "cavities created by loss" (1). According to Roach, new surrogations step into these openings, performances that reframe memory and reset networks of relations. One can view the current North Side Skull and Bones Gang in this light, as a new iteration of a traditional form, and draw insight from how the skeletons function as a kind of a proxy, registering change, resisting erasure, and recasting their street performance for a changing Treme. This revival also elicits questions regarding authenticity, self-awareness, and the formalization of practices, as North Side has gained a surprising new prosperity, upheld as an icon of Carnival itself.

Many Carnival traditions experienced a reaffirmation and reinvigoration following Katrina, and such was the case with the North Side Skull and Bones Gang. The group has grown from two or three in number to over a dozen—where membership has been capped. This resurgence can be attributed on one level to the leadership of Barnes, who assumed the role of chief after the death of Al Morris in 2007. It can also be credited to a renewed appreciation for the gang itself, which—like much in the wake of Katrina—threatened to disappear altogether. Many more now wish to participate, though its ranks are not open. This feature adds to the enterprise's sense of selectivity and mysterious allure—it is an honor to join in this tradition, and skeletons see themselves as something of a secretive, priestly order.

The North Side gang has emerged as a reinvigorated representative of Treme, and the skeleton street theatre has stepped forward, addressing need, refiguring itself for present times. Perhaps chief among the gang's current service is its affirmation of tradition and insider belonging. Given the rapid changes to the neighborhood and the numbers of those who have not returned, the gang emphasizes a sense of unbroken continuity. According to Barnes, this performance aims at a connection with forebears, with an honoring of African American ancestors, giving "honor to the family spirits that went before them" (qtd. in Litwin).

The skeleton parade seeks connection with the dead but also celebrates the living community. Barnes is adept at working neighborhood crowds, throwing smiles and grimaces, engaging in easy banter. Residents gather on the streets to watch and cajole the gang, who give focus to Mardi Gras antics and play. Barnes cites a family on Villere Street he visits every year, where five generations of women prepare food for the day's celebration— each year they await the arrival of the chief (Barnes interview).

Though the performance of the gang remains energetic and exuberant, the workings of the group have given increased importance to protocol and pattern, as the gang seeks to keep its practices intact and protected. The skeletons as a matter of course visit the Backstreet Cultural Museum (devoted to African American culture and located across the street from St. Augustine Catholic Church, one of the country's oldest black Catholic churches) in the morning and the Mother-in-Law Lounge in the afternoon

(Swenson and Etheridge 37). They keep to long-held methods of costume construction—using wire, newspaper and flour to make the skull-heads; they wear sweatpants or long johns ("long-handle drawers") with bones painted on the chest, hips, arms, and legs. The gang holds to the tradition of all-male membership.

A new layering of ritual has added to this increased sense of regularization and formality. Barnes gathers the gang in the dark of Mardi Gras morning and spends twenty or so minutes in a nearby cemetery before returning to the Backstreet Cultural Museum. There the gang does "ceremonial things" and shares a drink before heading out the door (Barnes interview). Wandering the Treme neighborhood, going into homes, knocking on doors, the skeletons follow the spirit of the day, logging up to fifteen miles in the procession (Cox); throughout, Barnes requires decorum and dignity, "everything on point"—he will "put up with no stuff" (interview). Barnes has introduced new wrinkles, composing songs for the event, including "Prayer Song," "Too Late," and "Ashes to Ashes," which according to Barnes are now part of the tradition.

North Side and its performance protocols also serve an instructional function. Partaking in the gang's rituals serves the younger members as a vehicle of inculcation. Treme residents have one of lowest life expectancy rates in the city (Somosot); crime and incarceration plague many of the neighborhood's youths. Barnes sees the gang as a positive form of role-modeling. He wishes to connect his young maskers with their lineage and for them to revere and take pride in their African American legacy. He affirms: "you have to know who you are . . . you don't need the outside world to validate you" (interview).

Barnes and the North Side gang have enjoyed great success in bringing this Carnival tradition back from near extinction. It is not surprising that—unlike prior gang leaders, working-men of the neighborhood—Barnes is a professional cultural ambassador. Arriving in New Orleans in 1987 (he first masked with North Side in 1999), Barnes gained employment as a National Park Ranger, assigned to the French Quarter, where he gave lectures and performed with other ranger musicians. Barnes possesses wide knowledge of the area's Creole history and its legacy of enslaved Africans. He has conducted extensive fieldwork and interviews documenting the city's musical traditions.

Beyond dancing the streets for the black community of Treme, the gang functions in a much broader and more complicated way than its predecessors. Despite Barnes's admonition to the young skeletons regarding outside validation, the skeletons today very much perform to the "outside world." Al Morris and his few followers before Katrina operated under the radar, in almost guerrilla fashion; Osborn's documentary shows a small cadre of skeletons secretively lurking about the neighborhood. Today their performance has become a widely attended public event. Their marches are greeted by scores outside the Backstreet Cultural Museum, and throngs follow their wanderings through the course of the day. Those who witness the event extend far beyond a coterie of insiders—they are diverse in makeup, from partying tourists to hipster newcomers, to culturally informed locals, to academics, and the list goes on. Barnes shares that when he and the skeletons go on their march, they are now followed by "ethnologists, musicologists, anthropologists, and all the other -ologists" (qtd. in Walenter).

On some level the rise in profile experienced by North Side draws from the same energy and interest driving other expressions of Downtown Mardi Gras; however, there are also factors particular to this practice. Scholarship reflects robust interest in black Carnival; Lynnell Thomas documents the increasing importance of black culture to local tourism (8). And without question Hurricane Katrina raised New Orleans's African American community and culture to international awareness—furthered by the HBO series *Treme*. The city's infusion of newcomers has also contributed to this phenomenon. Catherine Michna points out how many transplants come from white suburbia and are thus drawn by the exoticism of New Orleans; they desire involvement with local culture and seek contact with "black authenticity" (qtd. in Rivet 18). In this regard the bones gang draws outsiders seeking proximity, hoping to draw close to the source—the skeleton signifying a formerly secretive, hidden, quintessentially black realm of Carnival experience.

This increased interest has accelerated the visibility of North Side in recent years. The opening credits of HBO's *Treme* feature a marauding skeleton reveler. The North Side appearances on Mardi Gras morning are announced and promoted in local publications. An increasingly large number of blogs chronicle the skeletons. *Lonely Planet* cites the group. *National Geographic* recently displayed images of the North Side gang. In 2013 Loyola University documentary filmmaker Jim Gabour held a public presentation on black Carnival, featuring the North Side Skull and Bones. A masked bone-gang figure wearing a Baron Samedi–style hat now appears on the front of Abita Purple Haze beer cans.

This popularization of the bone gang indicates the power of media attention and the forces of consumption that seek to capitalize on the skeleton's performative fascination. Demands and pressures pull on the gang in new and different ways; however, on some level the gang has contributed to this exposure. The group maintains a Facebook site. Barnes allows his skeleton image to be reproduced widely for print and internet Mardi Gras advertisements. In 2015 a contingent of the group traveled to Portland, Oregon, to showcase black Carnival for that city's Mardi Gras celebration. Barnes regularly appears as an ambassador at different events, such as the 2017 Treme Festival, where he strolled alongside a Mardi Gras Indian, as iconic representations of black Carnival culture. The bone gang also annually meets on Mardi Gras day with the Black Storyville Dolls (discussed in chapter 6), marking the convergence of two revived traditions.

Barbara Kirshenblatt-Gimblett has written of how the "context of presentation" can affect local heritage performance, how audience or framing can change the event, adding a kind of estrangement, or "Brechtian" element (157). The revels of the North Side Skull and Bones Gang can demonstrate this kind of odd, alienating performance. In recent years the gang has gained in dynamism and appeal, though it finds itself undertaking numerous and perhaps at times conflicting surrogations. An insider-outsider tension requires performers to recognize two audiences simultaneously, and to manifest differing degrees of approachability.

Barnes can be an intense, commanding figure, and in one sense he provides priestly, cultlike leadership, guarding over the mysteries of the bones. He is likewise quite garrulous and affable, willing to engage large numbers and facilitate wide enjoyment. This predilection perhaps reflects Barnes's gifts as a skilled, charismatic performer—former pro football player, musician, and sometime film/TV actor. With his band Sunpie and the Sunspots, Barnes performs "blues, zydeco, and Afro-Louisiana music" ("Bruce 'Sunpie' Barnes"). He has five notable CDs and has appeared around the world (having toured with Paul Simon and Sting in 2013).

The present-day North Side performance thus retains its ritualistic function while simultaneously offering widely anticipated public entertainment. North Side member Royce Osborn voiced mixed feelings about this alteration and new visibility. He feared that the skeletons might now be too public, that the bone-gang performance had become a "reenactment" (interview). In fact, Osborn broke off from the North Side gang, feeling that it had become overly formalized, and started his own gang-practice, one he hoped would be more in keeping with its Haitian roots, secretive and sexualized, open to intoxicated, hedonistic play (e-mail to Wade, February 19, 2014).

Bruce "Sunpie" Barnes. Photo by Robin Roberts. Permission of Robin
Roberts.

Osborn's contention raises issues of tradition and authenticity, alteration and authority. Ironically, Barnes is himself a transplant, a native of
Benton, Arkansas (Ramsey). Folklore scholar Regina Bendix argues that
in all claims of authenticity there resides an element of anxiety (10), an
observation that holds particular relevance for present-day New Orleans,
as cultural contestations rise from shifting landscapes, shifting populations,
and shifting desires.

Today, performance of the skull and bones is a vibrant, entertaining,
sometimes menacing event that serves multiple surrogations. It is a living
ritual of the Treme community, connecting residents to a storied past.

It is a powerful, assertive incarnation of racial pride. In this Mardi Gras enactment, Barnes and his skeletons physically traverse the streets and lay figurative claim, retaking the neighborhood for their own.

In quite a different way, the performance also functions as a kind of folkloric display, almost as an exemplar of itself, as the skeletons playfully pose for photographers and filmmakers. This exchange need not be considered an instance of touristic consumption, though for some it may be; the encounter can manifest a gesture of goodwill, as skeletons stand before onlookers, on their own terms, evincing power and pride as they advance appreciation of their singular skull and bone performance. Smiling, the gang offers invitation, pulling back the curtain of black Mardi Gras; scowling, the skeletons act as protectors and sentries, in face of forces that threaten to dislocate and dispossess.

Skinz n Bonez: Bones in Migration

The North Side Skull and Bones Gang occupies a position of prestige as the essential New Orleans bones gang. It continues to vivify the streets of Treme on the early mornings of Mardi Gras, showcasing black Carnival performance and African American tradition. Recent Carnival seasons, however, have seen the elements of skulls and bones conducting a strange migration, moving from one Downtown neighborhood to another, serving new users and new communities. In *Folklore Recycled: Old Traditions in New Contexts*, Frank de Caro examines how "folklore becomes transmuted or transported" (3) and generates uncanny new manifestations. De Caro emphasizes that attention to the resituation of folkloric activity can be "as important as the study of folklore's prime contexts themselves" (4). This claim suggests how one may honor the North Side pride of place but also recognize the importance of new skull and bone incarnations, that may operate in much different ways, with differing significances and implications.

Following Hurricane Katrina, the dance of skulls and bones has traveled beyond the realm of Treme, inciting new performance in the neighborhood of St. Roch. Embraced and transformed by a new set of practitioners, the bone-gang tradition has inspired the enterprise Skinz n Bonez, an all-female gang founded and spearheaded by Claudia "Mardi Claw" Gehrke, a white New Orleans resident and artist. This novel surrogation celebrates African American precedents while conveying its own sense of neighborhood identity and, importantly, its own commitment to female solidarity.

Gehrke's new gang offers a rich test case for the investigation of reimagined tradition and its utilization by new and different populations, especially given the vibrant and competing energies at play in the post-Katrina
context. Skinz n Bonez on a basic level reveals itself as a kind of hybrid
performance, a fusion that champions the revival of the city, and the female
sensibility. Carolyn E. Ware has written insightfully on the reformations
of folkloric practices in her book *Cajun Women and Mardi Gras: Reading
the Rules Backward.* She emphasizes the renewing and nurturing outcome
of women's involvement: "As they refashion once-male Mardi Gras roles,
women offer their own critique of gender relations, suggest alternatives,
and offer new meanings to the festival" (2). Ware's valuation of "new meanings" invites examination of how Claudia "Mardi Claw" Gehrke and the
Skinz n Bonez have encountered and resituated the long-practiced male
performance tradition of the skull and bones, and how their efforts may
variously champion, displace, affirm, transform, and/or appropriate this
African American ritual.

As with many of the new manifestations of Downtown Mardi Gras, in-
novation comes from the drive of a strong inspirational figure, in this case
Claudia Gehrke, who almost exclusively goes by the moniker "Mardi Claw."
Gehrke is a multitalented, gregarious individual who exudes warmth and
easily draws others into her sphere. Her efforts to launch and lead Skinz n
Bonez reflect her guiding motivation to seek connections, to build bridges.
A fierce advocate of New Orleans, she is a socially conscious woman who
gains enjoyment from bonding with others and participating in the city's
rich cultural offerings.

Mardi Claw is a transplant, originally from Portland, Oregon (interview
with Wade, August 8, 2012). Her story is a familiar one, as she visited New
Orleans in Mardi Gras 1995 and "just fell in love with it" (Gehrke e-mail
to Wade, September 11, 2017). She moved to the city in 2002 and has continued to value the unique and original character of New Orleans, which
she describes as "the last bohemia of America, the dirty Paris of the South"
(e-mail, September 11, 2017). Rather than the popular, touristic aspects
of New Orleans, she celebrates the city's more personal, neighborhood-
centered sensibility, its corner-bar culture "filled with friendly faces and
rich foods" (e-mail, September 11, 2017). The open and affable manner of
New Orleanians draws her appreciation and respect (though it provided
a culture shock early on).

Gehrke venerates New Orleans for its openness to various forms of
artistic expression, which has nurtured her own creative efforts. Mardi

Mardi Claw self-portrait. Photo by Mardi Claw. Permission of Mardi Claw.

Claw is a professionally trained artist who began art lessons at the age of six; in the course of her education she studied at the Portland Art Museum, the Seattle Art Institute, and the University of Oregon. She consciously associates with Mexican art and describes herself as a Day of the Dead artist; she became fascinated with Mexican culture and its skeleton imagery upon her father's death in 1990. Gehrke recounts a revelatory experience that led her out of depression following the loss of her father: walking through Pike Place Market in Seattle, seeing skeletons in a Latino store window, she recognized that the bones "were smiling, laughing and carrying on ... filled with LIFE not remorse" (Gehrke). Gehrke now sells skeleton handicrafts online and creates skeleton-themed paintings that she exhibits in neighborhood galleries, including the popular Surrey Juice Bar on Magazine Street. Her painting of a skeleton eating oysters (pronounced "ersters" by the locals) typifies her work. As with the Day of the Dead figurines, her paintings dramatize skeletons in daily activities—often in recognizable local bars and eateries.

The trauma of Katrina and its challenging aftermath have had a profound effect on Gehrke, galvanizing her affection for the city and her commitment to its unique cultural life, subsequently informing her founding of Skinz n Bonez. Her description of New Orleans as "the modern day Atlantis" (interview 2012) highlights the near-mythic associations she feels for the place (and the fragility of its future well-being). Having put aside her art for a period of time, she was inspired in the aftermath of Katrina to return to her painting with new vigor and emotion; she relates that the event "changed me and still is changing me" (interview with Wade, September 7, 2017). Her first painting in years was a skeleton blowing water from a saxophone. Many of Mardi Claw's subsequent efforts have been Katrina-themed, with skeletal images inhabiting a flooded and derelict environment. She honors the magnitude and vast suffering of the event and consciously connects her work to the post-Katrina renewal. Mardi Claw in fact calls her art "post K." It is significant that she keeps in close communication with other artists and experiences a consequent sense of solidarity. She has been an active member in art organizations, such as the NOLA Rising Artists Front.

It was also in the aftermath of Katrina that Gehrke experienced significant encounters with African American performance that would inform her launching of Skinz n Bonez. These experiences, along with her continuing personal and artistic fomentation, helped the incipient idea of a skeleton-inspired performance come into focus over the course of the next five years. A central, galvanizing element in this process was Mardi Claw's friendship with Wildman John Ellis, a member at that time of the Wild Tchoupitoulas Mardi Gras Indians. Gehrke recalls meeting him at the Healing Center on St. Claude: "It was at the Anba Dio festival that I met a Mardi Gras Indian by the name of Wildman John. I was selling skeleton maracas, and he wanted one for his suit. We exchanged numbers and within weeks I was talking with him, and planning on checking out his tribe the Wild Tchoupitoulas" (Gehrke). In subsequent years Wildman John would in effect provide tutelage for Mardi Claw, inviting her to accompany him on many festive events, giving her entrée to black culture.

She was in fact with Wildman John at the St. Joseph's Parade in 2006—Mardi Gras Day and St. Joseph's Day are the two traditional times for Indian marches—when she first encountered a black skeleton. A member of the North Side Skull and Bones gang was following at the end of the parade, serving as a soul-sweeper. This first sighting was entrancing and powerful for Mardi Claw; she had found another manifestation of the skeleton. This experience stirred her emotions and activated her imagination: "And then I saw it. A lone skeleton stepped out onto the street with a broom and began to sweep away the souls left behind, and now my mind was really thinking . . . drums . . . bones . . . bonez" (Gehrke).

Gehrke continued to enjoy rich and powerful experiences in African American street performance. For the ensuing years she proved a regular cohort of Wildman John, marching alongside him at numerous Indian events. She was marching in the 6t'9 Social Aid and Pleasure Club's annual Halloween parade when she first made the acquaintance of a North Side member. Ronald Lewis, gatekeeper of the North Side gang, was riding atop a float shaped like a huge bone; Mardi Claw initiated conversation and an acquaintanceship followed between the two. Gehrke's fascination with North Side continued to evolve and deepen. She met and got to know Sunpie Barnes, North Side chief, at the Hi-Ho Lounge on St. Claude, where she was employed at the time (his band Sunpie and the Sunspots often performed at the club).

The Hi-Ho Lounge played a significant role in the origin of Skinz n Bonez. Owner John Hartsock proved a passionate devotee of New Orleans culture. The club served as a meeting point for individuals struggling with Katrina recovery, screening each new episode of the HBO series *Treme* for its patrons. He expressed appreciation for the city's African American culture and regularly booked black performers; he also opened up the space for various Mardi Gras Indian meetings and practices. Importantly, Hartsock acted in a catalytic way for Mardi Claw. While she had long been imagining a new kind of skeleton enterprise, Hartsock's cajoling brought fruition. He suggested that Mardi Claw should start a new performance group; he offered the Hi-Ho Lounge as a sort of headquarters for meetings and rehearsals. In the summer of 2011 Mardi Claw, took Hartsock up on his proposal.

Recalling Roach's notion of surrogation, how cultural gaps or cavities open up for filling, one here recognizes a literal gap that called for attention and enlistment. Mardi Claw tells of doing Mardi Gras day 2007 with Wildman John and Queen Yolanda and finding that they marched without attendants, "with no drum line behind them" (e-mail, September 11, 2017); this same experience occurred on St. Joseph's Day of that year, as the Wild Tchoupitoulas paraded with no drummers. This lack, in effect, precipitated a new surrogation, a supporting entourage of drummers, what would become Skinz n Bonez.

Mardi Claw originally envisioned her new enterprise in an affiliate sense, assisting the Wild Tchoupitoulas, but the idea took new life and new dimensions. The skeleton motif was always a prominent and informing element of Mardi Claw's thinking; however, according to Gehrke, it was Hartsock who advertised this incipient group as a "skull and bones gang ... presumably to get more attention" (e-mail, September 11, 2017). Though she greatly admires the efforts of North Side leadership, it is significant that Mardi Claw never sought to directly replicate North Side practices; Skinz n Bonez was not launched as a rival gang. Greg Kutcher, a Skinz n Bonez soul sweeper, emphasizes this point, explaining that the female krewe "acts as an homage to the tradition ... but does not claim to be an actual bone gang itself" (e-mail to Wade, November 7, 2017).

In fact, the emergence of Skinz n Bonez derived from a hybridization of influences that represent an eclectic array of performative elements. With the influx of workers laboring to rebuild the city, Gehrke became sensitive to the increasing number of Hispanics present and sought to honor their contribution—by invoking Day of the Dead skeleton imagery in street performance. The yoking together of disparate motifs and cultural inflections characterizes Mardi Claw's artistic work, and Skinz n Bonez manifests this melding, which she describes as "the marriage of Hispanic culture and the second line" (interview 2012). With prominent African American and Hispanic influences in play, Skinz n Bonez consequently emerged as a sort of surrealist, cross-cultural, kinetic collage.

Gehrke's artistic interests, activist outlook, personal relationships, and involvement in black Carnival all found convergence in a serendipitous fashion, leading to the launch of a new performance experiment, one that would gain sharper focus and materialization over time. Mardi Claw's boyfriend came up with the group's name: Skinz/drums and Bonez/bones (e-mail, September 11, 2017). She began publicizing notices for women who might be interested in a new Carnival enterprise to meet at the Hi-Ho.

In June 2011 she posted: "Looking for women to form new krewe playing drums and running with Indians" (Gehrke). Soon she had twenty members. Skinz n Bonez made its first appearance shortly thereafter—a small, uncoordinated contingent of women, wearing skeleton face-paint, danced alongside Wildman John in the 2011 Midsummer Mardi Gras Parade.

The celebration of Mardi Gras in New Orleans has largely been a male-dominated enterprise, especially in respect to the traditional krewes chiefly associated with the city's affluent and socially prominent. Robin Roberts has examined the gendered aspect of Carnival and has revealed the patriarchal dynamics operative in the Krewe of Rex, where the king reigns supreme and his court manifests a nineteenth-century mindset (310–15). It is a significant turn in recent Mardi Gras history that New Orleans has witnessed the rise of many all-women krewes. Muses has emerged as one of the more popular women's organizations; recognized for their saucy and playful disposition, the members highlight politically topical themes (and throw hand-painted shoes to parade-goers). In addition to the new women's krewe Nyx, the city has seen an explosion of all-women social—and walking/dance—clubs, including the Muff-a-lottas, the Amelia EarHawts Cabin Krewe, the Sirens, the Organ Grinders, the NOLA Cherry Bombs, the Dames de Perlage, the Merry Antoinettes, the Black Storyville Baby Dolls, and the list goes on (see "31 marvelous Mardi Gras"; and Roques).

This female upsurge in Carnival activity represents a widening of participation and a challenge to what has been perceived as the staid, conventional male order of Carnival. Having already been an active member in many neighborhood social organizations, including the Good Children Social Aid and Pleasure Club, Mardi Claw was already open to communal activity in the post-Katrina environment. It was her association with Wildman John and the Wild Tchoupitoulas that provided her the opportunity to launch her own version of a marching club, one involving drums and exclusively for women.

Unlike other emergent female groups, Mardi Claw consciously connected her krewe to African American traditions, resulting in an unusual alliance of styles—what one member has described as "straddling the walking krewe/bone gang threshold" (Dhani Adomaitis e-mail to Wade, November 7, 2017). This choice evinces Gehrke's regard for and appreciation of black Mardi Gras, and also her desire to counterpoint the Skinz n Bonez to Uptown krewes (and their sense of exclusion and hierarchy). In addition to accompanying Mardi Gras Indians as a drumming ensemble, Skinz n Bonez its first year embraced the skull and bone gang practice of neighborhood meandering. In homage to the North Side Skull and Bones Gang, female krewe members in 2012 marched through neighborhood streets in the early hours of Mardi Gras morning in skeleton masquerade (with butcher aprons), making noise and general mischief. In its inception the group also self-consciously modeled its organizational structure on that of the Mardi Gras Indians and its notable functionaries—big queen, spy boy, flag boy, wild man; the group invented a new position named "voodoo doll."

Following its somewhat slapdash participation in the Midsummer Mardi Gras Parade, Skinz n Bonez came out in full force on Mardi Gras day 2012 (they have made an appearance every year since). Mardi Claw has recounted the experience of their first parade and how the gang worked to explore and establish its sense of self, its own practices and protocols. On this first Mardi Gras, the meeting spot for the morning gathering was only posted online twelve hours before the start time, to make the event "a little secretive" (Gehrke interview 2012). The gang assembled at the home of Ann Lynn at 5:00 a.m., where they ate cupcakes and drank Bloody Marys. By 6:00 a.m. they were out on the street—approximately fifty-five in number. Mardi Claw led the group, ringing a cowbell, followed by members holding a Skinz n Bonez banner. Members joked with onlookers and handed out champagne corks—painted as skulls—as souvenirs, serving as the group's signature "throws." While meandering through the St. Roch, Bywater, and Marigny neighborhoods—waking up the inhabitants—from time to time the group would stop at a welcoming home, for more food and drinks. They also made stops at many of the local bars, including the St. Roch Tavern, the Saturn Bar, Kajun's Pub, Schiro's, and the R Bar. In the course of the day Skinz n Bonez joined up with the Bywater Bone Boys (another emergent bones gang) and made a drum circle. They also entered the flow of the Society of St. Anne, which led them into the French Quarter. Moreover, in tribute to the original North Side Skull and Bones Gang, they made their way to the Backstreet Cultural Museum in Treme, where they encountered Sunpie Barnes and his followers. The women meandered for the remainder of the day, making their way to the Frenchmen Street and St. Claude areas for further partying. An inner circle monitored the group for any incapacitation brought by drunkenness and saw that the intoxicated were delivered home safely.

While inspired by the skull and bones tradition, Skinz n Bonez has departed in significant ways from the practices of the North Side gang. Unlike North Side, which wears large papier mache skulls, members of

Skinz n Bonez paint their faces Day-of-the-Dead style—they then wear skeleton masks on the backs of their heads (and this has become the loosely agreed-upon custom). They wear no standard costume per se, such as butcher aprons or long-handled underwear. While the North Side gang keeps predominately to a strict black-white color scheme in attire, Skinz n Bonez often dresses in vibrant, bold colors, with floral accoutrement. And unlike the North Side gang, which maintains clear gender distinctions, the all-women krewe welcomes their male friends to join as attendants; they are known as "soul sweepers." The krewe also abides intoxication and sensuality, while the North Side gang keeps attentive to its serious function (although there is much playfulness), and Sunpie Barnes discourages any public drunkenness. Skinz n Bonez has also cultivated an open and welcoming attitude to other groups. They welcome into their own parade those involved with such outfits as the Bearded Oysters, the Paradice Tumblers, and Krewedelusion.

Just as the North Side gang serves as an incarnation of the Treme neighborhood, Skinz n Bonez originated with a strong sense of place and geographical identity, as a Downtown phenomenon, conveying the energies of St. Roch and the adjacent neighborhoods of Marigny and Bywater (Gehrke at the time lived on St. Roch Avenue). The krewe and its colorful street performance may be seen as participant in the burgeoning art enterprises of the St. Claude corridor, which threads through this area and has emerged as one of the most potent creative incubators of post-Katrina New Orleans.

Mardi Claw and her krewe members give high regard to local bars and music clubs as focal points of community cohesion. A fundraiser was held at the Hi-Ho Lounge, attended by David Simon and other associates of HBO's *Treme*; Simon bought drinks for all in the bar. Mardi Claw identifies herself as a community activist and has been involved with the Healing Arts Center at the corner of St. Claude and St. Roch. She has done work to help Hispanic newcomers to the area. She has invested much time and energy into the neighborhood, leading clean-up projects, inaugurating a community garden project, and working to solve issues facing St. Roch—drug abuse, poverty, encroaching gentrification.

Early in its history, the Skinz n Bonez webpage proclaimed the following: "Bringing back a tradition long held only by male bone gangs in New Orleans, Skinz n Bonez bring a feminine element to the mourning [*sic*] with song and dance, chant and drum, and smiles on our faces" ("Skinz n Bonez"). This assertion is a bold one, highlighting the krewe as a new surrogation of bone gang tradition, and as a new place for female empowerment; it is enlightening to examine the aspects that support a female sensibility and that provide sanctuary for its all-women membership.

On a fundamental level, the krewe has created an environment that is warm and embracing; it prizes community and relationship. This outlook is evident in their attitude to other krewes, which is supportive and not adversarial. Skinz n Bonez emphasizes a kind of interconnectivity between themselves and other groups. In addition to the Wild Tchoupitoulas, the krewe supports pyrates and wenches (cosplay groups), the Sisters of Perpetual Indulgence, and the Radical Fairies (LGBTQ groups). Its Facebook site has amassed over three thousand friends.

Within the group, Mardi Claw works to create a safe space, one that allows shy members to step forward, for all members to share and grow. In this light Mardi Claw sees Skinz n Bonez as a vehicle for personal actualization, valuing "freedom of expression and creativity" (interview 2012). Members gain experience in community building, enjoying makeup workshops, rituals of initiation, and rhyming games practiced in a circle. While most Carnival organizations meet infrequently in the off-season, Skinz n Bonez maintains a regular weekly schedule: Monday evenings are given to craft creation (where they produce their now signature throws, bonez Barbie dolls), while Thursday evenings are for drumming practice.

The gang takes pride in its diversity. It is mostly white though racially and economically mixed. Members include visual artists, clothing designers, schoolteachers, musicians, burlesque performers, a botanist, and a belly dancer. While there are younger and older members, most are in their thirties and forties. The membership is open; annual dues are $50. Though anyone can join, they must go through a probationary period as one of the wishbonez. The krewe now numbers about a hundred, though around sixty regularly parade. About a quarter of the group resides out of town and participate when they can (Gehrke e-mail, September 12, 2017). On the rare occasion a member has been barred, this is usually for "drinking, picking fights doing things publically that didn't reflect well on the group" (Gehrke e-mail, September 12, 2017). Mardi Claw relates, "with a group of women that big . . . there's a lot of drama going on" (interview 2012). She nonetheless remains pleased with the emergence of Skinz n Bonez and the relationships that have ensued. Drum Captain Dhani Adomaitis understands that participation requires an "emotional investment" but affirms that the krewe can bring great personal reward: "your fellow members become your family" (e-mail, November 7, 2017). Skinz n Bonez takes pride in fostering this sort of solidarity. For Mardi Claw, the gang is a great group of women who have become a great group of sisters.

Gehrke's efforts have led to the creation of a new female space in Mardi Gras, and she has in essence claimed a place for women in the predominantly male tradition. The group stands as an assertion of female pride and support, an embodiment of feminist values that has gained visibility in the public arena, typically coded as masculine in wider culture. This commitment to women recently led Skinz n Bonez to participate in the Women's March in Washington, D.C., in January 2017, the only women's krewe representing New Orleans. The krewe paraded down the National Mall and drew encouragement and cheers from onlookers. In full skeleton regalia, they launched into their own homegrown version of the classic "St. James Infirmary," and "blew a lot of people's minds":

> I went down to king trumps infirmary
> where I saw my country there
> tied to a rusty flagpole, so cold so lean so bare.
> Let her go, Let her go, god bless her
> The lady Liberty
> people the whole world over, know this, was stolen from me
> (Gehrke e-mail, September 12, 2017)

Drum Captain Dhani Adomaitis confesses that this performance represented one of her "proudest moments ever leading a musical ensemble" (e-mail, November 7, 2017). Mardi Claw ranks this event as one of the highlights of the gang's history.

Bonez Connected to Bones

Mardi Claw and Skinz n Bonez reveal themselves as committed, generous individuals, deeply fond of their city, who are participants in the upswing of female-oriented Mardi Gras phenomena. The hybridity of their efforts, however, raises questions about New Orleans culture, and its complex nexus of gender, race, and class. Carolyn Ware has argued that the higher profile and involvement of women in country Mardi Gras—practiced in Cajun Louisiana—have brought salutary effects, "creating a continuum of alternatives" (153). However, in country Mardi Gras the women are insiders, helping refashion a tradition and community into which most were born. One could make the case that new female groups such as Skinz n Bonez parallel the resurgence of the Baby Dolls, a Carnival practice that originated circa 1912, where African American women would dress in infant attire and sport large pacifiers, parading in bold and often sexually candid demeanor. This practice experienced a steep decline, yet has returned in recent years with new popularity and enthusiasm—especially post-Katrina, another instance of women taking a larger arena in Carnival activities. As Millisia White, founder of the New Orleans Society of Dance, notes in her prelude to *The "Baby Dolls": Breaking the Race and Gender Barriers of the New Orleans Mardi Gras Tradition*: "we are carrying the torch of our ancestral traditions ... like our forebears, contemporary Baby Doll groups personify womanhood through dance" (v). Importantly in this instance, it has been African American women reviving and advancing an African American tradition. What are the consequences of white female artists taking elements of long-lived African American practices and recasting them for new purposes and populations?

Inequitable participation in the city's recovery has justifiably raised alarms and caused concern regarding racial interplay. While the flood brought suffering across the racial and economic spectrum, many in the African American community point out that the benefits of recovery have largely passed them over—the difference between white and black median income has risen 18 percent (Roig-Franzia, "Rebirth" 36). Activist Jordan Flaherty has voiced African American resentment in strong terms, identifying blacks as "the ones who get pushed out, disregarded and forgotten" (Flaherty).

Mardi Gras 2014 witnessed a controversy that brought issues of racial and cultural tension to the fore when a new female, mainly white Mardi Gras krewe, the Glambeaux, performed in the Muses parade. The group cited African American performance, incorporating the dance moves and accoutrement of the flambeaux (Carnival's black, working-class torch carriers). Gianna Chachere voiced harsh criticism for the Glambeaux—and for other "new incarnations" of black performance rituals—what she described as an exercise in "privilege and entitlement" (Chachere). The controversy played out on social media, targeting the women as "mostly white, mostly transplanted, grafting themselves onto an ancient tradition because it seems fun" (anonymous in Johnson). In short, this new Carnival practice revealed another instance of white arrogation and encroachment, an affront to African American tradition.

While the worst fears regarding a decimated black populace have not materialized, New Orleans has changed. Though still predominantly African American in makeup, the city has become younger and more affluent. It is ironic that many newcomers, who have in fact been drawn to the city for its unique culture and strong African American aspect, have been complicit in bringing strains and changes to African American New Orleans—rising housing costs, heightened competition for jobs, and increased worry over cultural commodification. One commentator in the Chachere exchange, well aware of black resentment and suspicion, offered this advice for newcomers: "I understand wanting to participate but you gotta be careful. the black folks of this city have payed their dues in the way white transplants haven't. so if you're a bywater bohemian or a mid-city young professional . . . don't elbow your way to the street, yield. you symbolize invasion" (anonymous in Johnson).

This chapter's largely affirmative reading of recycled skull and bones must acknowledge and address the continuing question of appropriation, of outsiders practicing performance forms originated by those of a different race and class. This conversation commonly invokes citations of Elvis or Mick Jagger, of those "attracted to the culture they plundered" (Lott 8). In light of the operations of "love and theft," so powerfully articulated in the work Eric Lott, the resituation of bone performance in the practices of Skinz n Bonez draws questions of accountability, how the women might address the harshest judgment: that they are purveyors of cultural theft, appropriating the African American skeleton ritual of Treme, for service in the whimsical hipster parade of St. Roch.

The migration of folkloric practice from one group to another can without question reveal inequalities of power, in practices that exploit, displace, and demean. Strong voices rightly point out such asymmetrical dynamics. Yet, there are instances of migration that may work in more multifaceted ways, that do not readily allow easy, clear-cut assessment and judgment. As one so often hears in conversations of race and racial politics in New Orleans, the matter can be "complicated." This chapter acknowledges its supportive reading of Skinz n Bonez, highlighting the group's dialogic aspect, and the validation the krewe has received from black culture-bearers.

In her *TDR: The Drama Review* essay chronicling her experiences in the street life of the city following Katrina, Rachel Carrico introduces a fictional companion character in her adventures—known as "the good thief." This savvy narrative device raises questions of cross-racial encounter; it also signals a warning, how even the most well-intentioned admirer of African American performance practices can bring unintended, deleterious consequences. With that cautionary note in place, the essay raises—but does not answer—the question of how one might participate in and draw from a different culture, while not enacting opportunistic motive or biased hierarchical relations. She introduces the possibility of "good-natured borrowing" (81).

Carrico's question opens up a range of viewpoints that invite complication and do not readily fit either/or categorization. In their essay "From Ritual Ground to Stage," which primarily explores the migration of tradition practices into theatrical and media forms, DuBois et al. relate how rituals are frequently recast for new audiences, and how some regard this recontextualization negatively, as something that causes the original performances to "lose value" (37). Following their examination of many test cases, however, they conclude that the "transformation of ritual into a commodified piece of art [or, by extension, new Carnival street theatre] does not necessarily devalue it culturally" (37). Rather, they suggest that different iterations of the performance can have different standings for different audiences, even different meanings, all of which can recognize the tradition as "important." They relate that local practitioners do not necessarily "see aesthetic transformation as commodification ultimately destroying their traditions" but rather as a validation, including their ritual in wider discourse, showing that their "tradition has become a value in its own right" (52).

When asked about the North Side Skull and Bones Gang maintaining proprietary claim over their unique street performance, Osborn responded with some humor: "What are you going to do? You can't put a copyright on a skeleton" (interview 2012). Osborn's comments underscore the fact that, despite any attempt at cultural policing, change is inevitable, and that iconography and enactments migrate and evolve, often resisting attempts at ownership. That noted, how might it be possible to understand the relation between the North Side tradition and the current practices of the Skinz n Bonez in a way that does not simply give over to the perambulatory inclinations of symbols, as an inevitability, or to accusations of cultural looting?

While such questioning may have no easy answer, it may be possible to cite more positive aspects of cultural exchange, where the implications are not strictly seen as deleterious or self-serving but rather indicative of a complex and multivalent encounter. In respect to the African American tradition of the skull and bones gangs, white female reiteration may have the capacity to work in a mutually supportive manner, as benign borrowing, where the assertion of one does not predicate the diminishment of the other.

The conception of an all-female bone gang can readily invite stereotypes and contentions of racial/class arrogance, casting members as out-of-touch interlopers. This assessment in many respects misses the mark with Skinz n Bonez. The demographics of the gang is not that of more notable and costly female krewes, such as Iris, Muses, and Nyx, whose membership comprises many well-positioned, highly paid professionals. Skinz n Bonez exhibits a varied social range, though many are creative, self-employed artists, teachers, service-industry workers—both transplants and natives. Their members often experience the economic challenges of wage inequity. Many struggle to maintain livelihoods and families in a time of gentrification; Mardi Claw herself has been a victim of gentrification, as her apartment jumped from $275 a month to $1400 overnight (e-mail, September 12, 2017). She subsequently moved to Gentilly, where she enjoys living on the same street as a former Zulu King, with the home of Royce Osborn around the corner.

Importantly, Gehrke has experienced close affiliation with black Carnival practices and their culture bearers. The group's employment of bone gang elements did not come from afar, as haphazard citation, but from close participation and involvement. Mardi Claw has nurtured and developed a productive friendship with the Wild Tchoupitoulas, especially with Wildman John. The two have sustained a relationship of mutual respect: "if he said don't do it, I didn't do it" (Gehrke e-mail, November 7, 2017). He has led a number of Skinz n Bonez parades, while Mardi Claw has supported the Wild Tchoupitoulas as a backup drummer on events ranging from Super Sunday to the New Orleans Jazz and Heritage Festival. Mardi Claw has gained emissary status, appearing before groups in league with Indians, skeletons, and baby dolls. She once stood alongside Ronald Lewis in the ceremonial kickoff of a 6t'9 Halloween parade.

Skinz n Bonez has largely avoided controversy; certainly it has not been embroiled in anything like the Glambeaux dispute. Mardi Claw is aware and sensitive to issues of exchange and appropriation. She, in fact, posted a statement of the krewe's website in 2014 that spoke to the phenomenon of the "culture vulture" and how she has tried to operate outside the dynamics of opportunism or entitlement.

According to Gehrke, "if there is one community that makes this city what it is, it would be the African American community" (e-mail,

September 12, 2017). Skinz n Bonez does not take its relationship to black culture lightly. The group honors and gives pride of place to the North Side Skull and Bones Gang, exhibiting reverence and an attitude of marked deference. One reads on the group's website: "All Hail Big Chief Sunpie Barnes and the North Side Skull and Bone Gang" (Gehrke). On Mardi Gras day Skinz n Bonez makes its way to Treme to encounter Barnes and the North Side gang. However, there is no face-to-face square-off, no confrontation; rather, Skinz n Bonez makes a show of backing off, bowing down, and paying respect. Mardi Claw's krewe pays homage to North Side in other ways. They have enlisted the North Side gang in costume and mask-making lessons. Mardi Claw is in fact particularly proud of the special decree granted by Ronald Lewis, North Side gatekeeper, that recognizes Skinz n Bonez as an "official" skull and bones gang. Gehrke affirms: "I have a very large respect for the North Side Skull and Bone Gang. . . . We did learn much from them, and to this day that is the ultimate experience on a Nola level. THEY ARE the bone gang" (Gehrke).

To a great degree, Mardi Claw and her female street performers have heeded the advice: "Be careful, don't elbow your way to the street" (anonymous in Johnson). Gehrke expects the krewe to exhibit respect and reverence. She, in fact, mandates a kind of inculcation of new members, where they learn the history and traditions of black Carnival. Initiates must visit the House of Golden Feathers in the Lower Ninth Ward and gain instruction from Ronald Lewis. While doing crafts on Monday evenings, the group will often watch films and documentaries that provide historical information, such as *All on a Mardi Gras Day* and *Bury the Hatchet*. Mardi Claw affirms that those who do not "catch on" must "move out" (interview 2017).

A strong racial awareness and sensitivity mark the group and its membership, evidenced in a recent barroom conversation at Poor Boy's, where the gang regularly meets for drum practice. When the subject of cultural appropriation surfaced, bartender Morgan Farrington voiced the importance of "respecting what came before" (interview with Wade and Roberts, September 28, 2017), a view readily endorsed by gang members. Drum Captain Dhani Adomaitis shares: "Personally to me, there is only one bone gang in New Orleans: North Side. We're given permission to do what we do and understand the precariousness of our place" (e-mail, November 7, 2017). Member Maria Brodine, who joined the krewe in 2011, echoes this sentiment, underscoring the need to watch assumptions and proprieties: "it's messy . . . feminist groups and new groups all walk that line" (interview with Wade and Roberts, September 28, 2017).

Gehrke deserves acknowledgment for working to bring about a notable enterprise of cross-cultural encounter. In consort with Toronto-based writer Cherie Dimaline, who had received funding from the Canadian Arts Council, Mardi Claw brought a gathering of First Nation tribal members from Canada to New Orleans to meet and share with the Wild Tchoupitoulas, for each to learn about the other's history and performative culture (the tribal members also visited the Backstreet Cultural Museum). Gehrke was instrumental in making this event happen; she also provided artwork for a prospective book about this project and hosted a party at her home for the two groups, which was attended by other culture bearers, including a number of baby dolls. A contingent of Mardi Gras Indians is expected to make a reciprocal trip to Canada in 2019.

Mardi Claw and the Skinz n Bonez hardly fit the profile of self-centered thrill-seekers trampling on long-held traditions. While the members enjoy their camaraderie and the excitement of their parades, "fun" is not the primary or dominant motivation. Aside from their commitment to drum training, craft creation, and regular weekly meetings, the women have participated in numerous community-directed activities, including animal rescue, aid to flood victims, and singing in the Treme Community Choir. On the recent untimely death of Royce Osborn, members organized meals to be delivered for the family and for the wake.

The last years have seen an evolution in Skinz n Bonez, in both orientation and practice, indicating a changing relationship to bone-gang precedents. Dhani Adomaitis shares that when she joined in 2014, Skinz n Bonez "pretty much existed as a support team for Indians—the Wild Tchoups" (e-mail, November 7, 2017). In large measure the krewe has grown beyond this capacity and has worked to establish an identity in its own right, as it has gained more confidence in its own performances and protocols. Mardi Claw has in fact signaled a desire to no longer conceive of or name the group as a skull and bones gang but to represent the krewe as a female drum corps. Consequently, group members no longer wear the butcher aprons in the manner of North Side, and they have reframed their organizational structure, dispensing with such functionaries as the big queen, spy boy, etc. A group of "inner bones" now serve as krewe captains. Mardi Claw explains that the group has tried to follow "a more feminine approach" and to give greater impetus to further creativity (e-mail, September 12, 2017).

In light of this turn, Skinz n Bonez has developed as a serious-minded group of women drummers. They hold two-hour practice sessions weekly

Skinz n Bonez marching in the Okeanos Parade. Photo by Rick Moore. Permission of Rick Moore.

at Poor Boy's, a bar on St. Bernard in Treme, and gain mastery of various drum rhythms and styles. They practice under the expert guidance of Drum Captain Dhani Adomaitis (a.k.a. Indiana Bones), who has emerged as one of the krewe's central figures. A skilled musician and teacher, Adomaitis moved to New Orleans from Massachusetts in 2002. She travels in the summer, leading drum-building workshops at festivals and community events. Her personal outlook well accords with the vision of Skinz n Bonez, as she views "rhythmic facilitation as a tool of community engagement" ("Presenters and Performers").

The performance practices of Skinz n Bonez have consequently transformed significantly since the group's appearance in 2012, when the krewe presented itself as an entourage of skeleton celebrants meandering through Downtown New Orleans. Skinz n Bonez has become a skilled and impressive performance ensemble. Numbering sixty or more, they march in powerful, arresting alignment with choreographed dance steps and gestures. With faces painted as skeletons and drums sounding loudly, the krewe creates a powerful, affecting impression, one that engages onlookers in a visceral and compelling way. The marchers are accompanied and followed by a formidable, talented walking band, with musicians such as Dobro Bone, Bonerella, and Skelle Belle. Often headed by a stilt-walker (Glitter

Skinz n Bonez marching in the Joan of Arc Parade. Photo by Kim Welsh. Permission of Krewe de Jeanne d'Arc.

Bonez) and True—outfitted with an oversize, intimidating skull (Gehrke e-mail, September 12, 2017)—Skinz n Bonez marches as an impressive array of skeletal performers, giving vitality to the streets and piquancy to Carnival celebration.

Skinz n Bonez has become a highly visible, popular krewe, increasingly sought-after for an array of events. They have marched for a number of main-line Mardi Gras parades, such as Okeanos, Toth, and the Femme Fatales. They regularly perform in the Halloween parade Krewe of Boo and the Southern Decadence Walking Parade. They have also been enlisted for specific staged events, such as the Anne Rice Lestat Ball. On several instances they have participated in film shoots, including *Jack Reacher* and *Benjy*. A Skinz n Bonez Barbie doll found its way into an episode of *NCIS: New Orleans*. Any monies the krewe make ($250 for marching in Okeanos) go back into the organization, to help pay for supplies. The group is not seeking profit or commercialization, just the opportunity to continue its activities and to strengthen the relationships they enjoy.

The emergence and new independence of Skinz n Bonez highlight the fertile context of Downtown Carnival, which supports and feeds energy to new enterprises. The success of the all-women krewe, significantly, has in no way limited or diminished the repute of the North Side gang, as its profile and performances continue to rise in popularity. Sunpie Barnes feels no threat from the group, assured of the North Side pride of place, and laughingly refers to such capillary efforts as "mimicry" (interview). In the recent book *New Orleans Remix*, Jack Sullivan cites the collaboration of the Wild Tchoupitoulas and Skinz n Bonez as "a delicate balancing act," though he credits the women for "adding layers of sound and a female vibe" (140). The efforts of Skinz n Bonez, their visibility and their manifest reverence for black Carnival traditions, might serve in a beneficial manner, as a kind of homage, affirming the importance and value of these traditions. Susan Beeton, in researching the Mardi Gras Indians, has recognized that not everyone views the popularization of black Carnival as desirable; "on the other hand," she writes, "exposing their culture to a wider audience on their own terms may well contribute to their cultural survival and well-being" (201).

Beyond viewing Skinz n Bonez as either a rival to or a devotee of the North Side gang, one can see the women's efforts as an independent enterprise, one that affirms the breadth of Downtown Mardi Gras and the expansive stage of its street theatre, its ability to host a wide array of performance, so that one need not cancel or detract from another. Perhaps one may see this arena in Carolyn Ware's terms, as "a continuum of alternatives" (153), where there is no zero-sum game.

Marching for a Better New Orleans

Before Katrina New Orleans was a city in decline, steadily losing its population and struggling with an eroding economy. In many respects the city has made tremendous headway in the twelve years since, with population gains, economic diversification, rising tourism, a booming film industry, a new medical center, a new system of bicycle pathways, and the list goes on. *Offbeat* editor Jan Ramsey has praised New Orleans as "a strong, resilient and capable community that's come back from almost being wiped off the face of the planet" (8), and such resilience should be celebrated. However, renaissance optimism bears tempering. As *Crisis Cities* reminds us, policies undertaken for recovery in almost every measure only increased inequalities already present before the storm (Gotham and Greenburg ix). Following Katrina, it has been "either the poor and/or blacks" who have borne "the brunt of change" (Burns and Thomas 161).

The history of New Orleans Mardi Gras itself can on a basic level be understood as a chronicle of racial encounter, as William Piersen explains:

Mardi Claw and friends before the Krewe of Boo. Photo by Kim Welsh. Permission of Kim Welsh.

"the original French Mardi Gras and other European holiday activities were revitalized by being grafted to a hardier rootstock out of African American culture" (135). It is a common perception that the unique vitality of New Orleans has issued from the diversity of its population and the cross-fertilization of its cultures. Photographer Chris Bickford writes of "the strange and beautiful fermentation of a whole host of ethnic influences that have made New Orleans one of the most culturally significant cities in the world" (Bickford).

The fecundity of cultural encounter and its resultant artistic expressions cannot obfuscate a history of racial domination and violence. Deep racial tensions remain in New Orleans, along with stark disparities of wealth. Lynnell Thomas has extended a challenge to those who celebrate African American performance, that they not simply enthrall themselves in its performative beauty and pleasures but that they recognize the deep-rooted social inequities faced by African Americans in New Orleans today; she calls for visitors, transplants, and natives to undertake the "abnegating task of sustained antiracist work to create economic, educational, and environmental parity" (14).

While Skinz n Bonez operates in many capacities, involving women from a wide array of backgrounds, it is not a political entity; it is not a civil rights organization. However, the group does manifest, in outlook and actions, a desire for a better New Orleans, one that eschews racial bigotry and values social cooperation. Time and again, Mardi Claw speaks of "creating bridges"; she and her krewe foster social awareness and an attitude of social responsibility. She has shared that sexism, homophobia, and racism are not welcome in her group—Mardi Claw tells of combatting instances of racial slurs during one recent parade (interview 2017), an instance that caused consternation but strengthened resolve.

In embodying a fundamentally feminist outlook, one valuing relationships over individualist self-seeking, the krewe looks to build community and embraces opportunities for outreach and encounter. Skinz n Bonez has welcomed children from Treme (who participate in the arts program of St. Anna's Episcopal Church) and has included the youths in krewe events, involving them in Halloween and Carnival parades. Mardi Claw raises funds for school supplies distributed to children of the Big Nine Social Aid and Pleasure Club, headed by North Side gatekeeper Ronald Lewis. Such ventures underscore a central mission of the group—to "give back" (Gehrke).

Skinz n Bonez member Dhani Adomaitis affirms that "there is unity in community engagement" (e-mail to Wade, November 7, 2017), and this perception speaks to what is perhaps the strongest achievement of the female bone gang—the opening of cross-racial dialogue, the creation of bridges. In repeated instances Mardi Claw has taken the opportunity to engage in open and mutually respectful relationship with members of the Wild Tchoupitoulas and members of the North Side Skull and Bones Gang. When guiding group members, Mardi Claw emphasizes a humility of engagement and underscores this sage advice: "ask permission, show respect, ask questions" (Gehrke). This kind of posture promotes exchange, promotes listening. While the repositioning of traditional cultural practices can sometimes cause unease, Dubois et al. suggest that this dynamic can also have productive results, serving "the cause of dialogue across differences" (53). From its inception Skinz n Bonez has worked to pursue this end.

While recent years of recovery have certainly failed to meet ideals of inclusion and racial acceptance, Skinz n Bonez has operated in a manner that works to recognize difference, in a way that does not divide. Carol Bebelle, director of the Ashe Cultural Arts Center, relates a striking phenomenon in a post-Katrina story-telling circle, multiracial in membership, where "a new sense of 'we-ness' emerged . . . a temporary willingness to admit to the reality of institutionalized racism" (qtd. in Michna 49). For Bebelle, the participants experienced a "consequent solidarity and heightened aware-ness of racial bias," generating hope for "social transformation" (qtd. in Michna 49). This kind of solidarity building can be a positive tool for a shared sense of purpose, of civic vision. Carnival ventures can themselves operate in such a manner, as productive sites of exchange and racial healing. Recent Carnivals have seen Zulu inviting Muses to ride in their parade, the Black Storyville Baby Dolls complemented by their white support group the Basin Street Players, Skinz n Bonez parading with the African American Femme Fatales. The latter instance speaks to the outlook and actions of the female gang. In Mardi Claw's words, "We have taken the time to build bridges, not burn them" (e-mail, September 12, 2017).

Skinz n Bonez offers illustration of New Orleans's resurgent creative energy, an example of cross-racial interplay, as traditional forms find new expressions—bones rising, animating the city streets on a Mardi Gras morning. The efforts of both this krewe and that of the North Side Skull and Bones Gang confirm Chris Bickford's contention that the cultural life of the city "remains a living, breathing, continually evolving way of life–and serious business" (Bickford). These enterprises act as the vehicle for differing identities but also for a shared identity, that of being a New Orleanian, of being a participant in the city's kaleidoscopic civic experi-ment, a belonging Mardi Claw unabashedly celebrates: "come hell or high water, I'm a nola daughter" ("hello, mardi gras!").

CHAPTER 3

Size Matters: 'tit Rəx

Robin Roberts

While it is small both in numbers of participants and in the size of its floats, the 'tit Rəx parade has been described (along with the Chewbacchus parade, which runs the same night) by the New Orleans *Times-Picayune* writer Doug MacCash as "My number one, not-to-miss 2013 Carnival occurrence" ("The former 'tit Rəx"). The unique features of 'tit Rəx make it *the* parade for many New Orleanians. To MacCash, these parades are "much more amusing than most major Carnival krewes.... To me, they will always represent the bottom-up, come back spirit that is the silver lining of New Orleans 2005-to-present recovery" ("The former 'tit Rəx"). 'tit Rəx offers an ironic twist on the gigantic, expensive, and traditional krewe and parade, Rex, whose king is *the* King of Carnival, and whose parade runs the traditional Uptown route. These parades, like the other Downtown Parades discussed in this book, reflect the historical divisions between "downtown" and "uptown" in New Orleans. What Richard Campanella writes about historical New Orleans remains true today: "uptown ... is generally wealthier than downtown. Racial distributions are different as well; uptown is more 'clumped'; downtown is more intermingled" (*Geographies* 165), and these two areas manifest very different approaches to Carnival.

Through interviews and images, this chapter analyzes 'tit Rəx by examining representative participants and floats. While the parade shares some features with the other parades featured in this book, 'tit Rəx provides an example of how the parades can explicitly and overtly resist by revising traditional Carnival. Like the other new parades, 'tit Rəx raises issues of gender and class. Like the other new parades, 'tit Rəx fits Errol Laborde's description of Carnival: "like all downtowns, inherently adult" (55). While 'tit Rəx floats are tiny, evoking schoolchildren's Mardi Gras floats made from shoeboxes, the floats are political and often sexually explicit. What makes the krewe unique is its focus on dimension, its insistence on diminutive floats, implicitly rejecting the massive, excessive, and inherently masculine extravaganza of Uptown Mardi Gras. 'tit Rǝx presents itself as the opposite of Rex, the Uptown parade. In so doing it articulates a defiant and sometimes explicitly political stance. Re-centering Carnival on tiny, artistic floats and throws, the krewe valorizes art, and not surprisingly, numbers professional artists as a significant part of its small organization.

In addition to sharing a post-Katrina genesis, this parade shares the features of the other new downtown organizations. Like them, 'tit Rǝx comments both explicitly and implicitly on Carnival, class, and local politics. The krewe also displays an emphasis on art and creativity, humor, and accessibility that defines these new Carnival groups. Gender also plays a key role, though in this krewe it is gender as a part of culture, where certain styles are coded as feminine rather than masculine. Due to its diminutive floats and throws, and its emphasis on an alternative to the massive and masculine floats of uptown parades, 'tit Rǝx itself is implicitly coded as a feminine alternative to traditional Mardi Gras. How this transformation came to happen requires some history of traditional Carnival.

Rex, King of Carnival

To appreciate the extent of 'tit Rǝx's creativity and commentary, it is necessary to know something of the krewe of Rex. Rex is seen as central to Carnival: its king is known as the King of Carnival. Focusing primarily in Uptown Mardi Gras, Jason Berry describes Rex's preeminent position: "At one level, Mardi Gras can be seen as a vast hierarchy with Rex, Comus, and the white patrician society at the top, like figurines on a wedding cake, followed by a pyramid of descending faux royalty" (312). Parading on Mardi Gras Day, Rex is considered the apex of Carnival season. Confusingly, the word "Rex" is used for the krewe and its king. Never called "King Rex," but simply, Rex, the word indicates the position's prominence and centrality in traditional Mardi Gras. It is not too much to say that being Rex is a position to which one is born; the krewe's other royalty also run in family lines. For example, Eli Tullis, Rex of 1997, had numerous Rex connections: his father, grandfather, and great uncle had been Rex, his aunt and daughter had both ruled as queen. Multi-generational lines of Mardi Gras royalty are common. Eli Tullis also served as a page in the Rex parade as a boy. This pattern demonstrates what Joseph Roach describes as Mardi Gras's transmission and conservation of "the exclusionary hierarchies of the social elite" (243).

James Gill explains that "To reign over the Rex parade, as king of all carnival" is "the highest honor of Mardi Gras" (7). The honor's importance is underscored by its being kept a secret until Mardi Gras morning, when the man's photograph and name is revealed in the *Times-Picayune*. In addition, the krewe's presentation of debutantes and royalty is displayed in the newspaper and in the Rex Room at the famous restaurant Antoine's, and one of the actual parties is shown on live local television. While Rex's response to a 1992 anti-segregation city ordinance directed at Mardi Gras krewes was to integrate nominally, it remains an all-male organization, with women's roles, even that of the queen, subordinate to the men's active participation. In the parade, for example, the queen does not ride on a float, though in many other Mardi Gras parades the queen does. Rex's critical position has been described as "the Keeper of Carnival," with author Ian McNulty describing Rex as "essential to the celebration as king cake and bead throws" (1), and "the repository for the public image of Mardi Gras" (61).

Rex has the historical advantage also of being the oldest still-parading organization. Founded in 1872, the krewe features elaborate and expensive floats and costumes. Rex's costume in particular typifies the excess of Carnival. His red wig is imported from France, and his bespoke costume is made of the finest materials. The scepter, crown, and other aspects of costuming, as well as party invitations and favors, are works of art. A permanent exhibit in the state museum, the Presbytere, focuses on Rex, and has numerous cases featuring the spectacular beadwork and jewelry from more than one hundred thirty years of Rex events. The krewe even boasts a historian, Henri Schindler, author of a number of books that laud Rex's parades and artistry (and those of a select few other uptown krewes) over the years. In addition to all these other features that emphasize Rex's prominence, it also has the distinction of being the first parade to throw trinkets to the crowds (in 1921). Today, a rider's bead package, as they are called, can cost thousands of dollars for one ride. Rex throws distinctive beads, marked with a crown insignia and an "R." Rex himself, however, rides grandly on a throne, and waves a bejeweled scepter. Members on other floats throw the beads, though Rex has a few pages who distribute largesse from his magnificent float.

Rex, then, typifies the class distinctions sometimes said to be reversed during Carnival. But in its repetition of class structure through faux royalty, the parade reinscribes distinctions. Since you must be wealthy to be a member of Rex, and wealthy and connected to historically prominent families to become royalty in most instances, the krewe reminds New Orleanians of its everyday power structure and the dominance of elite white men. This portrait of Rex might not be recognized by its members, who prefer to emphasize the krewe's motto, "pro bono publica," for the public good. Like other traditional Uptown Mardi Gras organizations, Rex has a charity foundation, and makes substantial contributions to local causes, especially education. Its parade themes focus on myths and legends, with recent parade themes being "Gods of All Ages" (2014) and "Royal Gardens–Horti Regis" (2016)—the use of the Latin itself functioning as a class marker. While in the nineteenth-century it sometimes had been overtly political, Rex has in the twentieth and twenty-first centuries selected ostensibly neutral literary or historical themes. Nevertheless, Rex's hierarchy and class position is unassailable, and it forms a base for the creation of its polar opposite, the krewe of 'tit Rəx.

An Alternative, Feminine Vision

In its extreme and overt rejection of the enormous size, expense, and excess of traditional Mardi Gras, 'tit Rəx offers an alternative, feminized version of a parade. 'tit Rəx has miniature floats so small that parade-goers have to walk up to and bend over to see the themes and decorations. In its diminutive size and its intimate interactions with parade-goers, the krewe evokes traditional stereotypes about masculinity and femininity and art from the nineteenth century that persist today (Tansley). Jane Austen, for example, famously wrote about her work as writing "a little bit (two inches wide) of ivory on which I work with so fine a brush" (Chapman 469). More recently, commentator Rebecca Solnit, in discussing women artists in the 1980s, remarks, "I remember all the women art students I met in that era, who made tiny, furtive things that expressed something about their condition, including the lack of room they felt free to occupy" (Solnit). 'tit Rəx's choice of miniatures can be seen as embracing a similarly feminine aesthetic as a reaction against the aggressive and exclusive masculinity, size, and cost of traditional Mardi Gras.

Stereotypes about masculinity and femininity and art from the nineteenth century persist today. This analysis draws on the idea, from folklore studies and anthropology, that "material objects are indeed agents of social relations" (Scheld 222). Since all social relations draw on gender, in explicit and implicit fashion, this chapter focuses on the aspects of Rex that are masculinized and those of 'tit Rǝx that occupy the feminine side of the social binary. The argument could be made first in terms of membership, for Rex is limited to men, and 'tit Rǝx allows women and men to be members, but as this chapter focuses on the floats and throws, it is relevant to look at how discussions of art have also been gendered. The characterization goes back centuries, as, for example, Martin Danahay argues in *Gender at Work in Victorian Culture*: "Male writers and artists in particular found their labors troubled by class and gender ideologies that idealized 'man's work' as sweaty, muscled labor and tended to feminize intellectual and artistic pursuits" (book jacket). In another artistic context, critic Robert Morris asserts that "big [art] is not only always better but also the only hope against its nemesis, the decorative" ("Size" 477). The decorative, he explains further, is "the feminine, the beautiful, in short—the minor" ("Size" 478). While Morris focuses on the art of the 1960s, his words still carry relevance today for Mardi Gras parades and their ever-growing floats and throws: "The artwork must carry the stamp of *work* [emphasis in original]—that is to say, men's work, the only possible serious work, brought back still glowing from the foundries and mills ... this men's work is big, foursquare" ("Size" 478). He concludes saying, "Big is what matters" ("Size" 482). 'tit Rǝx's choice of miniatures functions as an obvious and extreme reaction against the aggressive and exclusive masculinity and cost of traditional Mardi Gras.

In its evocation of children's floats created in homes, versus the massive traditional Mardi Gras floats created and stored in warehouses, 'tit Rǝx's version of Mardi Gras evokes the domestic, again allying the parade with the feminine. That the 'tit Rǝx's krewe members are forbidden to wear masks shows another form of resistance to barriers between float rider and parade-goer that characterizes traditional Mardi Gras. Uptown parades require masks—there are even fines levied by the city and krewes for not wearing a mask at all times during a parade. As Frank de Caro and Tom Ireland explain about Mardi Gras, "On one level Carnival does emphasize hierarchy and social division. Yet in another way it serves to break divisions down and to mock their very existence" (34). 'tit Rǝx provides a strong example of "the other way," mocking the very existence of class as it appears in Uptown Mardi Gras. The enormous size of Uptown floats, some city blocks long, and all towering above the people on the street, mark another significant separation between performer and audience. 'tit Rǝx, by contrast, is a stop-and-go parade, where its members stop and talk, hug, and pose for photos with people they know, and people they don't know, all along the route. Finally, while the krewe's tiny size (limited to thirty floats, each with three participants) means it cannot be as inclusive as, for example, Red Beans or Chewbacchus organizations, the krewe contains gender and some racial diversity, as well as a commitment to promoting what they see as New Orleans values of openness and acceptance.

Parading as Protest, Affirmation, and Art

'tit Rəx began parading in 2009, a new krewe generated from the experiences of its founders during Katrina. To the question of whether there should even be parades after the levee failures that followed Hurricane Katrina, 'tit Rəx, like the other parades discussed in this book, is New Orleanians' vehement, passionate response. As David Rutledge characterizes it, "the locals remember what they are rebuilding. It is not just a city, not just houses—it is a culture" (Rutledge, "Preface" 10). Running in the still-not-completely gentrified downtown St. Roch neighborhood, the krewe is peopled by artists who create floats with witty, clever, and often political and subversive themes. What Sherwood Anderson says about New Orleanians is particularly apt for Mid-City: "There is something in the people here that makes them like one another, that leads to constant outbursts of the spirit of play" (qtd. in Rutledge, *Where We Know* 121). 'tit Rəx, like other new downtown krewes, embodies the description of New Orleans as "in this city, culture is something you live" (Rutledge, "Preface" 139).

The emergence of 'tit Rəx after Katrina provides an example of how the city has recovered by embracing its subversive sensibility, which requires public engagement and participation either as a parade participant or parade-goer. As Rutledge asserts, "This story of resilience is one that America needs: culture can still be connected to home, something one lives, not merely a product one purchases or a program one tunes in to watch. The culture of New Orleans is not a culture for the sedentary" (Rutledge, *Where We Know* xxvii). 'tit Rəx lives up to a 2011 review that describes it as "hysterically witty on so many levels" ("'tit Rəx Parade"). A more recent New Orleans newspaper headline captures the parade's resistance to super-sized Mardi Gras: "In its own small way, tiny parade 'tit Rəx changes Mardi Gras" (Bynum). Through its inversion of uptown parades that emphasize bigger is better, mass-produced throws, and larger floats every year, 'tit Rəx reinvents Mardi Gras by returning it to a human scale. Its artistic excess

'tit Rəx throws. Photo by Robin Roberts. Permission of Robin Roberts.

is embodied in vision and individual creation, versus the mass-produced, for-hire professional floats used in Uptown parades.

Distinctive in terms of its miniaturization, 'tit Rəx's vision is resolutely art-focused, with its members required to make their throws and floats themselves. The floats and throws are fashioned from inexpensive materials, and their uniqueness is part of the krewe's resistance to the mass-produced and China-made throws that characterize traditional uptown Mardi Gras parades. The annual parade theme and individual float concepts reinforce an anti-capitalist approach, with floats in 2017, for example, criticizing the giant Airbnb corporation and the human cost of short-term rentals in the city. By satirizing a very real housing crisis, as residents are pushed out of affordable housing, 'tit Rəx ensures that distressed New Orleanians are given voice even in Carnival.

Integral to its anti-capitalist slant is the krewe's emphasis on creativity and art. Many of its members make their living as artists or teachers, and the results are evident in the krewe's high standards of float and throw construction. Jewelry, miniature books, and other tiny works of art appear on the floats and are distributed to the crowds. The krewe requires that all floats and throws be handmade, thus ensuring not only personal invest-ment in the work, but also making the throws unique and irreplaceable.

Their audience is not only the parade-goers, but also themselves, as each parade concludes with a runway show of the floats in a local bar.

The satirical element that appears other Downtown parades, such as Krewe of Red Beans and The Intergalactic Krewe of Chewbacchus (discussed in the next two chapters) is very much in evidence in 'tit Rəx. Playful humor defines the krewe's themes, and even their name, a riposte to the traditional Uptown krewe of Rex at the same time that the "tit" evokes a conventional idea of Mardi Gras as being all about women baring their breasts. In the analysis of floats that follows, the krewe's unique perspective and satirical humor emerges clearly. It is not only that humor itself is innately resistant to dominant culture, but also that the krewe directly satirizes aspects of the city's growth and emphasis on wealth and capital. Ridiculing traditional Uptown parades, the krewe suggests an alternative to "bigger is better."

The krewe's website maintains the light, humorous, and ironic tone that is a feature of its parades. Under the heading "US," the krewe proclaims: "The world's first micro-krewe, 'tit Rəx was founded in 2008 by a group of artists, teachers, businesspeople, workers, and bon vivants. Some say it took place in a kitchen, others on a porch in Mid-City, while still others just can't remember anything from that night" (titrexparade.com). Under "The Vision," the krewe asks, "When the size and velocity of throws has become at times physically hazardous to the recipients, could New Orleans not benefit from one krewe that takes the opposite approach?" (titrexparade.com). The answer to this question, as this chapter will reveal, is a resounding "yes."

The assault on traditional Mardi Gras begins with the krewe's name. A clever play on words, 'tit Rəx contains a number of regional allusions. "'tit" is a Cajun abbreviation of the French word for small or petite. Often used before a person's name, for example, 'tit John, the word might indicate a smaller or younger person. 'tit Rəx, the founders explain, is "Cajun wordplay on one of Carnival's hoariest parades" (titrexparade.com). Carefully not using the word "Rex" because of a legal issue," the 'tit Rəx website still makes its ambitious scope clear. Rex, after all, boasts the King of Carnival, and its activities mark it as a high-society, very exclusive organization. Many members of Rex are more or less born into the group. Other allusions embedded in the krewe's name include an ironic one to the giant dinosaur, T Rex (whose likeness has been featured on 'tit Rəx floats), and whimsically, the website also points to the rock band T. Rex. While 'tit Rəx floats are far more elaborate and complicated than children's art projects from which 'tit Rəx takes its format, actual shoeboxes are employed.

That its name has significance can be seen in the reaction to it by the Rex organization. A controversy involving the prestigious krewe of Rex and lawyers threatened to put an end to 'tit Rǝx. In the fall of 2011 ('tit Rǝx had then been running for three years), the krewe's president was contacted by lawyers who, though they "reiterated it wasn't anything personal but brand (or name) protection" (Evans), threatened 'tit Rǝx with a lawsuit. The objection was to the use of the word "Rex." The controversy was covered widely in local and even national media, with a piece airing on NPR. Ironically, it may have been the inclusion of 'tit Rǝx's parade in the venerable *Arthur Hardy's Guide to Mardi Gras* that brought little Rex to the attention of big Rex. After meeting with two Rex representatives (where else but in a bar!), the board of 'tit Rǝx met to ponder its fate. Because they did not want to change the name, the board debated a number of solutions, before one of the krewe's founders, Brett Evans, proposed changing the "e" in "Rex" to a schwa, an inverted e. As Evans describes it, "the schwa seemed the sort of vowel underdog that just added one more layer to what was already the triple pun of our name" (Evans).

The 2012 parade featured many jokes incorporating the schwa, including one float that focused on the "'little man syndrome' called Chi-schwa-ua, which depicted a toy dog squared off against a much larger dog" (Evans). While there were times of serious concern about Rex's assault on 'tit Rǝx's name, in general, the krewe members found it to be a positive experience, as it emblematized their desire to comment on larger krewes and a certain type of Mardi Gras practice. In addition, 'tit Rǝx received extensive publicity. As one founder described it, "we reveled in the publicity. I loved it—we all did" (Nancy Dixon, interview with Robin Roberts, November 30, 2016). As the negotiations dragged on, the krewe was heartened by an insider who reassured them that Rex did not truly want to eradicate 'tit Rǝx. A former student of one of the 'tit Rǝx founders was also in Rex, a coincidence that highlights how small and interconnected New Orleans Mardi Gras can sometimes be.

Despite the compromise solution to the krewe's name, the group still finds that it is treated differently by city authorities. While older, established Uptown krewes can reserve their parade night a year ahead of time, 'tit Rǝx cannot do so until a few weeks before the parade. In addition, the required police escort has been vexing. In 2012, despite having been paid, the police did not even show up, and parade revelers had to step in and block a city street so that the parade could cross St. Claude, a busy thoroughfare. In 2014 the police showed up, but they attempted to hurry the parade; "they were cramping our style," Bill Lavender, one of the founders, complains (Bill Lavender, interview Robin Roberts, November 30, 2016). The police escort left after an hour and half, Lavender thinks, so that they could go make money escorting Chewbacchus, which runs the same night. Although there is never any trouble with parades that run in the Marigny neighborhood, Lavender says the police do not appear to like working at the smaller parades.

In their choice of neighborhood and their assertive response to having the parade without the police escort, Downtown parades like 'tit Rəx enact the resistance aspect of Carnival, as depicted by C. W. Cannon: "It's all a symbolic act of occupation of public space at a time when the rest of America advances toward the total privatization of everything" (qtd. in Rutledge 139). 'tit Rəx fits Jennifer Laing and Warwick Frost's analysis of rituals as "reacting against this trend, toward homogeneity, [that] communities strive to preserve and even recreate their traditional events, which may require rituals to be resurrected or reinvented for a new audience" (frontispiece). A more humorous but apt description by Martha Burton fits new downtown parades: "In London, they say if two people stand on a corner, a queue forms. In New Orleans, a parade starts" (qtd. in Fitzpatrick). 'tit Rəx offers an example of a few people creating a parade from a small neighborhood group.

Parade-goers are notably more enthusiastic about 'tit Rəx than are the police, and relish the krewe's oppositional stance and artistic merit. A recent review by a visitor praises the floats by contrasting them to the larger parades: "My heart goes out to the craftiness and uniqueness of parades such as this. For most parades, riders can just hop on to these beautifully crafted floats, throw their beads that were put on the float for them, and go to sleep knowing they had a spectacular time with no need to pick up their discarded beer cans, empty bottle of Crown or crumpled Zapp's potato chip bags off their float.... [in] This parade ... each float and throw is handcrafted to go with that year's theme, and then tugged through the Marigny" ("'tit Rəx Parade" Joi B., February 27, 2015). Yet another review of the parade identifies a high-art resonance to 'tit Rəx: "My favorite artist, Joseph Cornell, would highly approve of this diorama and miniatures parade" ("'tit Rəx Parade" Matthew B., January 30, 2013). It is probably not a coincidence that the New Orleans Museum of Art has a room dedicated to Cornell's work. One of the founders sees Cornell's work as an appropriate analogue, explaining that, like Cornell, 'tit Rəx artists create "little miniatures, little tableaus," that tell a story (Lavender interview). Yet another

Yelp review describes 'tit Rəx as "Clever and cute. Who doesn't love a good satirical parade?" ("'tit Rəx Parade" JJ S., May 13, 2014).

Floats and Politics

Examining two floats from the parade provide a salient example of the artistic vision and insouciant attitude of the krewe. Two recent 'tit Rəx floats that deal with housing develop a critique of a politically specific, community-based issue of short-term rentals. Short-term rentals are part of the so-called "sharing economy," which might be more properly characterized as the "rip-off economy." The enormous multi-billion-dollar company Airbnb (referred to in one of the floats) runs a service that connects short-term renters and private property. In its idealized version, seen in Airbnb ads, a homeowner raises needed extra income by renting out a room or a house. The seller of the property is presented as a "host" or a "guide." The reality of this service, in marked contrast to the misleading ads, is emptied-out neighborhoods turned into de facto hotels, huge increases in cost of homes and rents, and a sharp decline in the quality of life for residents. San Francisco and other tourist cities like New York have been hit hard by these unregulated services, not merely losing tax dollars, but also raising the specter of safety hazards, and most critically and immediately, driving residents out of entire neighborhoods due to the astronomically increased cost of property. New Orleans has had bans on short-term rentals in the French Quarter for years, but the bans were rarely enforced, and gradually short-term rentals became a problem throughout the city. The City Planning Commission in New Orleans proposed new regulations with stronger enforcement on short-term rentals, which were then weakened for every part of the city except the French Quarter. A heated public debate ensued, including an ad campaign by Airbnb, and several contentious public hearings in which hundreds of residents participated; the fear of losing service workers, artists, young people, and longtime residents became a key part of the debate. In the public hearings it was revealed that many of the hosts own more than two dozen properties, paying large prices because they can fill the spaces with people paying hundreds of dollars a night (for homes in the Marigny and Bywater that used to rent for a few hundred a month).

A float from the 2015 'tit Rəx parade, whose theme was "L'Enfant Terrible," used the krewe's typical use of humor, size distortion, and artistry to criticize the impact of short-term rental and capitalistic greed on New

Janine Hayes's float. Photo by Robin Roberts. Permission of Robin Roberts.

Orleans. In Janine Hayes's float, a terrible large baby sits on top an adult figure, dominating the neighborhood of homes. Holding an adult figure in its hands, the infant evokes King Kong. As the tiny adult figures flee windows and doors, a sign in huge letter announces, "Rent $2100." The terrible infant then, is short-term rentals, driving locals out of their homes in terror. Its neighborhood-destroying power is underscored by the well-known sign, "Be Nice or Leave," by the Bywater artist known as Dr. Bob.

A 2017 float created by Dana Embree, a white female professional costume designer for film and stage, shows a more recent commentary on the same anti-capitalistic topic. As Embree explains, "I always choose a local issue to illuminate with my float" (Dana Embree e-mail to Robin Roberts, March 30, 2017). The float depicts the iconic St. Louis Cathedral as up for rent, saddled with two large Airbnb signs on its flanks. The map in the middle depicts in red the neighborhoods affected by short-term rentals listings. The human cost of this displacement is shown in the two tents, alluding to the large number of homeless people in New Orleans. The juxtaposition of the cathedral with the allusion to Jesus having "no place to lay his head" comments on the lack of care for the displacement short-term rentals cause. The float asks its viewers to think about the community's

Dana Embree's float. Photo by Robin Roberts. Permission of Robin Roberts.

values and actions, criticizing them directly. Mayor Landrieu intervened, insisting that short-term rentals be allowed. The float criticizes him through the use of the cathedral building, for Landrieu is an avowed Catholic and usually progressive in social issues—New Orleans is a sanctuary city, for example. Landrieu's critical role in legalizing short-term rentals appears on the back of the float (not pictured). The plain silver back of the float sports a bumper sticker with a photo of Mitch Landrieu looking serious and the legend "Resting Mitch Face," an uncomplimentary play on the common catch phrase "resting bitch face."

As Embree makes clear, the political message was quite deliberate, and a cause near to her heart and to her experience of living in New Orleans. As she explains: "The past couple of years, we have been battling the loss of our neighborhoods to tourists in short term rentals. I was very much against whole house rentals and having air b and b's in every neighborhood; we fought the battle with city council and lost. The city council and mayor, in their infinite money grubbing wisdom, had been allowing the influx of Air B and B rentals to proliferate" (e-mail). In contrast to Airbnb ads that promote the idea of friendly hosts sharing the city with visitors, Embree complains, "We've seen a direct effect on the locals who are trying to make a living here. Out of town developers are buying up whole neighborhoods and turning them into essentially hotels. People who live and work here can't find affordable houses, and those of us who are lucky enough to already own property are watching our neighborhoods turn into weekend long frat parties; strangers are pissing off of balconies and wandering around at all hours being annoying" (e-mail). In contrast to Rex members whose Carnival participation involves endless parties and numerous social events, Embree uses her Mardi Gras experience to create pointed political commentary. She describes her float: "my float this year was a reflection of the sellout and then fallout from that. The theme was "tit Rǝx Takes a Nap." My float was 'No Place to Lay His Head.'... I think you have a picture of it which drives the point home" (e-mail). This float was selected to be on display at the New Orleans Jazz and Heritage Festival Heritage Folklife Tent, an honor that reflects its cleverness and artistry.

Two Founders' Perspectives

Throws and floats demonstrate the artistic products that define 'tit Rǝx, but interviewing participants reveals the krewe's backstory and its importance to its creators. Two of the krewe's founders are a couple, Bill Lavender and Nancy Dixon, and they exemplify many of the qualities valued by 'tit Rǝx. Longtime white New Orleanians (both have lived here since the mid-1970s), they like many other members of 'tit Rǝx, live in Mid-City. Dixon is an academic, a writer, a licensed New Orleans tour guide, and the author of *NO Lit*, a historical anthology of New Orleans writers. Bill's set of professions is equally impressive: he is a writer, poet, publisher, former academic, and a rock musician. The couple's love for New Orleans in general, and Mardi Gras in particular, is intense and compelling. It was Brett Evans, a poet friend of Bill's, who brought them into the founding of 'tit Rǝx. The idea for a new walking krewe was Jeremy Yuslim's, but its eventual shape and size was the result of a group of people. While both Dixon and Lavender have participated in other Mardi Gras parades, they both evince a particular affinity for 'tit Rǝx, exemplifying as it does for them, what is best about Mardi Gras. Lavender rode in Krewe of Underwear which became Krewe du Vieux, a French Quarter parade; Dixon was well known for the parties she threw for Uptown parades when she lived on St. Charles Avenue, a street down which all large parades roll. Dixon also has ridden with a large Uptown parade, the all-female Muses.

Dixon sees a specific moment that sparked her interest in joining a new Carnival celebration. For years, there had been a local bonfire on Orleans Avenue in Mid-City, signifying the end of Christmas (people contributed their defunct Christmas trees to the blaze), and indicating the approach of Carnival. A spontaneous and time-honored tradition, it was shut down, and then allowed in a much-reduced form, by city authorities, who, perhaps rightly, feared the fire could turn into a conflagration. To Dixon, the spontaneous neighborhood celebration represented what was essential to New Orleans, and to her, 'tit Rǝx fills some of that anarchic, fun-loving space. (Lavender and Dixon have also, since 2009, held their own bonfire to replace the one on Orleans Avenue.) In addition, both Dixon and Lavender noted with dismay the increasing "Disneyfication" of the large Uptown parades, with floats getting bigger and more grandiose every year. The so-called "super krewes," Dixon and Lavender believe, have lost some of Mardi Gras' homegrown, artistic feel. In particular, Dixon recalled when one of the super krewes two-block-long floats couldn't make a turn, stopping the parade for hours. To Dixon, the final indignity was that the super krewe "blamed the delay on the revelers" (interview). This same krewe, Dixon noted, dropped Woody Harrelson as a king because of his opposition to the Iraq War. Endymion, she explains, "is the epitome of everything we don't like about Mardi Gras: no political satire, all about the fancy costumes, no emphasis on a theme, military and popular stuff" (interview). In Lavender's words, "everything has gotten bigger and definitely not better" (interview).

Both see that 'tit Rǝx makes a unique contribution to New Orleans Mardi Gras. Not only, Lavender says, do "we contribute a kind of philosophy that bigger is not necessarily better and more is less sometimes," but also, "a certain attitude and a kind of nostalgia for Old New Orleans, the New Orleans that was beginning to be lost even in the 1970s" (interview). For Lavender, the "bigger is better" attitude, against which 'tit Rǝx defines itself, is also a piece of gentrification, currently a big issue in New Orleans. He compares it to another new parade Chewbacchus (discussed in chapter 5), whose approach seems to be "to take over, to be bigger and bigger" (interview). Lavender sees this as being similar to numerous proposals in New Orleans for larger apartment complexes.

For most New Orleanians, Mardi Gras is a family event, and Lavender and Dixon's experience of 'tit Rǝx fits this description. Lavender and Dixon tailor their parade schedule to their granddaughters' schedules and preferences, and the girls always watch 'tit Rǝx. Initially limited to two people (called riders, even though they walk the tiny floats), Lavender and Dixon were glad when the krewe opened each float up to a third "rider," who could be an artist who was involved in the float's creation. Since Dixon and Lavender do all the work on their float themselves, they decided to invite Bill's son, Ben Lavender, to be the third rider. Will Lavender, his wife Beth Rosch, and their children determine what other parades Lavender and Dixon attend, and 'tit Rəx remains a centerpiece of Carnival for Lavender and Nancy's grandchildren.

With two fundraisers a year and eight to ten throw meetings to decide the theme and create throws, 'tit Rəx is very much a social group. They vote on their theme in July. While the theme isn't revealed officially, the krewe's attitude toward their theme reflects their laissez-faire, "let's have fun" attitude to Carnival. In contrast, for example, the Krewe of Chaos keeps their theme confidential until the parade, and Rex's identity is not revealed until just before his parade. Dixon explains about 'tit Rəx's theme "it really doesn't matter that it does get leaked." Dixon had an experience that reveals the krewe's relaxed attitude: "in fact, I couldn't for the life of me remember this year's theme, and got called out on in a public e-mail, but one member e-mailed me privately to make me feel better. He not only had the wrong theme, but he also had already built his float!" (e-mail to Robin Roberts, November 20, 2015). 'tit Rəx meetings are usually held at a member's house: Dixon and Lavender have hosted meetings at their home in Mid-City. The float's construction is divided, with Lavender creating the structure, and Dixon usually doing all of its decoration.

Most people work from a shoe or boot box, and reuse the base every year. This practice reflects that of larger parades, where floats are decorated for a theme, and then stripped of those decorations for the next parade. In 2014, as a fundraiser, the krewe auctioned off numerous floats. All sold, so there were many more floats built from a new shoebox bases in 2015. Members usually build their floats in their own homes, and at krewe meetings, gather together and make throws. Dixon and Lavender obtain their materials from several local stores, including Jefferson Variety, the Dollar Store, and other purveyors of inexpensive products. Two years ago, Lavender and Dixon were chosen to have the king float, and Lavender built the king's platform, which Dixon then decorated with satin feathers and gold (e-mail). Ben Lavender, Bill's son, also parades with Nancy and Bill.

Of their tiny, handmade throws, all created by Dixon, she immediately exclaims with a laugh there are "never enough!" Every year, she takes tiny cocktail umbrellas and decorates them with small plastic babies customarily placed in Mardi Gras king cakes. She usually adorns the umbrellas

Ben Lavender, Nancy Dixon, Bill Lavender. Permission of Bill Lavender.

with one white and one black king cake baby, often adding a tiny pecan to symbolize the Zulu coconut (a prized throw on Mardi Gras day). Decorated miniature umbrellas are Dixon's conscious "shout out to second line um- brellas (which are brightly colored, often branded, and used in dancing)" (e-mail, August 30, 2017). The king cake babies, small plastic dolls found in the seasonal cake, are a signature item of Mardi Gras. Dixon explains

The 'tit Rəx audience. Photo by Robin Roberts. Permission of Robin Roberts.

that deciding to use these dolls was "a no-brainer. It's carnival, they're wee, and we dress them up" (e-mail). She recalls that her friends Alex Rawls and Kat Gasparian "were making tiny umbrellas one year and we joined them" (e-mail, November 20, 2015). The king cake baby throws, Dixon says, "are always a favorite among revelers" (e-mail, November 20, 2015). Miniature plush toys called Shrinky Dinks are also a favored feature of her throws, which are often decorated in accordance with the parade's theme that year. Dixon also creates throws that are tributes to another venerable Mardi Gras tradition, the Zulu coconut, and she also was inspired by Muses to decorate Barbie doll shoes (as Muses does with real shoes) with glitter. She describes this as "riffing on other krewes' throws." As Dixon notes, at the krewe meetings, it is mostly women who make the throws (e-mail, August 30, 2017). Their throws mostly are related to their own floats, and thus are original concepts rather than spin-offs or homages. While the throws are tiny, the amount of work that goes into creating the largesse is not: "I usually start around Christmas," Dixon says, "and make throws every night for two weeks before the parade" (e-mail). But the work is appreciated by parade-goers. "Our 'beads' are tiny, so they're more like bracelets, and little kids LOVE our tiny throws" (e-mail, November 20, 2015).

The crowd has also gotten involved with the idea of creating small tableaus, with a number of revelers holding up tiny 'tit Rəx signs, sometimes including dolls as erstwhile audience members. One enterprising group even replicated the Uptown experience in miniature. Altered ladders with seats at the very top are a fixture of Uptown parades, and every year people create their own tiny stepladders with dolls, arms outstretched, begging for throws. As you can imagine, the riders of 'tit Rəx very much appreciate this homage, and stop and pay tribute. The website even has a section encouraging people to create miniature viewing stands. So, despite the long waiting list (eleven years!) for 'tit Rəx membership, parade-goers have an opportunity to participate in the parade through their own handiwork.

Dixon and Lavender describe the experience of being in the parade as communal and interactive, the opposite of other larger parades in which they have ridden. As Lavender explains, "'tit Rəx has exactly the opposite feeling than that of a large parade: [in 'tit Rəx] the crowds are large and are looking down on the tiny floats" (interview). In Uptown parades, the floats are huge, and parade-goers look up at the floats and riders. The larger parades are more anonymous, for by city regulation Uptown parade-riders must be masked and keep their masks on throughout the whole parade. As Dixon notes, "It is a very different way of experiencing the crowd. We're not masked, so if people know us, they see us." 'tit Rəx can be like a reunion, she explains: "I see people I haven't seen in years" during the parade (interview). The parade's space allows for interaction; Dixon says, "I stop and hug and kiss people. It's a real personal affection for the crowds" (interview). The first time they paraded, Lavender's son Ben commented, "I didn't know that you knew everybody on the route!" Lavender states: "At no point in the parade am I not in front of someone I know. . . . I like masking but that's not what this parade is about. . . . you're right there" with the crowd (interview).

Although Dixon spends hours making hundreds of throws, she usually finds that most of them have been distributed in the first third of the parade. Her guiding principle is to only give throws to people who really want them. Anyone who has ridden in an Uptown parade has watched with chagrin as a cup or standard bead is dropped to the ground as the drunken reveler rejects it. Or the parade-rider may see she has just thrown a special bead to someone who already has a dozen of that bead around his neck. That rarely happens with 'tit Rəx throws, because of their relative scarcity and uniqueness.

To Dixon and Lavender, who stayed in their Mid-City home through Katrina's landing and the levee failure, "There is a reason ['tit Rəx] started after the storm. Many people became closer after the storm" (Dixon inter-view). Not coincidentally, Lavender and Dixon weathered the aftermath of Katrina with two of the other founding members of 'tit Rǝx, Jonathan Trevius, a photographer, and Brett Evans, a poet. Using their boat, Dixon and Lavender paddled over to the American Can condos, where they found the other two. Breaking into a friend's condo, they got food and drink, and distributed it to others in the neighborhood. Bill's powerful book of poetry/ prose poems, *I of the Storm*, vividly details New Orleans before the disaster, and a long series, "Katrina Series," describes their experiences, including seeing on television evacuations by helicopter of the American Can build-ing. These intense experiences bonded the people who were there, fueling their commitment to the city and the bohemian way of life they had and wanted to help return.

In the concept meetings held by the founding members, they struggled to define how the krewe would identify itself, but all were in agreement that the parade should emphasize the floats, that there would be no costuming. (Costuming plays a large role in Uptown parades and krewe balls, with elaborate costumes for royalty. Rex, for example, wears a red wig imported for him from France.) Most of the founding members of the krewe are art-ists, and the majority live in Mid-City, and the first meetings were all held in this area, often at Brett Evans and Jeremy Yuslim's house on Dumaine Street. The first parade emphasized art; the parade took place in front of the Front Gallery on St. Claude, the after-party was held there, and for some time after the parade the floats were on display, and offered for sale, in the gallery. A recent acknowledgment of the 'tit Rǝx floats is the request to the krewe by the Historic Collection of New Orleans for one of the floats to be a part of the museum's permanent collection. The request was honored, but not without some difficulty, as the krewe had to identify a float that would be suitable for viewing by children. While not as raunchy as the larger French Quarter parade Krewe du Vieux, 'tit Rǝx floats are often political and sexual in nature. Another sign of the cachet and significance of the krewe's handiwork is their inclusion in the New Orleans Jazz and Heritage Festival (JazzFest). Every year members of the krewe demonstrate their unique float construction techniques in the Louisiana Folklife Tent. (Other Mardi Gras practices featured at JazzFest include the African American krewe of Zulu hand-decorating coconuts, and female Muses decorating women's shoes.) While it is an honor to be included in the Folklife Tent, the arrangement also helps participating members create their throws. This year, Dixon participated, with the result that she made more than a hundred throws. "I have never had so many throws by this time," she says (e-mail, November 20, 2015).

For Lavender, a resident of New Orleans since 1975, it is very important that all of 'tit Rəx's throws are handmade. To him, it evokes the spirit of earlier Mardi Gras, when it wasn't about collecting tons of plastic. For his early Mardi Gras, he recollects, "if you came back with three tiny beads, you'd brag about it . . . and doubloons were actually collectable" (interview). The old tradition of the Mardi Gras parade as political commentary is a tradition Lavender cherishes, and one that he finds mostly absent from Uptown parades. An early member of Krewe de Underwear and Krewe du Vieux, Lavender regrets that this parade has become more scatological than political in its emphasis.

Located Downtown in the St. Roch neighborhood, and then moving into the Marigny, the parade's location is, Dixon and Lavender insist, more important than where the participants live. Lavender had owned a home for many years in Bywater, and he and Dixon both identified the area as being populated by artists, edgy and countercultural. They exhibit a typical New Orleanian attachment to place. "It is a well-known fact that New Orleanians are temporarily insular about their city and even more so about the neighborhood in which they live" (Martinez and Le Corgne 15). In a touching indication of the parade's desire to be wild and out of control, or at least out of the city's control, the first floats were mounted on radio-powered cars, which, as they discovered, ran wildly amok as the radio signals crossed each other. All subsequent parades have been low-tech, hand-drawn with fish wire, rather than powered by electricity.

The krewe has changed its route a number of times, but has always been Downtown (unlike Chewbacchus, which began Uptown and moved its parade Downtown). The St. Roch route used in 2015 was selected because a member's friend owns the Firehouse in St. Roch and, for the cost of the required insurance, the friend allows the krewe to use the space to set up and gather before the parade rolls. Keeping the cost of participation reasonable is a goal of 'tit Rəx. The fees have been $85 for the float maker/ owner, and $60 for the riders. This cost is extremely inexpensive compared to the thousands that Uptown parades charge. In addition, the krewe holds regular "fun-raisers" to pay for costs like insurance and the police escort. One "fun-raiser" recently made thousands of dollars, as krewe members offered their unique, handmade floats for sale. Every float offered was sold, a sign of their collectability and artistic value. That Bill Lavender's press, Lavender Ink, also publishes poetry, including a volume titled *T. Rəx Parade* by Brətt Evans (a founder of 'tit Rəx) and Chris Shipman, provides another measure of the krewe's values and interests. The collection of poetry takes its inspiration from the parade, and those poems not about Mardi Gras carry the irreverent, fun-loving, and earthy perspective of the krewe. Lavender Ink also published Nancy Dixon's anthology of New Orleans literature, *NO LIT*. These books reveal the artistic practice of New Orleanians who express themselves through Carnival but who also live and produce art every day of the year.

An Artist's View

Dixon and Lavender's insights as founders reveal a great deal about 'tit Rəx's history and vision. Yet the insights of a parade participant who joined after its creation are illuminating, revealing that it is an artistic world view that sustains the group's membership. A newer member, Claudia Lynch, a white Uptowner, reinforces the importance of art and artists to the parade. She believes she is the only member of the krewe who lives Uptown, emphasizing the krewe's neighborhood roots. Many Mardi Gras participants ride in more than one parade, and Claudia, who moved to New Orleans in 2005, just before the levee failures, exemplifies this pattern. As she says, "I want to be in everything" (Claudia Lynch, interview with Robin Roberts, August 12, 2015). Her enthusiasm recalls David Rutledge's explanation that in New Orleans, "culture is something you live" (Rutledge, "Preface" 11). The parade is important to her, as is Mardi Gras generally. She and her husband, Jim Gelarden, decided to live on a parade route, because "otherwise, why live here?" (interview). She describes her participation and creation of Mardi Gras floats and throws as "a public service." She explains that, especially because she was "not originally from here, that when she moved here, it was like going to Candyland. There were so many creative things to do, and I wanted to do them all, right away" (interview). Her words typify the enthusiastic transplant, "the outsider who comes to New Orleans is often transformed" (Rutledge, *Where We Know* xxvii). Lynch has experienced firsthand that New Orleans has a mix, and "the message of the mix [is]: you too can be a part of this place; New Orleans is here to accept you" (Abrams 231). After seeing the 'tit Rəx parade, Lynch asked to join, but was told she couldn't because the number of floats were limited. Her friend Karen Crain remembered Lynch's interest, and as soon as the krewe opened up the number of participants in 2014, Crain asked Lynch to join. Lynch realized it was a rare opportunity, and immediately agreed. "A lot of people want to be in it," Lynch explains.

Lynch also rides in the nighttime, Uptown, all-female parade Muses. As an artist who has long used shoes as a feature of her art content, Lynch enjoys Muses. In comparing the larger, more expensive parade to 'tit Rəx, she notes that in the downtown parade, "there are fewer rules, more freedom, a more open experience. You can see more immediate creativity" in 'tit Rəx (interview). In 'tit Rəx, the emphasis remains on the floats and the handiwork. Riders are expected to don formal wear, which like that worn in dog shows, is meant to keep the emphasis on the object, not the "handlers." Even wigs are discouraged, and keeping the paraders' costumes simple has become an issue for the parade organizers. Lynch sees an important difference in 'tit Rəx in that, unlike other parades, the riders in 'tit Rəx do not wear masks or headdresses or themed costumes.

Lynch notes that she may be the only Uptown participant in 'tit Rəx, and her journey to be in the parade reveals the importance of connections and artistic talent in obtaining a place in this very exclusive organization. She joined the krewe in 2013. Originally, each float had only one "rider" (a conventional term, but recall, in this case, the "rider" pulls a miniature float). As interest in participation had grown tremendously, the krewe decided to allow one additional member per float. In 2014, the parade expanded to its current size, with three people assigned to each tiny float. Claudia's friend Crain also creates art; and in 2014, as the float's "owner," Crain also invited her boss, a custom software consultant, Steve Walkup, to join the float, too. Each has a specific role, with Lynch "doing the creative stuff—making, Steve does the bells and whistles" [logistics of the float's movement and lighting, for example], and Karen, as their float captain, is the organizer. In a sign of how connected the parade is, Karen lives around the corner from Dixon and Lavender in Mid-City.

A professional artist, Lynch characterizes 'tit Rəx as "like all Mardi Gras—you just want to make things." She explains that "a lot of people are artists" (interview) in 'tit Rəx, and she sees the openness and the number of artists as a defining quality of New Orleans itself. With its economical and handmade floats and throws, 'tit Rəx has "a starving artist quality to it," she explains. When Lynch lived in Ohio, she found that when she told people she was an artist, that they would get "the deer-in-the-headlights" look: they wouldn't know what to say next; because they didn't have a clue what it meant." By contrast, in New Orleans, people "are not afraid to identify as artists" (interview). If they're not artists or musicians, "they know someone

Claudia Lynch. Photo by Robin Roberts. Permission of Robin Roberts.

who is." In addition, people know who she is, art is everywhere—it's really a very good place to be an artist," she continues. "Even though you're doing it [art] by yourself, you can always see art in New Orleans" (interview). Claudia's immersion in 'tit Rəx reflects an attitude expressed by another New Orleanian, David Rutledge: "It's the people from elsewhere who care most about preserving the city. . . . We know how different New Orleans is from the land of stripmallconcrete. We value the music in the streets, as well as the oaks and palms at their borders. We work to keep it . . . Even more important is the message of the mix: you too can be a part of this place; New Orleans is here to accept you" (Rutledge, *Where We Know* 231).

Lynch's art influences her work on 'tit Rǝx, but she sees the work for the parade as art in a different, nonprofessional context. "It doesn't have to be as perfect as what I do every day," she explains. "It's a one-shot deal. I am able to be a little more free." Claudia's own work involves language, so she was particularly drawn to 'tit Rǝx's play on words. As she says, "I also enjoy the writing part" (interview). Like some of the other participants, Lynch, Crain, and Walkup create miniature throws that play on the specific theme of their float.

Every year, according to Lynch, someone running the krewe chooses the theme, and it is communicated to the krewe through e-mail. The common thread is some kind of play on words, perhaps a pun, as it was one year, on the concept of "small." For example, in 2013, the theme was "Wee the People"; in 2015, "L'Enfant Terrible." Her float in 2015 involved a complicated play on an Edward Gorey book, *The Gashleycrumb Tinies*. A twentieth-century writer and illustrator, Gorey is well known for his creepy and haunting artwork and themes, so choosing his book as a theme echoed the parade's overall theme. Lynch's first reaction to her teammates' proposal was that it would be too difficult to materialize. However, floatmate Walkup found a Weeblie House, which they were able to use for the haunted house on their float. "We doctored that up and cut up the house, attached it to the float, and built a lake with an iPad that showed a pond that had moving goldfish on it." During the parade, people came up and touched the float iPad, making the pictured fish move. Lynch describes the interactivity as one unique feature of 'tit Rǝx. "In Muses [a large Uptown parade with large floats]," Lynch says, "half the time you can't hear or see anybody" (interview), because of the size of the float and the crowds. In 'tit Rǝx, you have more personal interaction with the crowd. People who want to see and touch the floats unimpeded come to the beginning of the parade, because as they line up, the floats are there for a long time. It's easier then, to take pictures and see everything close up.

"I like the contrast of the small floats, the immediacy of the crowd and the interaction with my team." Self-described as "a person who doesn't play well with others," Lynch nevertheless says one of the important features of 'tit Rǝx for her, is that "she loves her team." She enjoys the prestige associated with being part of a small parade, with fewer than one hundred members. "It's a very different group than the people I normally hang out with" (interview). She and her float don't usually make their throws with the rest of the krewe at throw-making parties, as they are often early, before the individual float themes have been settled. While many other floats throw generic tiny items, Lynch and her float-mates create specific items that relate to their float's theme that year. "Every year I get to know one or two more people a little better. On parade day, they tell us to go the firehouse at St. Roch, because somebody who rides owns it. Then we all 'ooh' and 'aah' over everybody's float. It is the first time that riders get to see the other floats." While some members imbibe during the parade, Claudia explains, "I never drink, for the same reason I never drink on the Muses float. I can't imagine. It's a long day. I think of it as a long work day . . . it doesn't end until the parade ends at 8 or 9 p.m. I feel some responsibility [not to be drunk]; I don't want to trip over my float or anybody else's" (interview).

On the parade night, someone from the krewe takes professional quality photos of all the floats before the parade begins. Then they start lining up at 4:00 p.m., along St. Roch on the neutral ground. The position isn't as important as it is in larger parades, where it can be hours between the first and last floats. Each of the riders take turns pulling the floats. Lynch decides how to give throws out, deciding that, "I don't give them to kids because they get enough. I will give them to people if they have good costumes or if they say please."

The first year Lynch rode, her float had five hundred throws with tiny certificates of authenticity that were numbered. The second year they made a thousand, and in 2014 it was almost two thousand, and they gave them all away. It is up to each float to decide how many and what the throws should be. The labor, skill, and sheer inventiveness in these throws make them works of art.

Many of the comments on the parade praise the artistry involved in creating the floats and throws. In "Krewed Art: Four Mardi Gras Must-Sees," Shawn Fink describes the parade thusly: "an antithesis of sorts to the pomp and spectacle of major Mardi Gras parades, all 'tit Rəx floats began life as a shoebox before dozens of hours of work transform them" (Fink). In 2015 a cherished throw was the 'tit Rəx comic book. Only an inch and half high by and inch wide, this tiny book is a hand-drawn and Xeroxed comic, in this instance featuring a wry commentary on the relationship of film director Werner Herzog and actor Klaus Kinski. The bright orange front and back cover feature the krewe's name and drawings of a tiny float. The uptown Rex parade throws beads featuring a crown; another prize throw in 2015 was a tiny handmade pin, in blue, with a crown perched over a schwa; the entire item is less than an inch in circumference. A tiny bracelet or ring on elastic with a miniature letter "t" is another throw Lynch herself crafted, a clever play on the krewe's name.

The after-party is in the theatre of the Allways Lounge, which they call Gallier Small (after Gallier Hall, the mayor's hall on St. Charles, where all Uptown parades stop). Each float enters, with an announcer reading a paragraph description of each float. The riders only are in the space, as it is too small to accommodate spectators. There's no prize because it's not a competition, but the announcer in 2014 said, "although we don't have a prize and we shouldn't have a prize, I am declaring the Gashly Crumbtinies the best in show" (interview). All riders stay until the end, as each float is paraded on a little runway. Then, riders go into the bar and have a drink. Lynch explains, "I am pooped by the end; I think I stayed an hour which was a long time for me" (interview). Then 'tit Rəx is over for Lynch, until Crain calls her in the fall with the new theme for the parade.

The creation of 'tit Rəx floats and throws fits in with Lynch's previous occupation of costume designer. "It's very easy to think three-dimensionally and think what kind of pattern you would have to make to have it turn into what it is supposed to be turned into." She sees the floats and throws as "every one was a little sculpture." The collaborative aspect of the work also appeals to her. As a professional artist, her own practice is "so solitary. You do it mostly by yourself. You don't get feedback until it's finished." By contrast, the process of selecting a float theme and related throws and executing it is collaborative. Lynch explains, "you don't get defensive," as she might with her own professional art; instead, "everybody's ideas count" (interview).

Like her professional art, 'tit Rəx has qualities that could be described as "feminine": the work is tiny and whimsical. Although Lynch doesn't identify explicitly as a feminist artist, she recalls that while she was in art school, people kept pushing large-scale art. "It wasn't my thing," Lynch explained; she preferred to create "tight and small" art. Her professional style is, as she characterizes it, "detailed and perfect" (see her website for examples of her art work: shoestories.com). She sees her participation in both 'tit Rəx and Muses as very good for her "regular work," as "advertising for her art." "I couldn't make a perfect float the size of a Muses float (a large float carrying 44 women), but I can make a perfect float the size of a 'tit Rəx float" (interview).

The year before, when Lynch and her husband were moving to New Orleans, she wasn't able to be here for 2005 Mardi Gras (she was working on the gates in New York City with Christo). "My first Mardi Gras was the first Mardi Gras after Katrina, in 2006. . . . I think we went to every parade, every one. It was the only thing to do." She went to the first 'tit Rəx parade with a friend who also introduced her to Muses. This friend invited Lynch to a shoe decorating party for Muses; Lynch was a self-described "glitter bitch" who helped others decorate their shoes. With exasperation, Lynch describes decorating with other women, some of whom say, "Oh, I'm not an artist like you." She explains her feelings thus: "You're here with me, doing the same exact thing I am doing—what do you think art is? Everybody is an artist if they identify as one or not. They are making something for Mardi Gras—therefore they are an artist" (interview).

'tit Rəx, Lynch explains, "is like the antithesis of the uptown krewes, it really is. Everything is home-made . . . they're not afraid to make anything and to identify as artists, more than for example, Muses would" (interview). Claudia's perception is that 'tit Rəx is roughly half men and half women, and that it is a mostly white krewe. Lynch says the other people on her float are successful businessmen, but she insists that if you saw her krewe members, you would think they were artists and bohemians.

'tit Rəx, according to Claudia, contributes to New Orleans culture in many ways: first, she says, with a laugh, "Rex cannot win," referring to the upper-class krewe that runs on Mardi Gras day, and whose king, Rex, is considered to be King of Carnival. By its very existence, and certainly its name and size, 'tit Rəx offers another way to look at Mardi Gras, one that is more participatory and accessible. Lynch continues: "Look at what a fortune it costs to run in the big uptown parades—it isn't even economically feasible. I don't know how we do it" (interview). 'tit Rəx, in contrast, as Lynch says, remains accessible and promotes individual handiwork and creativity.

Conclusion

'tit Rəx, then, provides a vivid example of New Orleans culture at work reinventing itself, and including both old and new New Orleanians. The krewe, like the others discussed in this book, demonstrates the flexibility and responsiveness of Mardi Gras traditions. At the same time, the krewe and parade shows how the city incorporates newer residents into older traditions. 'tit Rəx both refashions and revives Carnival traditions. Its oppositional world view is open to a diverse group, including women, and 'tit Rəx has been racially integrated since its inception, reflecting the more mixed nature of the Marigny, Bywater, and Treme neighborhoods in which it parades. While the more established parades run an Uptown route through the city's most expensive real estate, 'tit Rəx parades through

The 'tit Rəx parade. Photo by Robin Roberts. Permission of Robin Roberts.

lower-middle-class streets. In its emphasis on small is beautiful, the parade reverses the top-down dynamic of Uptown parades, where the multi-level floats tower over the crowds.

In contrast, 'tit Rəx values intimacy and close examination of their work. The parade moves slowly, and stops for extended periods of time. People can come up to the floats, bend over them, touch them, and make eye contact with riders. While masks are required for Uptown parades, 'tit Rəx participants are encouraged to minimize their costuming and eschew masks. In the handiwork and creativity that goes into each float and set of throws, this parade suggests that everyone can and should be an artist. In its emphasis on art, satire, and whimsical play, 'tit Rəx keeps alive what they see as the heart and soul of Mardi Gras. 'tit Rǝx, then, like the other Downtown parades, reveals the tension related to size, to capitalism versus art, to different visions not only of Mardi Gras, but of the city's future and mission. In emphasizing an alternative to the Uptown excess and emphasis on enormous and enormously expensive parades, 'tit Rǝx like the St. Joan Parade, looks to the past and rejects the ways that New Orleans has become gentrified and profitized.

The pointed contrast between Rex and 'tit Rǝx reflects the tension between old money and power, and the celebration of an alternative to traditional hierarchies, that of artists. What 'tit Rǝx prizes in Carnival is its celebration of beauty on a human scale, and an insistence on active individual participation. At its core, 'tit Rǝx and Rex represent fundamental differences in world views, and contrasting views not only of what Mardi Gras is, but also of what should be central to city life. That both groups use Mardi Gras as a vehicle to assert their values is not surprising. Yet some of the same issues of exclusivity also appear as a concomitant to 'tit Rǝx's closed membership, with its eleven-year waiting list. In its determination to stay small and intimate, the krewe lives up to its values and mission, but then also sends those wanting to join the krewe a message that if they want to parade, they should perhaps create their own new Downtown Mardi Gras parade.

CHAPTER 4

The Red Beans Krewe: An Iconic Dish and a New Parade

Robin Roberts and Frank de Caro

Another new parade that has success and visibility, created by a transplant who moved to New Orleans in 2006, also first ran in 2009. The Krewe of Red Beans parades in the neighborhoods of Marigny and Bywater. Its first year, as Devin De Wulf recalls, there was virtually no audience. In 2017 the audience was estimated at ten thousand people. In a sign of the group's importance and reputation, De Wulf was contacted by the *Arthur Hardy's Guide to Mardi Gras* for inclusion in its 2018 edition. The krewe began with a small group who pay varying dues, but by 2017 increased to 165 participants. Red Beans has been so successful that it has created a second parade, marching on the same day, but in a different neighborhood (Mid-City), known as the Dead Beans krewe.

Perhaps this rapid expansion has occurred because it has been so instrumental in letting newcomers to New Orleans participate in the city's great festival celebration. The parade's policy of open participation, effective leadership by De Wulf, and eccentricity has made it a highly popular event. Krewe members decorate (with beans and rice) a car; the most recent car had a Louis Armstrong theme, including a side which featured his famous sign-off, "Red Beans and Ricely yours." The car has been provided by the Camellia Brand, which commercially packages red beans and has become a sponsor of the group; it will be used in an upcoming parade (unless there is rain) and the company also uses it for other public relations purposes.

This chapter explores the ways that this new parade draws on New Orleans culture, from its signature red beans and rice dish, to the Mardi Gras Indians' costumes, to the second-line tradition. Like the other new

Devin De Wulf, founder of Red Beans. Photo by Rosan Augusta Jordan. Permission of Rosan Augusta Jordan.

Downtown parades, the Red Beans parade fosters artistic expression (and competition); displays whimsical and political humor based on local culture; and valorizes the domestic (a common meal and foodstuff), and thus the feminine. And like the other new Mardi Gras parades, the Red Beans krewe wrestles with the changes in New Orleans and the role of transplants to these changes. In addition, like the 'tit Rəx organization, the krewe has had to deal with rapid expansion, due to rapidly increasing interest in the parade. The krewe's unique focus on red beans as its material for costumes typifies the innovation and creativity of the Downtown Mardi Gras scene.

Focusing on the founder Devin De Wulf's vision, the costumes, parade, and throws, and the signal importance of red beans to New Orleans culture, we will explore how and why this extraordinary adventure came to pass and to flourish. The Red Beans krewe (officially the Red Beans Social Aid and Pleasure Club, though as of 2017 the group is not incorporated as such and is only organized in the loosest sense) is registered with the State of Louisiana as a parade organization. Like the St. Joan Project, this krewe was founded by a single individual who has thus far been the dominant force in how the group has developed. And like the founders of the St. Joan of Arc and Chewbacchus parades (discussed in the first and fifth chapters), De Wulf is a newcomer to New Orleans, a native of South Carolina who moved to New Orleans in 2007. De Wulf had visited New Orleans earlier, after Hurricane Katrina, to work as a volunteer, primarily doing photographic work for several organizations, including a Mardi Gras Indian group. He had long-standing interests in cultural matters. He came to live in New Orleans full time in July 2007. As Halloween of that year approached, he was giving thought to his costume for that holiday; he came up with the idea of a suit decorated with red beans, a costume that attracted a certain amount of attention as he walked around the city. The enthusiastic response to his costume resulted in his photograph being taken numerous times; as De Wulf describes it, "people were taking pictures like I was famous" (Devin De Wulf interview with Robin Roberts, November 30, 2017). He would go on to organize the krewe that is distinguished by its decorative use of beans and rice on costumes. De Wulf had become fond of eating beans when he lived in Brazil, where both red and black beans are food staples, and he was well aware that red beans and rice were an important feature in New Orleans and Louisiana cuisine as well.

Like other transplants who have begun new Mardi Gras parades, De Wulf feels a strong sense of connection with New Orleans, and appreciate it as a special and unique culture. He describes the city as having a "culture and history, an appreciation of wackiness and carnival, that allows someone like me to create a parade" (interview). Loving "the magic of the city," De Wulf explains, "I would never want to live anywhere else. I don't think this environment exists anywhere else" (interview). Describing the city's unique features, De Wulf insists, "it's cool to live here because you can be a part of a living culture. It's out in the streets, ever evolving" (interview). The Red Beans' family-friendliness is a part of the group's evolving and growing as the city does. As De Wulf points out, he and his friends started this parade when they were in their twenties, ten years ago.

Children in the Red Beans parade. Photo by Robin Roberts. Permission of Robin Roberts.

Now in their thirties, many of them have children, and De Wulf includes his own two young children in the parade. While Krewe de Jeanne D'Arc formally permits children to participate, Red Beans does so informally, telling members that children are welcome. De Wulf sees this as another of New Orleans's unique qualities: that Mardi Gras and other festivals are all-age inclusive, with old and young welcome in the revelry.

Devin De Wulf at the present time lives in the Bywater neighborhood and is a full-time stay-at-home father. He lived in New York for two years, while his wife, Annelies De Wulf, an emergency room physician, participated in a program at the State University of New York Downstate medical school, and he ran the krewe from afar during those years (this was "pretty easy," he says, a matter of collecting dues and delegating some tasks), while he worked as a teacher in several New York middle schools. He has tried to keep the krewe open to newcomers by keeping the dues low, and by allowing members to pay what they can afford. It is, he thinks, the cheapest Mardi Gras organization, and participation is open to all; that is, there is no need to be a longtime New Orleanian to participate, nor is there any sort of waiting list. The members continue to make their own costumes but now meet at Seal's Class Act Lounge, a bar on St. Bernard Avenue, to work on making them. A video made of the parade in 2014, when the New Orleans police forgot to send an escort and the parade was briefly stopped because of a misunderstanding over the parade permit (the group had the proper permit, as it always does, though the lack of an escort caused someone to think they did not and they were reported to police), also includes some footage of costume making and of work on the second car made by the group, honoring Louis Armstrong. (The video is available at https://vimeo.com/121198481.) Particularly as families have grown, the group has also become more child-friendly, with a group of "kid beaners," including De Wulf's own daughter and son, now part of the parade; and there are other groups, including a troop of Girl Scouts, who now march with the parade as well. De Wulf met his wife, who is a member of the krewe, through involvement in the organization. As De Wulf wryly notes, "If I hadn't created the Red Beans krewe, I wouldn't have met my wife, and my children would not have been born. So, I owe my family to Red Beans" (interview).

Food and Carnival: The Meaning of Red Beans and Rice

Along with its music, New Orleans has long been heralded for its innovative and unique cuisine. With its use of a brass band and second-line marching, the Red Beans parade exemplifies its commitment to New Orleans culture through its celebration of red beans and rice. The group's webpage proclaims its mission: "we celebrate the importance of red beans and rice and carnival" ("Red Beans Parade"). Before discussing the parade's genesis and its splendid, unique costumes, a discussion of foodways in general and red beans and rice in the New Orleans culture is helpful. New Orleans native, columnist, and television scriptwriter Lolis Eric Elie describes red beans and rice as one of "the totemic foods of New Orleans" (Franklin 42), and argues strenuously for the centrality of food to cultural identity. "Part of the great thing happening in this country in the last ten, twenty years is a greater interest in regional, vernacular food. And food is a window into a broad range of other aspects of culture. Food is central to identity" (Franklin 35), Elie explains.

A recent essay by Daina Cheyenne Harvey, "'Gimme a Pigfoot and a Bottle of Beer': Food as Cultural Performance in the Aftermath of Hurricane Katrina," explores the importance of foodways in the construction of cultural meaning. While Harvey focuses on actual meals, much of her analysis can be applied also to the Krewe of Red Beans, as it employs a food product to create costumes, throws, and a parade that function as the meals she describes: to create communication and events between disparate groups of people. As Harvey explains, "New Orleans has always been a top culinary tourism destination, but in the aftermath of Katrina it [food] played a different role" as a "significant cultural mediator" (498). The Krewe of Red Beans, and the other new parades discussed in this book, similarly demonstrate an adaptation of food, to connect not only volunteers and residents, as Harvey discussed, but also residents and transplants, with the latter eager to demonstrate fealty and appreciation for New Orleans culture. Like the residents whom Harvey studied, some residents see the new parades as risking the danger of appropriation (499). Therefore, studying New Orleans performance and analyzing its impact on the city's rebirth and transformation is imperative. As Harvey argues, "Although the 'Disneyfication of New Orleans' (Southey 2007) has been largely avoided, the issue of authenticity and culture are still paramount" (501). Harvey notes the tensions in food events she studied, but she also concludes that they can be interpreted as "performances of social solidarity" (512), a description that applies to the intentions, and in most cases, the execution, of new downtown Mardi Gras parades like the Krewe of Red Beans. As she explains, "performances of social solidarity were first and foremost about belonging" (513).

The Krewe of Red Beans began in the Marigny neighborhood, with the then twenty-two-year-old teacher De Wulf presenting the idea via a PowerPoint presentation to several of his twenty-year-old friends. Loving New Orleans culture and longing to be a part of it, De Wulf filled a vacuum by honoring a number of New Orleans cultural practices, from the dish of red beans and rice, to the Mardi Gras Indians' once-a-year beaded costumes, to the African American tradition of the second-line, a style of marching. In so doing, he consciously aimed at bridging different neighborhoods and communities, separated by class, race, and geography (interview). In this way, his parade, as well as the others discussed in this book, enact performances of social solidarity.

As the krewe's name and signature decorative item, red beans and rice, suggest, food is key to this parade. In their book *New Orleans Cuisine: Fourteen Signature Dishes and Their Histories*, noted cultural critic and author Susan Tucker and academic S. Frederick Starr include a chapter on red beans and rice. Before delving into particulars of recipes and ingredients, the chapter's authors, Karen Trahan Leathem and Sharon Stallworth Nossiter, cite famous New Orleanians who claim a special association between the dish and the city. Leathem and Nossiter point out that Louis

Armstrong mentions red beans and rice "more than any other food in his autobiography" (128), and show that he "equates the dish with home" (128). The Krewe of Red Beans honors Armstrong on the side of their bean-decorated vehicle, which depicts him and his trumpet, with his sign-off on correspondence, "red beans and ricely yours—Louis."

Demonstrating the importance of the dish to the city, Leathem and Nossiter cite Ray Nagin, then mayor of New Orleans, who when asked about the exodus of New Orleans after the disastrous levee failures, famously announced, "Once . . . the red beans and rice are being served on Monday in New Orleans and not where they are, they're going to be back'" (128). Other New Orleanians, from writer Randy Ferrel to restauranteur Wayne Baquet, similarly proclaim the centrality of red beans and rice to the city's culture (129). In part because of its status as a weekly ritual on Monday, red beans has more import than other significant local dishes; in addition, as Leathem and Nossiter point out, red beans and rice is inexpensive, uses leftovers (such as the ham bone from Sunday dinner), and "is an easy and cheap way to feed a crowd" (130). Harvey describes red beans' class impact and its creation of community: "the special at many restaurants, particularly in working-class neighborhoods, is red beans and rice. Food in New Orleans is used to establish temporal rhythms and thus group cohesion" (511). The rituals and low cost of red beans and rice, Leathem and Nossiter argue, are central to the "communal aspect to red beans that is in large part responsible for its popularity" (130). In addition to the actual dish, the red bean has appeared as an icon for the city in works as disparate as sculpture (Soulas' public art) to jewelry (Mignon Faget). So Devin De Wulf could scarcely have chosen a more apt item to symbolize the city's heart. Its fluidity and complex origins also make it a suitable symbol of the diverse city. As Leathem and Nossiter explain, "it is difficult to trace the origins of red beans and rice . . . it seems to be a product of a number of influences. Like gumbo, it borrows from a number of racial and ethnic groups that make up the people" (132).

Anthropologist David Beriss also claims a key role for red beans and rice in the city's recovery from Katrina, as we in this book argue is also true of the new Downtown parades. He explains, "in planning meetings, political events and art installations, red beans and rice became a metaphor for home and an index of the city's ability to sustain a distinctive culture" (243). Noting that red beans replaced stars as a measure in restaurant reviews, Beriss points to this and other examples of how "red beans and rice . . . had provided key symbols between post-Katrina New Orleans and the rest of the United States" (245). Harvey notes that food in general has important cultural meaning. Building on this view, Beriss explains that red beans specifically offered symbolic force: "In a city sharply divided by class and ethnicity, red beans and rice represented a comfort food that crossed those lines. It is something that nearly everyone can enjoy, both at home and in restaurants" (248–49). Movingly describing his own typical experience at being unable to find the ingredients to make New Orleans–style red beans and rice when an evacuee in 2005, Beriss explains that for him and other New Orleanians, discovering that the brand of beans and other elements were not available elsewhere made it clear that the city's culture was unique. Red beans and rice exemplifies Beriss's claim that "the central element that makes food an effective symbol for New Orleans is a sense that they all share in a common cuisine" (245). Beriss mentions the Krewe of Red Beans, and includes a photograph of a "beaner" costume; building on his (and others') analysis of the dish helps contextualize the parade's hybridity and impact. Our focus in this chapter is on the Mardi Gras practice, which employs the iconic dish but also, through Carnival practice, evokes the sense of communal connection Beriss claims for the food itself.

Giving Back and Keeping the Focus on Red Beans

As a means of encouraging and promoting local foodways, especially red beans and rice, the Red Beans krewe developed a new activity in 2017, creating a charity event. As De Wulf notes, the group is a social aid and pleasure club, but "for many years, we mostly focused on the pleasure" (interview). Determined to give back to the city that has become a beloved home for him, De Wulf also wanted to do more than the usual party to raise funds. Since March is usually after Mardi Gras, he came up with the idea of a competition to be held that month between restaurants for the honor of serving the city's best red beans. Showing the same sense of appropriateness involved in creating a Red Beans parade running the day New Orleans people customarily eat the dish, De Wulf decided to parallel basketball's March Madness tournament. For $5, patrons could sample two dishes of red beans and rice in a blind taste test. Again reflecting the krewe's emphasis on democracy (as well as De Wulf's social studies education training), the winner was determined by participants' votes. Sixty-four restaurants and a few individuals were involved, with Cornet Restaurant winning the honor. Thousands of dollars were raised for two charities: Anna's Place, a children's foundation, and Make Music Nola, which provides support for children by providing them with music education. As a result of the success of this tournament, De Wulf plans to hold a charity event every March.

Learning New Orleans Customs

The practice of creating new walking Mardi Gras parades such as the Krewe of Red Beans and the other parades discussed in this book also relies heavily on New Orleans's famed hybridity, tolerance, and quirkiness. Red Beans' use of features from the Mardi Gras Indians provides one example of borrowing, in a fashion that reflects homage rather than appropriation. De Wulf had seen second-lines and was familiar with Mardi Gras Indian traditions and with the rich local history of costuming, particularly exemplified by the Indians, of putting much hard work into creating a costume to be worn only once or a few times. Members of Mardi Gras Indian groups (African Americans who "mask Indian," are organized into groups with hierarchies including such offices as Big Chief and Spy Boy, fashion elaborate costumes, and maintain their own song and dance traditions) may refer to their group as a gang. Following general usage that divides actual Native Americans into tribes, people also speak of the Mardi Gras Indians as tribes. They have such names as the Yellow Pocahontas and Seventh Ward Hunters. De Wulf's first job in New Orleans was as volunteer photographer for the Black Feather Tribe; he spent Lundi Gras night at one of the Indians' homes, and documented their activities that night and all Mardi Gras day in 2006. This experience led him to create a more domesticated parallel, crafting with beans rather than beads. But like the Indians, De Wulf aims for a high standard of artistry.

By Mardi Gras 2008 De Wulf had in mind creating a "cultural phenomenon" that incorporated some of these elements and that paid homage to earlier second-line and Indian traditions, and the Red Beans krewe and its parade came out of that. By 2008 he was recruiting friends, primarily transplants to New Orleans, for the group. He decided that the krewe would walk on Lundi Gras, the day before Mardi Gras, because there was relatively little else going on that day in the way of Carnival activities (although many people have the day off from work) and because Monday was traditionally the day of the week on which red beans and rice were served in New Orleans households. Calling the Monday before Mardi Gras Lundi Gras

("Fat Monday") is a relatively new local affectation, not an older French usage. The usual explanation given for this is that historically Monday was set aside as the household washday in New Orleans. Red beans could easily be prepared by being set on the stove to simmer while washing household linens preoccupied the time and labor of homemakers; the cook could also possibly make use of scraps of meat left over from Sunday dinner to flavor the beans. The serendipity of an open time slot on Lundi Gras and the parade's Red Beans theme offers it yet another anchor as a new custom into hallowed practices of the city.

The Parades

The first Red Beans second-line in 2009 included about twenty participants, whereas that of 2010 was larger, with over forty people. On February 15, 2010, the marchers gathered slowly outside a grocery store in Faubourg Marigny, the neighborhood downriver from the French Quarter, where they had originally intended that the group's king would purchase red beans as a ceremonial act (although this plan was abandoned when the store declined to loan a shopping cart for the parade). Then, accompanied by the Treme Brass Band, the group second-lined through the Marigny and on into the French Quarter, wheeling a shopping cart that carried supplies, led by De Wulf, whose costume evoked in part a drum major's (because of the hat he wore) and who moved in an appropriate dance rhythm just in front of the band. It was also accompanied by New Orleans musician Al "Carnival Time" Johnson, who had been declared the krewe's Grand Marshal for Life (a role he still performs) and who performs at the group's annual party. De Wulf's then-roommate had met Al Johnson at *Offbeat* magazine's annual awards event, and asked Johnson to consider participating. Johnson is known for his Carnival anthem "Carnival Time,"; as De Wulf explains, "it doesn't get more carnival than 'Carnival Time'" (interview with Robin Roberts).

For 2010 the group had printed and distributed small cards giving the time, date, and route of the parade (although the route was only fixed for Marigny, with the Quarter route being improvised [later the group dropped the Quarter part of their parade, going instead into Treme, where they are now hosted by the Back Street Museum], the card indicating that the termination point would be Frenchmen Street back in Marigny, a street lined by popular bars and music venues). The group was made distinctive

Crawfish costume. Photo by Robin Roberts. Permission of Robin Roberts.

especially by its costumes, clothing of various kinds featuring decorative motifs created through the use of beans and rice. Within the similarity of beans and rice grains as decoration, the costumes covered a considerable range of styles, from (despite the chilly day) the nearly naked (with strands of beans for cover) to Baron Samedi–like black formality with elaborate skeletal outlines (in later years the variety of costuming, based on the red beans and rice basics, has continued). Many of the costumes displayed an insouciant sense of fantasy, not portraying alternative identities so much as an amorphous wispiness.

The 2017 parade began with aplomb, as the group emerged from the Marigny Opera House, spilling out across the block. Four motorcycle

Political message. Photo by Robin Roberts. Permission of Robin Roberts.

policemen were waiting to lead off the parade. Incongruously, the first most visible parader was a man in full skeleton face paint, thrusting a fully bean-covered umbrella in a striking pattern up into the sky. Dancing, the Red Beaner sported a corset and several glass red bean necklaces. To his left, a more somber but no less gaudily red-bean De Wulf walked. Behind them marched the Bon Bon Vivant band, also made up with skeleton makeup, featuring a tuba and accordion. As they played, onlookers, many themselves in costume (though not beaned costumes) took photos and also danced. The costumes varied from a splendid crawfish decoration, with coordinated hat, to handheld masks in red beans painted black, red, white, and brown—with images of a fox and a tiger, to a political sign in beans and rice: "South Asians for Black Lives."

The Red Beans parade: Mary Langston in matador costume; Amanda Helm as Red Beans Joan of Arc. Photo by Ryan Hodgson-Rigsbee. Permission of Ryan Hodgson-Rigsbee.

Like those in other Downtown parades, the costumes seem to grow in complexity and artistry every year. Beans and rice bikinis, jackets, and jeans, as well as men's suits were to be seen on many. Amanda Helm, one of the leaders of Joan of Arc parade featured in chapter 1, wore a resplendent military outfit, fully beaned and including two cans of actual red beans and rice, of the brand "Joan of Arc," evoking her other Mardi Gras parade. On a beautiful sunny Monday, the parade brought smiles, and parade-goers joined in with the marchers, carried away by the music and excitement. De Wulf describes the parade as "magic . . . we create happiness" (interview with Robin Roberts), and that was evident from the parade's onset.

Creating Art with Red Beans

De Wulf stresses the importance of a high level of artistry in the costumes. He explains that it takes forty to fifty hours for the "beaners" to create a good costume. Thomasine Bartlett and Minka Stoyanova, a mother and daughter who were invited to join Red Beans by Mary Langston, explain that they were prepared to create bean costumes when asked: "we're from New Orleans, so of course we had multiple glue guns!" (interview with

Robin Roberts, July 5, 2018). Both artists, Bartlett and Stoyanova had also participated in Krewedelusion and Chewbacchus, as well as the Uptown parade Muses. Both Krewedelusion and Chewbacchus are much larger krewes than Red Beans, and Stoyanova notes that "Delusion and Chewbacchus occupy a space between the street party second-line feel of Red Bean and the large, tractor-drawn float uptown parades" (interview, July 5, 2018). They describe Krewedelusion and Chewbacchus as being more organized in terms of organizational structure and the parade experience. While they value their participation in other parades, both women enjoy the personal interactions and intimacy of Red Beans, and value its "celebration of New Orleans culture," explaining that "this is true of all the marching krewes—you are always drawing out some part of your identity" (Stoyanova interview, July 5, 2018). Their identities as artists are central to their participation and enjoyment in the Red Beans parade. Bartlett says parading "keeps me in touch with New Orleans as an active participant. To be an active participant and to create your city's culture is to be a builder" (Bartlett interview, July 5, 2018). Both draw on their artistic abilities and visions for the costumes and throws they create, but they also see that parading informs and energizes their art. Bartlett says participating "gets your creative juices going," and Stoyanova sees that "there's a dialogue between my carnival activities and my art . . . [Mardi Gras] costumes and throws are fun—less work than making more serious, high-concept art" (interview, July 5, 2018).

The members of the group also pride themselves on their hand-crafted throws, which range from small packets of red beans and rice to beautiful glass bead necklaces and even snow globes filled with glass red beans. The beads are created by one of the members, Nancy Thacker, who is a glass artist. She approached De Wulf with the idea, which he enthusiastically embraced. Now as part of their member package, all members receive ten packets of glass beads that they can use in their throws. To De Wulf, "It's cool that it's made here—not stuff from China" (interview), referring to the copious amounts of cheap plastic beads thrown by Uptown parades.

The red beans used to decorate costumes and the two vehicles are supplied gratis by the Camellia Brand, which also provides drink koozies for members to give to the audience. For 2018, the company donated over five hundred pounds of beans. De Wulf contacted the company by letter, and they responded by phone, telling him they would be happy to partner with him. A local company, Camellia Beans are part of the fabric of the city. In an instance of serendipity, De Wulf heard from the Camellia company while

Minka Stoyanova and Thomasine Bartlett. Photo by Robin Roberts. Permission of Robin Roberts.

he was in his school cafeteria, on a Monday, eating red beans and rice. He took the timing as a favorable omen for his new parade.

At beaning workshops, members provide instruction, assistance, and encouragement to each other. De Wulf explains that he is not "a micromanager," but nevertheless encourages members to work very hard on their costumes. As he tells them, "You will have more fun if you put more work into your suit. If you half-ass it, you will still have a good time, but not as much as the others [who did more work]" (interview). In addition, there is a competition for best suit—a competition held the night before, where the members vote on who has the best costume—with the winners becoming the Red Beans king and queen for that year. De Wulf explains his complicated voting system, attributable, he says, to his professional training as a social studies teacher. It's like the electoral college, where each member's vote is weighted, based on the number of years that they have participated in the parade. That the system is mostly about the costume was reinforced when Mary Langston became queen the very first year that she participated. Yet as De Wulf acknowledges, there is a wide variety in the amount of beaning and the level of artistry in the krewe. This variety

Beaners at work: Joycelyn Askew, Sheralyn Askew, and Janelle Brazile with Devin De Wulf.
Photo by Ryan Hodgson-Rigsbee. Permission of Ryan Hodgson-Rigsbee.

also applies to their marching, which often includes audience members joining in for a few blocks or longer.

The costumes of the group have taken on particular importance for the group's members, many of whom live in the "hip" neighborhoods of Bywater and Marigny but who come from many parts of the city. Each member makes his or her own costume (De Wulf estimates that the group is half men and half women and also that about forty to fifty hours are required to make a "suit"). Although members do work on their costumes individually at home, communal costume-making sessions are an important element of the group dynamic. Between Halloween and Mardi Gras the group meets every Wednesday. Originally participants met at De Wulf's' house at a long table, the focal point for the work.

Beaning at their Community Center, Seal's Class Act Bar

As it has grown, the group has met once a week, on Mondays, at Seal's Class Act Lounge on St. Bernard Avenue; the bar, which has a mostly African American clientele, has welcomed the "beaners" and even cooks red beans and rice for them. The number of members attending the meetings varies.

In this regard, the krewe resembles the Mardi Gras Indians, who not only put great effort into making their own costumes but also often work in groups. De Wulf is well aware of this similarity and sees the Red Beans krewe as emulating the Indians in this regard (although he acknowledges that the Indians see themselves as having a spiritual dimension which the Red Beans group does not beyond a certain "good feeling"). Not only did De Wulf act as a photographer for one Indian "tribe" for several years but he has had close associations with families active in the Indian tradition and so has firsthand knowledge of the Indian subculture; he sees the Indian families as a "point of inspiration." He wants the Red Beans members to put considerable personal effort into their costumes, which while individually distinct have the unity provided by the beans and rice as decorative materials (working as a sort of substitute for the feathers and glitter used by the Indians); this practice distinguishes the group from many walking clubs and requires a level of commitment to the group and its activities; indeed, at the costume-making session Frank de Caro attended in 2009, members arrived and immediately sat down to work.

The group formerly bought ordinary packages of beans and rice such as are used for household consumption, though now the Camellia company, acting as a sponsor of the Red Beans group, provides beans to the group (as well as helping with payments for the parade permit and the band, and supplying the car for decoration); the krewe still needs to buy its own rice but does not use as much rice as beans. The beans and rice are affixed to clothing which might consist of old jackets and such, whether from a member's retired personal wardrobe or given to a member by someone else or bought for the purpose. Some members make costumes from special cloth, in a few instances material left over from Halloween. Bartlett showed additional innovation when she took the Camellia bean sacks in from the beans the company donated to the krewe, and created a kimono for the parade. The beans and rice are put on by use of hot glue guns, and some members also use bay leaves, a food item used in cooking red beans, as well as non-food items like spangles. This construction makes for an especially ephemeral sort of costume (not only are the beans and rice themselves perishable but they tend not to stay on the garments for very long), requiring that new costumes be made annually. In this need to regularly make and remake costumes, De Wulf also sees a similarity to Indian costuming. Individual members create their own designs (at least one member starts from sketches), so that each costume is rather different within the use of similar decorative materials and may be more or less elaborate. For 2010 De Wulf, for example, created a jacket that included an alligator head, the beans affixed to a cardboard base that allowed for an open gator's mouth.

The beans, some of which may be spray-painted gold or other colors, are not difficult to work with (the rice is more difficult) and innovations in 2010 included soaking the beans to make them soft enough to be sewn. Members may also make throws using beans, and in 2010 handed out glue guns as throws characteristic of the group. In 2009 the Southern Food and Beverage Museum presented an exhibition of Red Beans krewe costumes as examples of food-related ritual clothing.

Red Beans Royalty

The parade's internal organization both reflects and revises traditional Mardi Gras. Where in an Uptown parade royalty is selected on the basis of family connections—you have to be born into the right family to be royalty in Rex—Red Beans has a looser construction, not tying the royal positions of king, queen, and princess to gender, and involving a vote by the krewe members. De Wulf notes that the group seems to be evolving its own traditions as time goes on (use of the word *beaners* to distinguish themselves, specialized conversations about glue guns, the selection of the group's princess, who may be man or woman, on the basis of that person's being the group's "most ridiculous" in terms of costume and "persona"). The princess, king, and queen are annually selected at the party that precedes the parade (there is also a photo shoot of members in costume on the Sunday before Lundi Gras), in part on the basis of costumes most liked by the group (De Wulf sees inspiration for this in the Indians' emphasis on the importance of the "prettiness" of costumes and the competitiveness that evokes). Some members tend to be a little secretive about the costumes they are working on, an attitude well within the traditions of the Indians and of Mardi Gras in general, with its secrecy regarding such matters as krewe affiliations and the selection of kings and queens.

Joining the Krewe of Red Beans can be simple, as evidenced by the example of Dianne Honoré, an accomplished costumer, whose work with other new parades is discussed in this book's last chapter. Honoré saw a Facebook post by a friend of hers, Margie Perez, about the Krewe of Red Beans the night before its 2012 parade. She sent Perez a message, and at 6:15 a.m. Lundi Gras morning, received the reply that she was welcome to join the krewe, but that she would need to show up in a red bean costume. Honoré went into her kitchen, grabbed a Styrofoam plate, and began hot-gluing red beans, rice, and a piece of French bread to the plate. She affixed the plate to a dramatic hat she had, and voila, dashed off to join the parade.

The very next year, Honoré was voted in as queen. With more time to prepare, she created a fabulous fusion costume, with an all-white under-garment covered by a red-checked tablecloth apron and headdress. Her towering tignon headdress was topped by a plate with red beans and rice, a piece of French bread, and an empty glass bottle of wine, and festooned with large red ostrich feathers and sprigs of Spanish moss. That alone might have been enough to win the competition, but in addition, she had a fully beaned artwork of a voodoo doll, a five-foot beaned snake that wrapped around her body, and dance shoes fully decorated with red beans. A five-foot staff, with a red bean decorated skull, and coordinating dancing shoes, also fully beaned, completed the costume. The experience was a whirlwind, for that year, 2013, the krewe still met before the parade to vote on the roles of king, queen, and princess. In the matter of an hour, Honoré found herself elected, decorated with a large sash that proclaimed her "Queen," and the parade began. While the costume led to Honoré's being honored as queen, she was an appropriate selection for other reasons, as she has a long association with red beans and rice from her family's neighborhood restaurant, where red beans and rice were served every Monday, to her own work as a culture bearer, which includes giving demonstration to large groups about the history of red beans and rice, as well as guidance in how to prepare the dish.

Mary Langston's experience in joining the krewe in some ways parallels that of Dianne Honoré's. She didn't hear about the parade the first year, but received the honor of being selected queen for the 2015 parade, her first year of participating. The selection of the queen is democratic, unlike the practice in many Uptown parades, where family connections are criti-cal. Red Beans holds its "after-party" or "ball" the night before the parade. Members wear their costumes, and all vote on whose is the best, most worthy of being honored as "queen" or "king." (The gender of the wearer is not the operative factor, as the queen in 2017 was a male.) Langston describes her vision of a fusion costume as "a dream idea" (Mary Langston, interview with Robin Roberts, September 7, 2017). Starting with a Frida Kahlo costume, Langston fused the pieces with a Día de los Muertos (Day of the Dead) theme. Langston did not know when she devised her costume that there was a sub-krewe in Red Beans, known as the Dead Beans, who created costumes based on the Day of the Dead motifs. Drawing on her experience as a member of Muses, an Uptown parade whose signature throw is glittered shoes, Langston glittered beans for her costume, introducing a new feature to the krewe's costuming. Langston describes the Krewe of Red Beans as "more like a bar crawl than a walking parade. We stop at bars, so there is more drinking at each stop" (interview). In contrast to the St. Joan Parade (in which Langston also participates), Red Beans has "more emphasis on costuming," with the group getting together for the very detailed work of "beaning" (interview), attaching the beans with hot glue to clothing, hats, and shoes.

Dead Beans

De Wulf has come up with a novel way to deal with the krewe's burgeoning popularity. While 'tit Rəx and other krewes have responded to growth by capping or closing membership and creating waiting lists, De Wulf resisted this idea. In part this issue was brought to a head by the krewe's gathering place, the Marigny Opera House, having strict rules on having no more than a one hundred people at a time in their building. Valuing the krewe's openness to new members, De Wulf decided to add an additional Red Beans parade, drawing on a sub-krewe. The krewe's 2009 king organized a sub-krewe of members decorating costumes with skull motifs in the manner of the Mexican Día de Los Muertos tradition. The organization does not have sub-krewes in the same sense that Krewe du Vieux is made up of independent groups; the king had announced to all members that they could join his "sub-krewe" simply by creating a costume with the day of the dead theme. The day of the dead theme has proved to be a regular aspect of Red Beans, so much so that De Wulf decided that this group could parade in the Bayou St. John neighborhood, and meet up with the Red Beans parade. De Wulf approached two longtime Dead Beans paraders to be in charge, Mark Steven and Chris Le Blanc. At first the two resisted the idea, but gradually began to see it as De Wulf does, as a positive development related to the growth of interest in Red Beans. To further develop this new offshoot, De Wulf purchased a used hearse that the group will be decorating, and hired the Panorama Jazz Band and the Bon Bon Vivant band to provide music. The experience, he says, thus will differ from the traditional brass band music that the Red Bean parade uses, the Treme Brass Band. The Dead Beans are still part of the Red Beans group, and De

Wulf says that that he could imagine handling additional expansion by adding a third parade that originates in the Treme neighborhood.

The Dead Beans suits first appeared in the second year of the Red Bean parade, in 2009. As Devin De Wulf explains, "there has always been a small group of 'Dead Beans' suits in the 'traditional' Red Bean parade. As the crowd size grew, we decided to create our second parade—one that would roll at the same exact time as our first parade" (e-mail, June 3, 2018). The reasons for creating an apparent competitor to the successful Red Beans parade were threefold, In De Wulf's words: "By forcing spectators to choose, we keep both parades on the smaller size. Keeping the 'specialness' of a small neighborhood parade [for both parades]" (e-mail). In addition, new members could be added to the Krewe of Red Beans for people who could parade with Dead Beans. Finally, as De Wulf emphasizes, the expansion continues the growth of new downtown Mardi Gras, in a manner sympathetic to the original new parades. Dead Beans, he asserts, "allows for a new tradition to be created—in a new neighborhood, with a new theme and musical genre" (e-mail).

But before the Dead Beans inaugural parade, there was a practice of sorts in October 2017. In an expansion of the group's activities, a call went out to Red Beaners who had costumes with Día de Los Muertos costumes to parade during Voodoo Fest, a large and successful music festival that takes place in City Park. Mary Langston, whose Frida Kahlo–inspired dress won her the honor of being named queen in 2016, answered the call. She explains, "It was a short parade through the Voodoo Fest grounds with members from another group who had skull and bones outfits. It was a very short second-line parade, but a nice warm up to the real thing on Lundi Gras. We were a visual treat for the fest goers. There were not any throws, but was spirited marching. It was a fun prequel to the real parade, and totally appropriate for Halloween/All Saints setting of Voodoo Fest" (e-mail, June 9, 2018). De Wulf explains that the gig at Voodoo Fest "got us a little cash to pay for our Hearse" (which they decorated with beans as they did with the Volkswagen for Red Beans) (e-mail, June 10, 2018). Dead Beans got the opportunity "through a krewe member who also works for the production company that puts on Voodoo Fest each year" (e-mail, June 10, 2018). While De Wulf believes such commercial opportunities are justified in the interest of keeping the krewe's membership dues low, he also comments, "In general, I believe such activity should be limited in nature because of the [importance of] authenticity in carnival—but every now and then seems fine" (e-mail, June 10, 2018).

Dead Beans Mark Stevens and Jessica Fontaine. Photo by Ryan Hodgson-Rigsbee. Permission of Ryan Hodgson-Rigsbee.

The Dead Beans parade of 2018 was a marked success, with "one hundred new krewe members and over fifteen-hundred spectators" (e-mail). While retaining the original krewe's use of red beans to create costumes, Dead Beans "welcomed any suit that dealt with death—from any tradition or folklore from around the word . . . or members could pay homage to someone who passed away—either someone they knew personally (like a father), or someone they wanted to honor (like Tom Petty, who passed away not long before the parade)" (website). Like Red Beans, the Dead Beans also have an annual theme. Like Red Beans, as De Wulf describes it, "Suits ran the gamut from the serious to the silly" (e-mail). His wife created a suit to honor her grandmother who passed away a week before the parade. "Another member honored the memory of her father who passed away long before the parade—he loved playing the banjo, so her suit was a re-creation of his banjo (but in beans of course)" (e-mail). Since the inaugural theme was "Tarot," some participants made suits based on tarot cards.

Since cultural appropriation remains an issue in any new parade, it is relevant to note the participation of Mexican American krewe members, who "tap[ped] into Mexican visual arts—both Aztec-inspired and Day-of-the-Dead inspired" (e-mail). While this participation doesn't eliminate concern about appropriation (for example, Mexican appropriation of Aztec culture), its appearance alongside another costume that "represented the 'dead' banana industry of New Orleans" (e-mail) suggests the range and playfulness of the Dead Beans theme. In a reference to recent political passings, one woman wore a bean jacket with a portrait of Sean Spicer, with the legend (in beans) "So Long Spicey."

Significantly, De Wulf chose to march with Dead Beans, letting someone else lead the Red Beans parade for the first time. He explains: "We figured the Red Beans Parade could run more easily without me there—vs. the new parade, where it was important for me to be there to troubleshoot (which I certainly had to do on a few moments). So a long-time member of the Krewe stepped up to serve as our guide for the Red Beans Parade. In fact, after learning of her task, Lucia decided to make her whole bean-suit themed around her role, she became a stewardess—guiding the parade with those two-finger-together-points" (e-mail, June 3, 2018).

Yet the parades' interconnected nature was emphasized by their coming together at the end of each parade; they converged by the Backstreet Cultural Museum in Treme. This is where the Red Beans Parade traditionally ended, due to its significance to the African American traditions and figures who feature prominently in the city's culture.

Costumed in a suit with a skeleton outline in beads, beaned boots, a detachable heart made of beans, and a small skeleton doll on his back, De Wulf took the beaned megaphone to lead the crowd in a series of toasts to krewe members' friends and family members who had died the past year. Moving slowly and somewhat somberly, the parade moved from Cabrini Bridge, where the toasts were made, along the Esplanade Ridge to the Treme neighborhood. This Mid-City location was significant, for as Doug MacCash noted in his nola.com live video coverage, "I think [this parade] is significant because there has been an enthusiasm for do-it-yourself marching clubs since Katrina, and I think they're spreading . . . this is an example of one spreading into a neighborhood where there hadn't been one before" (nola.com live, Facebook, February 12, 2018).

Bartlett and Stoyanova, the mother and daughter artists who partici-pated in Red Beans in 2017, compared their participation in Dead Beans to the original parade. Stoyanova approves of De Wulf's decision to cap both krewes at a hundred, saying, "You can't have a marching krewe of over one hundred [people]; it stops being a traveling street party and becomes Chewbacchus" (the parade with thousands of participants discussed in chapter 5) (interview, July 5, 2018). Both women noted the almost com-plete absence of tourists, in a much quieter neighborhood. Stoyanova, who coded the Red Beans surveys, noted a number of European tourists now attend Red Beans, and she believes Red Beans, unlike the brand-new Dead Beans, must be in a tourist guidebook or website. The women created special throws for the Dead Beans parade, including hair clips with unique skeleton faces and beans.

Members of the group (who tend to be in their twenties and some of whom have come to New Orleans recently, attracted by its current reputa-tion as a magnet for the youthful) have said that they appreciate the social aspects of the krewe, appreciate opportunities for meeting a wider circle of people, and for regularly getting together with creative, "artsy" types. They may see it as a means for creative expression. De Wulf sees it as combining several elements of New Orleans culture (a city, he says, "great for oddball ideas"; interview with de Caro) and New Orleans parading and second-line traditions. Certainly the symbolism of red beans and rice as a quintessential New Orleans dish ties the krewe into the local consciousness and rather deftly uses food to express local identity (perhaps all the more important for the group's members who have come from elsewhere and find themselves in a place not always easy to fathom or fit into). De Wulf himself likes the hodgepodge nature of red beans and rice the dish, as representing the hodgepodge of people in the krewe. Surely food, in a city obsessed by food and a city with a famously well-developed local cuisine, is a particularly fitting symbolic arena for a group tying together a variety of older local traditions to create its own and to connect with a place that has a unique sense of itself (for other comments on food symbolism and local New Orleans identity, see de Caro, "Legends"). The referencing of older traditions and local ways of life may be particularly important to relative newcomers to New Orleans who are coming to terms with this city and its often quirky culture. Indeed, involvement in Mardi Gras may itself serve as an important entry point into local life and belonging for newcomers.

Conclusion

The Red Beans krewe is, obviously, quite different from the other new parades, even though they share genesis in the whirl of Carnival events and history and tradition. The Red Beans parade seems much in the tradition of Mardi Gras walking clubs (with some inspiration from second-lines): The St. Joan parade, despite its secular nature, has almost the air of a religious procession, a spirit largely foreign to Mardi Gras despite its religious roots (foreign to the drinking and ceremonial nudity at least associated with Mardi Gras in the popular consciousness [see Shrum and Mayer], or even to the more innocent parade throws and ladders used for children's parade viewing). The Skinz n Bonez group references a historical Mardi Gras practice, of Skulls and Bones, and worked with current practitioners to develop their practices. Skinz n Bonez focuses more on drums and music than the other groups. The Red Beans group draws heavily on the New Orleans past, while the St. Joan Project references much wider historical and cultural roots.

A certain unity in costuming is important to the Downtown marching groups, whether it's beans and rice as decorative materials, medieval-style garb, or painted skeleton costumes and makeup. All tie into significant aspects of New Orleans culture, whether the North Side Skull and Bones Gang, the Mardi Gras Indians, social aid and pleasure clubs and second-lining, or French history and heritage. And certainly all play with important local symbols: the Red Beans members have made local food, in turn representative of local identity, central to their costuming and their own name and identity; the members of the Joan of Arc Project use an historical figure representative of the city's French heritage and details of her life and image to tap into a range of ideas; and the Skinz n Bonez reprise a new, respectful version of traditional African American Skulls and Bones gangs.

In the past, Carnival traditions have come and sometimes gone, such that Carnival, despite the conservative power of tradition, both innovates and lets innovations pass away. It may be the ability of the St. Joan, Skinz n Bonez, Red Beans groups to adopt and adapt important local symbolic meanings that will ensure the success, persistence, and further development of each organization and its emerging tradition. The emergence of the Dead Beans Parade from Red Beans, however, points to the perhaps unavoidable aspect of new Mardi Gras krewes: how to grow without engaging in harmful cultural appropriation. As participant Stoyanova explains, "Mardi Gras is not a dead thing for old white men, but it is a constantly evolving tradition, responsive to the culture, to the people who participate" (interview, July 5, 2018). Bartlett agrees, explaining that Red Beans is "do-it-yourself culture, anti-Rex" (the traditional Uptown, upper-class large parade) (interview, July 5, 2018). That new Latinx krewes have emerged raises issues about how to incorporate a variety of cultural traditions without generating conflict and animosity among the various parading groups. In its unique homage to the Mardi Gras Indians, of beading with red beans, and now of employing some of the visuals of the Mexican Day of the Dead, the Red Beans krewe points a way to expansion without dilution, to have new parades with nods to other artistic and folkloric traditions. How this convergence will fare remains to be seen, but Dead Beans successful and uncontroversial first year bodes well for this mode of creating even more new Downtown parades.

CHAPTER 5

Chewbacchus and Science-Fiction Carnival

Leslie A. Wade

Downtown Mardi Gras has witnessed an array of new formations and new Carnival activities, but the largest and most spectacular of these undertakings is no doubt the Intergalactic Krewe of Chewbacchus. The krewe launched in 2011; in 2012 the *New York Times* noted Chewbacchus as the "quickest growing" Mardi Gras organization (Thier). It has become a wildly popular Carnival event, of massive dimension, that populates the Downtown streets of New Orleans with a fantastic array of space aliens, fantasy players, and sci-fi aficionados. On the second Saturday night before Mardi Gras, one can stand on the corner of Franklin and Decatur and see a parade of dazzling otherworldliness that includes a large, furry creature sporting a head-wreath of grape leaves, the figurehead and inspiration of the event—the Sacred Drunken Wookiee (modeled on Han Solo's companion in the *Star Wars* films). Onlookers fill the sidewalks of the route and cheer on this intergalactic stream of revelers, calling to familiar heroes and sci-fi icons, celebrating a strange and fascinating hybrid of Carnival expression, an uncanny amalgam of Mardi Gras and Dragon Con. This new enterprise highlights the playful whimsy of its participants and a joyful taking to the streets, where a passion for New Orleans conspires with fandom zeal to generate one of Carnival's most colorful, eccentric, and bizarre spectacles.

The origin and emergence of this sci-fi krewe offer rich opportunities for analyzing post-Katrina Carnival. The krewe may assume pride of place among new organizations in its degree of innovation and willingness to stretch the parameters of Carnival practice. In this respect the parade challenges traditionalists in an outright manner and brazenly explores new

The First Launching of the Intergalactic Krewe of Chewbacchus, 2011. Photo by Robin Roberts. Permission of Robin Roberts.

pathways and possibilities, appealing directly to nerds and geeks who love both sci-fi fantasy and New Orleans culture. Chewbacchus participates not just in the explosion of Downtown Carnival but in the broader changes witnessed in the Downtown neighborhoods themselves, where infusions of new residents have triggered contestation with natives and long-term residents, where educated and high-tech newcomers jockey with working-class neighbors, where the costs of living in post-Katrina New Orleans have inspired debate over the future development and identity of the city—particularly in the neighborhoods of Marigny, Bywater, and St. Roch.

The exceptional aspects of the Intergalactic Krewe of Chewbacchus—its massive membership, its spectacular array of contraptions and costumes, its embrace of otherworldly realms—draw curiosity and warrant analysis. This chapter illuminates the origins, mission, protocols, and organization of the krewe, introducing its longtime leader, Ryan Ballard; it also showcases two prominent sub-krewes (the group uses the designation "SubKrewe"), Sith Happens and the Redshirt Rebellion. Beyond documenting the origins and operations of Chewbacchus, the chapter looks at the krewe in the context of Downtown New Orleans, where dynamics of in-migration and gentrification are altering neighborhood geographies, often inciting civil war over cultural propriety. The chapter concludes by connecting Chewbacchus to utopian strains in Carnival and in science fiction, and by questioning how this often ungainly, fantastical parade of futurist imaginings might open up new, socially productive space in post-Katrina New Orleans—how utopian play might inspire pathways to better present-day material worlds.

Emergence of Science-Fiction Carnival

New Orleans has seldom curried favor for bold, forward thinking. The city rather has long traded in images and associations that evoke the past—gas lamps, banquettes, chicory coffee, etc. No one could mistake the city for one of the shining sun-belt metropolises in the mold of Charlotte or Atlanta. New Orleans has nurtured the impression of being out of step with change, unconcerned with trends and fashions, as though caught in an amber that conserves old-time habits and daily routines. In his acclaimed work *Nine Lives: Death and Life in New Orleans*, Dan Baum expounds on this New Orleans sensibility. He notes the problems that have reflected so poorly on the city—poverty, failing schools, violence, corruption—but points out a poll taken just before Katrina indicating that more New Orleanians, "regardless of age, race, or wealth," were "extremely satisfied" with their lives than residents of any other American city (xi). This finding, bolstered by his studied observation of New Orleans mores and social structures, led Baum to conclude the following: "New Orleanians really want nothing more than for everything to stay the same" (xi).

Given its predilection for the familiar, for cherishing long-held patterns of daily life (such as red beans on Mondays), the city does not by and large present itself in futuristic terms. It is thus not surprising that New Orleans has traditionally enjoyed little cachet or prominence in science-fiction circles. In fact, the genre can seem somewhat antithetical to the spirit of the city. That noted, one can nevertheless spot sightings of local sci-fi phenomena and expressions of futuristic imaginings. Science-fiction imagery appears in the songs of several New Orleans bands, including those of Rotary Downs and Egg Yolk Jubilee. Novelist Moira Crone has penned a futuristic tale of New Orleans in her award-winning work *The Not Yet*. Visual artist Dara Quick recently hosted sci-fi-themed installations in One Eyed Jacks and the Bywater Art Lofts. In Prospect 3, Dawn Dedeaux created a stunning outdoor environmental artwork titled *Mothership*. New Orleans has become a regular venue for Wizard World, a mecca event for lovers of science fiction and fantasy. MechaCon has served a similar function for devotees of anime. The city is home to *Star Trek* and *Star Wars* fan organizations. Recent TV/film shoots have included the comedy *SuperCon* and the Marvel comic series *Cloak and Dagger*. And upon the death of Leonard Nimoy, the city hosted a second-line honoring the revered actor and the beloved character Spock.

While such instances do not necessarily qualify as a trend or movement, this cultural bubbling does speak to new swirlings in the city, a readiness to engage the futuristic and the fantastical. Despite the city's perceived resistance to change, New Orleans has since its inception undergone continuous reinvention. In *Authentic New Orleans: Tourism, Culture, and Race in the Big Easy*, Tulane sociologist Kevin Gotham relates that symbols and icons of New Orleans culture "have always been in flux and transformation" (vii). The Intergalactic Krewe of Chewbacchus participates in this process of continued transformation, perhaps as starkly as any new krewe, as it takes Carnival traditions and New Orleans iconography and relocates them, recasting them in a science-fiction world, producing stunning new amalgams of Carnival hybridity. The enterprise has become a rallying cause for sci-fi fans and for Carnival revelers seeking the outré and the exotic.

The guiding figure in the emergence of Chewbacchus is Ryan Ballard, a forty-year-old arts educator and artist, a creator of puppetry and large-scale moving interactive artworks. A native of southern Missouri, Ballard received a BFA with an emphasis in sculpture from the University of Central Missouri. Taken by the travel bug following a study-abroad experience in Australia, he taught English in Asia and led tour groups. He shares that his most rewarding experiences include "sailing the Nile river; trekking in the Himalayas and Andes; and hitchhiking across Australia" ("Artist Guest"). His global travels fueled his sense of adventure, stirred his imagination, and whetted his desire for artistic experimentation.

After several years of a vagabond existence, in 2004 he came to New Orleans "with a fellow tour guide who would later become his wife" (Watercutter). He found arts-related employment, taking various jobs in museums and after-school programs. He set up a home-based puppetry company and studio, performing under the stage name Dr. Razzamataz.

His draw to and affection for the city relate to the uncommon aspects of New Orleans, its dissimilarity from other areas in the United States, its penchant for creating spaces and living environments that appeal to the eccentric—he was, in short, "looking for someplace weirdo" (interview with Wade, October 2, 2017). Ballard jokes that if he hadn't settled in New Orleans that he might have chosen a "Portuguese fishing village" or "somewhere on the Mekong River" (interview). Life in difficult places does not daunt Ballard; he is not fazed by the city's dubious infrastructure and often-noted third-world dimension. He has delved into the welter of the city and seized upon its unique aspects. Above all, Ballard credits New Orleans—as does Mardi Claw of Skinz n Bonez discussed in chapter 2— for its openness, as "a place to explore a creative lifestyle naturally, to do creative things" (interview).

Ballard is an energetic, exuberant individual whose raucous sense of play carries metaphysical inflections. The grandson of a fundamentalist minister, Ballard espouses no creeds but has retained a regard for spirituality, an interest nourished by his world travels. A blend of reverence and impertinence fuels much of his artwork. In 2012 he exhibited an electric sculpture project in an empty Uptown New Orleans church that included a "giant, throbbing, nail-pierced heart" (MacCash "Chewbacchus Is"). Many of Ballard's ventures exhibit unruly, contrastive, oppositional energies, what he describes as "the intersection between the sacred and the profane" (Ballard, *CONtraflow V*).

It is this intersection that in part accounts for the creation and emergence of Chewbacchus, as the irreverent, anarchic play of the krewe, in Ballard's estimation, connects Carnival revelers to mythic dimensions. The parade draws inspiration from the ancient Greek god Dionysus (Bacchus is the Roman equivalent), the god of intoxication and the unconscious, whose ecstatic rituals brought rapturous modes of community. Ballard holds that Mardi Gras retains its religious dimension and that Chewbacchus consequently functions as "half conceptual art project, half bacchanalia" (interview). Ballard moreover sees science fiction narratives and heroes as "mythologies of our time . . . Superman is Hercules, Batman is Orpheus" (interview). In this light Chewbacchus casts today's pop-culture gods in a ritual of ancient performance, drawing celebrants into new experiences of joyous encounter.

The Katrina disaster stands as a formative factor in Ballard's personal and professional life. Having lost all of his possessions to the flood, he relocated to Colorado Springs, Colorado, and accepted a teaching position (during this time he also completed an M.A. in education at the University of Colorado). Colorado Springs, however, did not suit his artistic and progressive outlooks; the city is a strong bastion of Christian conservatism. According to Ballard, there were "no freaks and geeks" there (interview). This time in exile was important for deepening Ballard's desire to return to New Orleans and its more tolerant environment. It was also significant

Overlord Ryan Ballard. Photo by Ryan Ballard. Permission of Ryan Ballard.

for introducing Ballard to the Burning Man Festival in northwest Nevada (where he would sojourn for renewal and experimentation in communal art). Ballard shares: "There is nothing better than camping with a bunch of beautiful, fun-loving, generous, creative people and enjoying spectacles of ephemeral art" (qtd. in Etheridge). Burning Man stirred Ballard's reflection on mass spectacle and began his thinking on how he might bring something of the ritualistic large-scale art experiment to New Orleans Carnival.

Ballard returned to New Orleans in 2010 committed to immersing himself in the art scene and cultural life of the city, to be an active force in the city's restoration. He became involved in Downtown Mardi Gras, parading in the well-established Krewe du Vieux and Society of St. Anne. This was a time of great creative foment in the city, as the energy of recovery proved a catalyst for artistic and musical expressions. Ballard was an active participant in this upsurge of creativity, open to new modes and avenues, eager to offer his own artistic contribution.

Perhaps not surprisingly, the concept for Chewbacchus came in a bar, the Big Top Circus, a haven for young artists and alternative performance.

Co-founder Kirah Haubrich recalls talking with a bartender, a newcomer from Indiana, about Mardi Gras and his remark that he "didn't see a lot of cosplay [sci-fi/fantasy costume play]" (qtd. in Matisse). This offhand comment stirred Haubrich, who engaged Ballard in conversation about this gap in the Mardi Gras landscape. Soon the idea for a new sci-fi venture took hold and prompted actual implementation. Ballard quickly designed and built Bar2-D2—a rolling android bar—for this anticipated event. Interest grew and activities were announced. A cosplay fashion show was held at the Big Top a few days before the parade. The Krewe of Chewbacchus subsequently rolled in 2011 with a group numbering near three hundred. In this enterprise Ballard found his unique contribution to the recovering city: a large-scale public art event, a new parade in the Carnival calendar—"for nerds, for popular culture" (interview).

This first parade marked the beginning of a new Carnival venture and, in so doing, set itself against (and within) Carnival tradition. The conception of Chewbacchus represents a mashup, the unlikely combination of Chewbacca from *Star Wars* and Bacchus the Roman god of wine. Beyond referencing classical mythology, the new krewe invoked the city's high-profile Krewe of Bacchus, which rolls with much pomp and adulation on the Saturday night before Fat Tuesday. In referencing this iconic organization, Chewbacchus was able to slyly invoke and tacitly critique established Carnival tradition and also gain its own place of distinction, as a kind of counter-Bacchus, as a Downtown upstart.

While one can examine the operations and iconography of Chewbacchus in contestatory terms, as a challenge to or inversion of Bacchus, it is also possible to see similar strategies and shared outlooks. The two no doubt represent different eras in Carnival history, different memberships, and different self-presentations. They also share the common experience of going up against the expectations and protocols of tradition. On some ironic level Chewbacchus is the progeny of Bacchus, as both have worked to open up the province of Carnival and to experiment with the pop-culture possibilities of Mardi Gras performance.

Like Chewbacchus, Bacchus raised eyebrows and ruffled feathers at its beginning. Spearheaded by the Brennan brothers, Dick and Owen Jr. (of the famous restaurant family), Bacchus from the outset was geared to an outsider perspective, intended "to cater to out-of-town visitors" (Tassin and Stall 26). Rolling for the first time in 1969, Bacchus functioned as a promotional venture, to tout the city and to stir business and tourism (not to massage patrician self-regard).

Bacchus proved to be an expansive and somewhat iconoclastic organization. It was quite willing to bring in out-of-town members and guests. It did away with protocols of the queen and royalty court. Instead of hosting a traditional, exclusive ball, the krewe threw a huge-scale "bash" at the Rivergate Convention Center, in a conventional hall that accommodated a procession of "oversize floats" (Laborde 119). This event was open to the public, offering six to ten thousand tickets (Elder 10). Eschewing the anachronistic trappings of other krewes, Bacchus selected images and themes that were "more popular and less literary" (Laborde 119).

Enlisting the services of talented designer Blaine Kern, Bacchus pushed the boundaries of spectacle and ostentation, evidenced in its showpiece float Bacchusaurus. Bacchus advanced the establishment of the "super-krewe," where riders would number over six hundred with two dozen floats (Elder 73); the parade experimented with double-tandem floats. Such expense and innovation drew some envy, as Bacchus made "the other nighttime parades of Momus, Comus, and Proteus look old and tired" (Huber 66).

Like Chewbacchus some years later, Bacchus mined the popularity and allure of TV and film. The krewe brought Hollywood notables to New Orleans. The first honorary king of Bacchus was Danny Kaye. Subsequent years saw a continuing line of celebrities: Jackie Gleason, Perry Como, Jim Nabors, Charlton Heston, Billy Crystal, William Shatner, Henry Winkler, and Will Ferrell. Bacchus profited from its embrace of media culture, raising its profile and expanding its audience, taking Mardi Gras from the local stage to the national stage. Criticized by some for coarsening Carnival fare, with lowbrow and circuslike antics, Bacchus blazed new ground and unabashedly embraced American popular culture.

Just as its predecessor, Chewbacchus can on one level be seen as a kind of play on or satire of long-established Uptown Carnival decorum, eschewing parochial mindsets. Like Bacchus, whose appearance "marked a new era of Carnival inclusiveness and extravagance" ("Birth of the Mardi Gras superkrewe"), Chewbacchus has attempted to expand Carnival participation with no elitist appeal to blood lines or class standing. Chewbacchus similarly revels in the realms of popular culture. As with Bacchus, Chewbacchus too in many respects views "bigger as better." Its parade boasts some sizeable otherworldly contraptions that awe and amaze. And the parade itself is immense, with a membership now of over 1,800, enjoying status Ballard touts as the city's largest walking krewe, doubling the size of its nearest competitor (interview).

Ballard shares that his krewe and Bacchus enjoy a cordial relationship and have discussed some collaborative activities (there are individuals who are members in both krewes). Bacchus and Chewbaccus indeed share common histories, as brash invigorations of Carnival. That noted, Chewbacchus is anti-commercial, anti-consumerist—anti-Bacchus, fundamentally counterposed. It is a vehicle for the bizarre and the eccentric, a haven for the geek. In fact, the first Chewbacchus parade strolled along St. Charles following the traditional Bacchus route, but reversed its direction—Chewbacchus in effect paraded Bacchus backwards.

Operation of the Krewe

New Orleans native Adam Karlin acknowledges the beauty and excitement that a spectator can enjoy watching traditional Uptown parades—"We have participated in that and it is a blast"; however, he points to the expense and self-aggrandizement of the Uptown krewes, how the riders traveling above the crowds comport themselves "as if they are Gods" (Karlin). Karlin shares that his "most awesome" Mardi Gras experience came at a Chewbacchus parade, where spectators were mostly locals, cheering on the motley krewe and their hand-crafted adornments. Noting the contrast of parades, Karlin continues: "[Chewbacchus] members do it for different reasons . . . a love of NOLA, a love of Mardi Gras, a love of the characters they are portraying, and a love for the people in the crowd who share their passions" (Karlin).

This glowing review and endorsement of Chewbacchus highlight the kind of delight the parade can bring; it also plays on the implicit differences between the Uptown and Downtown Carnival experiences. It is significant that Chewbacchus originally operated in Uptown's Lower Garden District, out of the 3 Ring Circus Arts Education Center at the Big Top Gallery. Its initial parades ran along St. Charles Avenue. Significantly, in 2013 the krewe moved its route to the Downtown side of Canal and established its den in Marigny, where it housed its contraptions. The upstairs dining hall of Frenchmen Street's Dat Dog in 2017 became a Chewbacchus shrine, the current site for various krewe meetings, including annual royalty dinners and award ceremonies. While in spirit Chewbacchus had always been in sympathy with the Downtown Mardi Gras and its insouciance—Ballard has characterized his krewe as "the red-headed cousin of Krewe du Vieux" (interview)—the krewe in 2013 made the physical, literal move to Downtown and in a figural sense joined the Downtown scene.

The emergence of Chewbacchus has exemplified the eclectic, improvisatory, and hardscrabble nature of Downtown Mardi Gras. In attempting to make room in Carnival for nerd and geek culture, Chewbaccus has issued a call to all branches of the sci-fi fandom community, characterizing its membership as "the most revelrous Star Wars Freaks, Trekkies, Whovians, Mega-Geeks, Gamers, Cosplayers, Circuit Benders, Cryptozoologists, UFO Conspiracy Theorists, Mad Scientists, and all the rest of Super Nerdom" ("About IKOC"). Ballard—operating under the moniker "Space Commander Chewbaccacabra"—has undertaken the daunting task of guiding this motley assemblage.

It has always been the aim of Chewbacchus to provide access to Carnival participation and to limit rules of governance. Chewbacchus is highly populist in outlook. Ballard has spoken of the cost and exclusivity of traditional Carnival, and his desire to "give access to Mardi Gras [to those] that they might not otherwise have" (interview). The group's website promotes this openness and cites its mission as "bringing the magical revelry of Mardi Gras to the poor, disenfranchised, socially awkward, and generally weird masses who may have never had the opportunity to participate in a Mardi Gras parade organization ("About IKOC"). Chewbacchus member Scott Simmons, who formerly rode with one of the super-krewes, has shared that the pre-Katrina costs of participating in the established group ran to over $5,000 (phone interview with Wade, December 1, 2017). Chewbacchus members join for the very affordable sum of $42, the number chosen due to its mystical status in *The Hitchhiker's Guide to the Galaxy*.

Chewbacchus has grown to be an extensive organization (the krewe operates under a 501c3 non-profit status). Maintaining the large membership of the krewe, overseeing the sub-krewes, and registering for permits demand a great time and energy commitment. Ballard is supported by two other "Overlords," Brett Powers and Brooke Ethridge, and a volunteer "OverBoard" support team. Each staff member is responsible for a specific task—such as website maintenance, throws, membership, etc. Ballard has remarked upon the juggling act of establishing order and regularity while attempting to maintain a Dionysian spirit.

Chewbacchus effectively exists as a colorful confederation of individual groups or SubKrewes, which comprise alliances of friends, neighbors, colleagues, relatives, etc. Each SubKrewe may set its own rules of operation or participation, as long as it conforms to both the Chewbacchus leadership policies and city/state laws (such as no glass of any kind on the parade route, no animals, family-friendly conduct, etc.). And each seeks to

The Sacred Drunken Wookiee, Intergalactic Krewe of Chewbacchus. Permission of Brooke Ethridge, IKOC.

establish and promote its own identity and its own creative contribution to the overall parade. These SubKrewes vie for attention and attempt to match one another in cleverness and originality. In artisan manner they build their rolling installations called contraptions (with few exceptions, no motorized vehicles are allowed—in keeping with the krewe's green consciousness). In 2016 the list of SubKrewes participating in Chewbacchus rose from 77 to 115 (Coviello). Ballard cites the current number at 200 (interview). The more established of these include: the Krewe of the Living Dead (zombies), the Rolling Elliots (a bicycle krewe—with ET dolls riding on handlebars—whose membership now exceeds 100), Sith Happens, and the Death-Star Steppers.

Headed by Scott Simmons, Sith Happens serves as a highly successful example of a Chewbacchus SubKrewe. Though already a sci-fi fan himself, Simmons credits his children with bringing him to membership—the parade has now for years served as a cherished family event. Simmons recounts taking his children to Wizard World and there encountering representatives of Chewbacchus, who won him over. At the behest of his son, who was "absolutely" stunned by the costuming, Simmons and family decided to participate in the next parade, dressing as Sith warriors (interview). A conversation with friend Scott Rivet led Simmons, who had immensely enjoyed the parade experience, to consider launching a full enterprise of Sith Lords. The idea became reality—the SubKrewe launched its inaugural march with twelve members. The group now numbers over fifty. They have also joined ranks with a sister group, the In Vaders, who are exclusively "Dark Side."

While the SubKrewe features Sith warriors—Simmons himself dons the costume of the evil Sith lord—the group welcomes others costuming in both "Light Side" and "Dark Side" gear. They begin their parade with shots of scotch and toasts to the Sacred Drunken Wookiee. They parade and prowl the streets with illuminated light sabers. Instructed by a Japanese sword master—from the Light Saber Dueling Society of New Orleans—members enact choreographed duels along the route. They pass throws out to onlookers and always give children with sabers the chance to slay an evil Sith.

The SubKrewe works to build camaraderie and strong relationships. The group maintains an active Facebook page, with friends from Mongolia to Madagascar. Sith Happens holds regular events outside of Carnival, such as an annual barbeque and a New Orleans library book fair. They also parade at the appearance of each year's new movie installment of the *Star Wars* series. Their most notable non-Carnival event is the annual Cantina Crawl, where saber-wielding members proceed through a series of bars in the French Quarter, plied with door prizes and specialty drinks, such as Vaderaid and Jabberslobber. Simmons reports that the pub crawl drew over 125 in 2017 (e-mail, December 3, 2017). The procession often stops traffic, as individuals step from their cars to take photos. Onlookers jest with the SubKrewe and often tag along, swelling the ranks.

Simmons celebrates Chewbacchus and the relationships that have ensued—many couples have formed in the membership. He lauds the parade's inclusivity and its LGBTQ friendliness. The vast expanse of the enterprise has allowed Simmons, a self-described "buttoned-down" type, to encounter

Sith Happens, Cantina Crawl at the House of Blues. Photo by Scott Simmons. Permission of Scott Simmons.

people from across the spectrum, from corporate executives to mechanical engineers to artists, to musicians, to those who "live completely off the grid" (interview). He credits the experience with opening up his own personal and political perspectives. Above all, he credits Chewbacchus for bringing fun and joy, for creating community (the group now even has its own dating service: Chube-love).

The enjoyment of the many SubKrewes during the course of the parade requires an overall regard for safety, which is the province of a special contingent—the Redshirts (officially named Redshirt Rebellion). According to leader Quincy Castillo, who works as captain with Lisa Weisert, this group serves a support and monitoring function; in 2017 the Redshirts numbered above 250 (interview with Wade and Roberts, September 19, 2017). Though involved with Chewbacchus, the group is an entity in its own right. It is allied with the local *Star Trek* fan club and has its own webpage, Facebook account, and membership. The group's use of red shirts is of particular significance. In the *Star Trek* universe, the Redshirts are anonymous characters who wear distinctive red uniforms with the United Federation of Planets logo—they are famously seen as expendable. The group thus plays on the awareness of this insider knowledge regarding the Redshirts' marginal and ironic role, often drawing shouts and jests from onlookers suggesting imminent death.

In many ways, the Chewbacchus parade is a giant cosplay event; the Redshirts serve a number of purposes and might be described as cosplay with a function. On an aesthetic level, the members provide visual continuity and focus—peppering red throughout—for an otherwise quite diffuse and diverse parade. More importantly, they act in service of security and medical aid. Described as "The brave volunteer security force for the Intergalactic Krewe of Chewbacchus," the Redshirt Rebellion sees its mission as one of safety, keeping "the drunken nerds in the parade separate from the drunken nerds watching the parade" (Redshirt). The Redshirts do, however, take their responsibilities seriously. They walk along the edge of the route, broken into thirteen zones, ensuring there is room for the larger floats and bands, marking the rather loose and fluid parade boundaries (Castillo interview). The members assist when there are mechanical failures, when contraptions need to be cleared from the parade path. They also are on the lookout for any contingencies—in a recent parade, the Redshirts were enlisted in moving a burning couch off the route.

While the Redshirt Rebellion undertakes important duties and watches for crowd safety, its members take the opportunity to enjoy the event's sense of cosmic play. They bring imagination and surprise to their costumes. The Redshirt Rebellion displays its own variation of the official *Star Trek* redshirt, featuring a Federation-style emblem that contains a dancing (some say inebriated) Chewbacchus with a second-line umbrella. Participants are encouraged to add their own touches to their uniforms, and many do so, incorporating smaller elements, such as a Dr. Who hat, or seductive accessories, such as tights and feather boas.

The individuals also enjoy banter and play with onlookers, as they consciously embody their genre identities. Frequent postings online and other fandom interactions (at science-fiction conventions) have fanned a rivalry between *Star Trek* and *Star Wars* followers. In a recent parade, two bemused male Redshirts guided a large R2D2 float through the parade—a jarring but humorous sight for those in fandom. In face of the critics who see the diminution of *Star Trek* influence, the Redshirt Rebellion demonstrates that fans are keeping the *Star Trek* universe alive and relevant into the twenty-first century, making it meaningful for a Mardi Gras context.

Highlighting the camaraderie and sense of delight taken by the Redshirts, Castillo, a native Texan who came to New Orleans to work in the film industry, remarks how the parade captivated him at first sight: "I knew

I wanted to be part of it" (interview). He has enjoyed his leadership role, assumed in 2015, but relates that krewe responsibilities are time consuming and ongoing throughout the year. Redshirts also conduct numerous events beyond Chewbacchus, including volunteer service at races held in the city, such as the Rock 'n' Roll Half Marathon. Participating in Chewbacchus has allowed Castillo to enjoy the communal aspects of the organization; it also has given him opportunity to indulge in his long-held science-fiction fascination. Castillo shares his sci-fi bona fides and boasts of the *Star Wars* items from childhood he keeps in his possession: "I may not know where I've put my birth certificate but I know where my Han Solo [toy action figure] is" (interview).

The SubKrewes and ancillaries together contribute to a remarkable and mind-bending Carnival experience. One of the parade's signature features is the procession of the Sacred Drunken Wookiee, the nominal head of the entourage, who weaves throughout the onlookers casting waves and blessings. Members often throw wookiee paraphernalia, such as golden bandoliers, and small wookiee teddy bears (loaded with king-cake babies). The parade has through the years presented a continuous flow of otherworldly creatures and contraptions, including Bar2-D2, a rolling bar and droid keg; a ten-foot, fire-breathing Mechagodzilla; a Reptilian DeLorean; and a Millennium Falcon (built atop a used golf cart). One of the parade's most memorable highlights came in 2013 when the Millennium Falcon served to convey the honorary king Peter Mayhew, the actor who originally starred as Chewbacchus in the *Star Wars* films. The event was hailed as "cosmic triumph" (MacCash, "Chewbacchus 2013"). Mayhew again participated in the event in 2015. *NCIS: New Orleans* star Scott Bakula, also noted for his roles in TV series *Quantum Leap* and *Star Trek: Enterprise*, made a special guest appearance at the krewe's 2016 after-party, Chewbacchanal.

Chewbacchus has established itself as a must-see event in the Carnival season, now regularly noted in the canonical *Arthur Hardy's Mardi Gras Guide*. After adjusting its parade route in 2016, the krewe winds through Bywater and Marigny, reaching a highpoint in the Frenchmen Street entertainment district. Crowds each year continue to grow, with numbers estimated in the tens of thousands. Ballard has indeed launched a remarkable enterprise, a socially aware, artistically captivating, infectious piece of egalitarian street theatre. The enterprise continues to exhibit its creative energy and guiding vision: "We are DIY, homemade, homegrown, totally sustainable, GREEN to the gills, and the 1st true OPEN SOURCE parade" ("About IKOC"). The achievement of Chewbacchus has not gone unnoticed. SubKrewes now travel from other states and countries to partic-ipate in the event. The *Washington Post*, the *New York Times*, the *Huffington Post*, and CNN have covered the krewe. Ballard takes deserved pride in the achievement of Chewbacchus and has garnered praise; in 2015 the *Gambit*, the local independent weekly, honored Ballard as one of the top civic lead-ers under forty making contributions to the city of New Orleans (Ricks).

Chewbacchus in Context: In-Migration and Geography

On many levels Chewbacchus illustrates in textbook fashion the insights of folklorist Frank de Caro. In "Emerging New Orleans Mardi Gras Tradi-tions," de Caro writes: "given the Carnivalesque nature of Carnival and its associated spirits of satire, disorder, and license to behave in unorthodox ways, there have always been possibilities for creating alternative struc-tures of participation" (2). Chewbacchus has certainly expanded the range of Mardi Gras possibilities; it has added significantly to the dimension and dynamism of Downtown Carnival. And importantly it has provided opportunity and access, regardless of income or social standing. While many natives enjoy membership, Chewbacchus has drawn into its ranks a significant number of transplants, particularly those who arrived after the Katrina disaster.

The wide appeal of Chewbacchus in New Orleans Carnival merits respect and admiration, as the krewe has proven itself one of the most inventive and egalitarian of Mardi Gras organizations, a do-it-yourself success. However, its emergence in the post-Katrina context invites inves-tigation that goes beyond particular practices and presentations. Chew-bacchus stands as a new iteration of Carnival parading; it also represents new populations and new perspectives. In this respect the krewe finds itself implicated in far reaching questions that concern the city, regard-ing demographic shifts, gentrification, and the hybridization of culture. Chewbacchus thus serves as an illuminating barometer of the present social climate. Its futuristic orientation moreover draws attention forward, to how New Orleans might evolve, how the city might negotiate its twenty-first-century challenges.

Following the disaster of Katrina and the widespread speculation that New Orleans was in a death spiral, residents concerned themselves with day-to-day realities and trusted that hope would prevail over despair. In these dark days many of the changes that have come to New Orleans would have seemed beyond the realm of belief. Given the legion of worries and fears rampant at the time, few voiced concern that the city would see an overabundance of new residents, particularly young, educated newcomers seeking to participate in the city's recovery. Nonetheless, this in-migration did occur, bringing change to New Orleans, fueling new activities and associations—including the Krewe of Chewbacchus.

In defining the term "hot spot," Lynda Gratton explains how some environments or locales create a magnetism, an "igniting" purpose that causes people to "flock to it—they want to be part of it" (13). In inhabiting such places, people feel "energized and vibrantly alive" (1). New Orleans following Katrina surprisingly found itself in such a position, as it became a hotspot for thousands of new residents who wanted to join in the city's rebuilding.

Brian Boyles notes this phenomenon as a series of waves (95), with the first newcomers being those involved in various aid activities, often volunteers, who worked to rehabilitate the city and being won over, desiring to put down roots in New Orleans. Many of these included health workers, teachers, and those in the not-for-profit realm. Artists and musicians also felt drawn to the energy and creativity spurred by the city's comeback. Another wave followed soon thereafter. As recovery gained momentum, city leaders made considerable effort to draw new residents who were involved in entrepreneurial activities. Tax breaks were offered for new investments, particularly in the field of digital media. Such inducements, along with the appeal of a New Orleans lifestyle, led to a surge of in-migration, including many educated newcomers with high-tech skills. Entities such as Launch Pad, the Idea Village, and GNO, Inc., stimulated an entrepreneurial environment. Between 2011 and 2013, start-up ventures in New Orleans "launched at a 64 percent higher rate than the national average" (Roig-Franzia, "Rebirth" 36). *Forbes* in 2014 noted New Orleans as first in the country's "new brainpower cities" (Kotkin).

The energy and appeal of the city proved a magnet to young people from around the country. New Orleans saw its "cool" cachet surge. Local writer Chris Rose observed: "Instead of dying, New Orleans is a city reborn. A work-in-progress to be sure, but a city renewed, rebuilt, and reimagined" ("Before" 33) Rose hailed the city's upswing in fortune, celebrating in half-playful tone: "Millennials, dreamers and visionaries are here creating the next new business model, designing the next great app, fusing the next landmark technology, mixing the next banging cocktail. We're the new Austin. The new Portland. The new Brooklyn. Hollywood South. Hipster City USA. The New New Orleans" ("Before" 33).

As a hot spot, however, New Orleans has found itself in something of an unanticipated double bind. Long experiencing outmigration and an eroding economy, New Orleans has happily welcomed new residents and economic diversification. The energy of recovery has spurred new businesses, heightened the city's national reputation, and enlivened the local arts scene. This turn has also raised many concerns, involving the shift of political influence along racial lines, the reach of economic prosperity, the escalating costs of housing, and the dilution of the city's cultural identity. "Hipster" and "gentrification" have become buzzwords. *Men's Journal* noted New Orleans in 2015 as one of the Ten Best Places to Live Now; however, the metrics for this designation—"a slew of inventive pop-up restaurants, an organic food co-op"—clearly reflect an upscale sensibility and furthermore invited speculative intervention—"a 150-year-old Creole cottage can be had for about $350,000" ("Ten Best Places").

This infusion of transplants has generated a backlash from many established residents. The matter of cultural continuance and change remains a prominent concern. Lance Vargas, Algiers resident and Jackson Square artist, has called it a "bad thing" to lose residents and replace them with newcomers who may clearly have a "passion for the city but don't have a hugely accurate knowledge of the history of it" (qtd. in Allman, "New New Orleans, Part 2"). Dahni Adomaitis welcomes the progressive attitudes and educated outlooks of many newcomers, but warns: "they need to tread carefully, to know where they can step and where they can't—and right now they're stepping wherever the hell they want and it's cutting off our cultural life support" (e-mail to Wade, November 7, 2017). Longtime resident and local writer Phil LaMancusa is most caustic in his appraisal: "those newly arrived are as far out of the loop concerning our funk and flavor as Liza Minnelli would be at a Big Freedia twerk party" (43).

The threatened changes in cultural practices relate and point to deeper changes in the material fabric of the city. This inflow of new residents has contributed to rising costs in the housing market and altered the nature of many neighborhoods. Those in Downtown New Orleans have been greatly impacted, perhaps Bywater above all. Significantly, Chewbacchus is closely associated with Bywater: its route proceeds through the neighborhood; many of its members are from this area; and the krewe's home, the Castillo Blanco, is on St. Claude Avenue, a Bywater boundary and one of the resurgent thoroughfares contributing to the changes in this Downtown part of the city.

It is illuminating to examine Bywater, as its shifting disposition aligns with the emergence of Chewbacchus and reflects upon the organization's outlook and identity. The pre-Katrina Bywater comprised a different community from that of the present. With its abundance of nineteenth-century Creole and Caribbean-styled architecture, the neighborhood had already been drawing new residents, though it remained more of a working-class neighborhood, racially and economically mixed, with affordable housing that attracted artists, musicians, the LGBT community, and service industry workers (Rose, "After"). Bywater enjoyed a reputation for its open, tolerant environment and creative energy; local resident Pearl Heart described the area as "delicate ecosystem for the arts" (qtd. in Allman, "The New New Orleans, Part 2").

Mainly spared from floodwaters, Bywater has increasingly gained status as desirable, high-value real estate. Many of the post-Katrina newcomers, specifically those identified as YURPs—young urban rebuilding professionals—have identified Bywater as their neighborhood of choice, seen as "an undiscovered bohemia" (Campanella, "Gentrification"). The *New York Times* has touted the allure of the Bywater scene, home to "punks and pinots" (Robertson). Another article notes new businesses popping up that cater to a hipster ethos, including a world-class vinyl record store and a highly popular New York–style pizzeria (Roig-Franzia, "Rebirth" 37). In fact, the neighborhood has been dubbed "Brooklyn South" due to the number of its New York transplants (Ball). With its music clubs, vintage-boutique wardrobes, and artisanal eateries, the new Bywater scene could be "picked up and dropped seamlessly into Austin, Burlington, Portland, or Brooklyn" (Campanella, "Gentrification").

These changes have had strong impact on the neighborhood. A Bywater cottage that sold for $80,000 pre-Katrina would now go for $200,000 (Rivlin 417). The neighborhood's racial mixture has changed, typified by one block where the black residential rate has fallen from 51 to 17 percent (Roig-Franzia, "Rebirth" 37). The neighborhood has seen an explosion of Airbnb rentals. Older residents are being forced to move. Local Bywater musician Peter "Sneaky Pete" Orr tells of getting mailbox notices of properties selling for $400k; he regards this real estate boom with dismay and regrets his neighborhood's loss of "grittiness" (qtd. in Rose, "After Hurricane").

Kirshenblatt-Gimblett explains how tourism (and by extension property development) desires distinctiveness, what cannot be gotten elsewhere, what she describes as "hereness" (153). Bywater possesses this quality to an enormous degree and has become one of the city's most intense hot spots. Many argue for the beneficial effects of neighborhood upgrading, that can eradicate blighted properties and draw new businesses; however, these same efforts can upset the delicate balance of neighborhood populations. The common dynamics of gentrification often lead to a "large-scale displacement" that disproportionately impacts minorities, low-income workers, and the elderly (Smith 28). And the urban adventurers who seek out such neighborhoods are often themselves displaced by more affluent newcomers, who see a once "risky" neighborhood as now "safe and sanitized" (Atkinson and Bridge 23).

Chewbacchus participates in this conversation regarding an evolving New Orleans and finds itself operating across numerous fields of influence and contestation. Some in the krewe, especially artists and service-industry workers, are increasingly finding themselves priced out of the real-estate market in the Bywater area, where the group houses its floats and conducts a substantial part of its route. Ballard currently resides in the Holy Cross neighborhood of the Lower Ninth Ward. He speaks harshly of developments and those "looting the charm of the city," fearing that the city will become a "playground for Californians" (interview).

In some respect, however, Chewbacchus has been the beneficiary of the tech boom that has brought scores of entrepreneurial transplants to the city. Ballard forthrightly acknowledges the impact of this group upon his krewe, that the arrival of tech-savvy newcomers—many with a love for science fiction—has brought an infusion of new members and new enthusiasm to Chewbacchus (interview). The krewe thus finds itself enmeshed in a multivalent artistic/urban dynamic, whose energies pull in various and sometimes contradictory directions. The success and allure of the krewe in some measure have added appeal and cachet to the area, unwittingly contributing to the rise in its popularity (and costs). In recent years, flocks of onlookers have come Downtown to see the parade, many of whom had never or infrequently ventured below Elysian Fields. Crowds now post ladders along the curbsides just as one sees along the Uptown parade routes. In this light, the krewe may be something of a victim of its own success, as its anarchic, anti-corporate expressions feed the reputation of the neighborhood, drawing in magnet fashion new young culture vultures and property speculators. Real estate companies recently have attempted to coopt this cultural cool, celebrating the neighborhood's funky edge, inviting prospective buyers to experience the "cross-pollination" of centuries and reside where "tomorrow's creations are nurtured in the warm glow of an intact and colorful past" ("Bywater"). Such instances alarm current residents, who worry that Bywater might succumb to forces of gentrification, which typically refashions unusual and socially tolerant neighborhoods into "playgrounds for the upper classes" (Brenner, Marcuse, and Mayer 78).

Culture Wars and the Future

Upon the tenth anniversary of Katrina, Mayor Mitch Landrieu championed the city's renaissance, extolling New Orleans "as a model of innovation and change" (Landrieu and Rodin). And certainly the city in this era experienced a rise in profile in scholarship and public discourse on topics involving urban frontiers, green investment, charter schools, racial inequity, cultural tourism, wetlands restoration, etc.—in short, the city distinguished itself as something of a test case for twenty-first-century urban centers. As Solnit and Snedeker recall in *Unfathomable City*, "one of the oddest turns post-Katrina" was how New Orleans "suddenly felt futuristic" (12). It is thus perhaps fitting that Chewbacchus emerged in these years, parading its ebullient energy and optimism, its sci-fi vision of a boundless future.

In many respects Chewbacchus has functioned as a flashpoint or lightning rod, drawing into focus many of the tensions and questions that confront New Orleans and its future. How will new residents impact the city and its traditional character? How will long-lived cultural practices survive? Who determines what is appropriate or inappropriate in the realm of Carnival? What does it mean to be a New Orleanian? The Krewe of Chewbacchus activates such questioning, and in some may evoke apprehension regarding an uncertain future—the wookiee seen as alien embodiment of anxiety and change.

Cautioning newcomers that New Orleans operates by a "whole different set of rules and traditions" (Tiggs 14), a local newspaper recently voiced concern over changes coming to the city and called for an awareness of and sensitivity to the unique New Orleans cultural environment. Local performer and native New Orleanian Ricky Graham voices similar concern and conveys a nostalgia for times past: "There's been a lot of attention to . . . guys in porkpie hats and there are girls on bicycles wearing ballerina skirts and puppy dog ears on their heads. And I am sure they are wonderful people, but to me that was never New Orleans, that was always Austin or

Seattle. It seems that aspect has been foisted on us. This is the new New Orleans? If it is, that's kind of sad" (qtd. in Allman, "The New New Orleans, Part 1").

Such sentiment is common in discussion of the changes impacting New Orleans, and Ballard has drawn censure from some quarters. Despite his deep affection for the city and commitment to the post-Katrina recovery, Ballard has incited controversy with his Intergalactic Krewe of Chewbacchus. He has spoken of the hostility targeting him and his efforts, though he understands that people have different histories and investments and that many glorify a pre-Katrina New Orleans. For these individuals, "change is threatening," and they see any kind of "melding" as controversial, considered a "sacrilege" (interview). He reports many encounters with "self-appointed culture czars" (interview), a type recently spoofed as "the culture cop" in a *Times-Picayune* cartoon on the most annoying people found in the city (MacCash, "New Orleans' most annoying"). Ballard recognizes that points of contention are not to be summarily dismissed, that they represent "serious, heart-felt identity investments" (interview). He nonetheless views himself as an iconoclast—"we represent a Rebellion against the established norms of Carnival Cultures" (qtd. in DeBerry, "Parades for celebrities")—and does not apologize for his experimentation or for his efforts to create a Carnival space for sci-fi eccentrics.

In December 2016 Chewbacchus found itself in a cross fire regarding traditional New Orleans culture and its performative practices. Following the deaths of David Bowie and Prince, fans in the city staged large-scale second-line parades in honor of these fallen icons. In like manner, Chewbacchus sought to commemorate Carrie Fisher (Princess Leia) with a second-line parade upon her untimely passing. Fisher enjoyed status as a sci-fi heroine, and her death saddened legions who had grown up seeing her in the *Star Wars* series. Beyond her achievement in the film industry, she had in recent years drawn visibility and honor for her work in feminist activism. Chewbacchus gained parade permits and the requisite police escort. However, shortly before the event a controversy flared on social media, indicting Chewbacchus for describing the parade as a "second-line." Opponents argued that the anticipated parade was not in keeping with traditional precedent and should thus not use the term. A back-and-forth ensued, drawing opinions from across the spectrum. The musician and radio personality Davis Rogan, who served to inspire the character of that name in the HBO series *Treme*, came out in vehement disapproval, writing online "that the Carrie Fisher parade was the one time he wished

The Leijorettes honoring Princess Leia. Photo by Allen Boudreaux. Permission of Allen Boudreaux.

somebody would shoot up a second-line," making reference to regrettable and tragic instances of violence on parade routes—Rogan later apologized (DeBerry, "Parades for celebrities"). Ballard defused the conflagration of opinion by withdrawing the term "second-line." The parade, which involved hundreds of costumed marchers and even more onlookers, proceeded along the Bywater streets of Chartres and Poland with much enthusiasm and emotion, promoted as a "tribute parade" to Carrie Fisher.

Kevin Gotham has noted and examined prior wrangling over cultural appropriateness in New Orleans; he writes that appeals to ownership or authenticity are often rhetorical acts "used by different groups to define urban culture" in a manner that is less about purity than potency (*Authentic* viii); that is, cultural battles signify contests of power between different interests and different populations that have a stake in cultural control. On the matter of second-line purity, *Times-Picayune* writer Jarvis DeBerry penned a column with the lead: "Parades for celebrities aren't the most questionable second-lines" ("Parades for celebrities"). In addition to citing the abundant number of official licenses for second-lines given to wedding parties, often destination weddings, DeBerry reported that between 2014 and 2016 less than 6 percent of all applications were "for the traditional New Orleans social aid and pleasure clubs or memorial second-lines" (DeBerry, "Parades for celebrities"). He concluded the article by relating that—on the cultural front—New Orleans was in a "period of civil war."

Chewbacchus again found itself at the intersection of controversy in the spring of 2017. This instance involved the murals of Los Angeles–based artist Muck Rock, who created a series of large-scale images of former presidents (those on money) along the St. Claude corridor. The murals were scorned on some fronts as the work of an interloper. New Orleans art critic Doug MacCash relates how Rock was reviled "by onlookers who would ordinarily welcome street art, but saw her as an insensitive out-of-town usurper who didn't understand the social politics of the city" (MacCash, "Controversial"). Near the time of Carrie Fisher's death Muck Rock had painted a large image of Princess Leia on the front door of Castillo Blanco, home of Chewbacchus on St. Claude. The artwork was vandalized on April 6. In response, Ballard determined to honor the Los Angeles artist and invited her to head the group's annual summer Shoeboxus parade—the 2017 theme: NOLAier than Thou. By invoking and satirizing the "holier than thou" posture, Ballard took aim at those claiming proprietorship of Crescent City traditions, implicitly raising the question—who can judge what is appropriate or inappropriate in the evocation of New Orleans culture?

These specific skirmishes in the culture war of New Orleans reveal resentments and contestations that percolate in the post-Katrina environment, and Chewbacchus has often been cast in the role of an outsider. Many look with suspicion on newcomers, seeing in them opportunistic invaders insinuating themselves in unwanted ways, playing out the stereotype of the carpetbagger. And clearly there are examples of outside influence that prompt the desire for pushback. C. W. Cannon, for instance, takes issue with those newcomers who would seek to shut down public performances, prohibiting street music and Jackson Square entertainments—newcomers he acerbically describes as "condo locusts from Dallas, Florida and the plain places beyond" (138). And there are developers who incite concerns of American homogenization, seeking to remake New Orleans in the image of other corporate capitals, or, in the arch take of urban sociologist Alan Blum, who wish to bring to the city center "that suburban development that you had always hoped would be Downtown" (87).

Debates over the identity of New Orleans are not trivial, as such contestation will inform the shape and direction of the city in years to come. That noted, the infusion of newcomers need not be viewed in apocalyptic terms. Many have welcomed those seeking to make a home in the city, and with good cause. Jan Ramsey, editor of the local music magazine *Offbeat*, writes: "I'm thrilled that so many entrepreneurs and young people have moved here (this wasn't happening pre-Katrina) and are strengthening New Orleans' intellectual infrastructure and support for the culture. They've brought much needed energy to the city" (8). Noting the "Brain Gain" of recent years, Chris Rose writes: "when young, smart and forward thinking people move in a place, and after 30 years of Brain Drain, I think it's an unequivocal win for the city" ("Before" 34).

Change is always threatening to a culture, especially in a place like New Orleans, which relies so heavily on tradition. Journalist Rob Walker, in fact, has opined that "the past is all that New Orleans has" (93). It is, however, relevant to note that recent cultural contestation—evident in the example of Chewbacchus—is not new to the city, though these current manifestations are heated and passionate. Certainly, Creole New Orleanians of the nineteenth century often found American newcomers distasteful, fearing "that hard-driving Yankees would turn their city into a tropical Philadelphia" (Starr 133). Waves of German, Irish, and Italian immigrants also often found an inhospitable welcome in the Crescent City. More recently Vietnamese, African, and Hispanic newcomers have worked to establish space in the city's cultural landscape.

To be sure, in-migration often has positive consequences. New Orleans has long benefited from its mix of peoples and its cultural contestations, which have generated unique blends and fusions. Oftentimes, transplants help conserve local culture, seeing value in things natives might overlook— a phenomenon that, as Mark Souther observes, frequently occurred in twentieth-century New Orleans history (13). Transplants can bring more enlightened social outlooks, more open and tolerant racial attitudes. Many are sensitive to gentrification and seek to minimize its impact. Owner of Barrister's Gallery Andy Antippas suggests the city should take heed: "perhaps we can learn something from their 'alien' ideas: how to eat healthier food occasionally, for example, and how to protect and better educate our children, how to end rampant social injustice, how to make use of public transportation and ride bicycles to the grocery store, how to care for our wetlands and how to build a sustainable economy in our city" (qtd. in Allman, "The New New Orleans, Part 1").

The future will bring many challenges to New Orleans, and it is appropriate to be wary, to consider the implications of change. The strength and forbearance of the city and the unique durability of its culture, however, can allay fears of diminution, of a diluted or ersatz New Orleans, of newcomers, of a wild-eyed furred creature that dances drunkenly amidst its Downtown followers. This perception perhaps calls for hope, but also a kind of faith that New Orleans possesses a sense of self that defies sabotage, that will allow for positive change while maintaining what distinctively makes the city one of the most interesting places on the planet.

New Orleans may take some confidence in the fact that those who come to the city often exhibit a willing and adaptive attitude. New Orleans clearly offers a different horizon-of-expectations from cities such as Dallas, or Austin, or Atlanta, and those who choose New Orleans over other options often do so because of inclinations (quirks) in taste and personality. Many come because New Orleans is New Orleans. As S. Frederick Starr noted over thirty years ago: "those who choose to move there [New Orleans] are precisely the ones most likely to adapt easily once there . . . [they] were already partly New Orleanians in spirit" (133). Richard Campanella corroborates this perception for the post-Katrina era, that those who choose to move to the city are often predisposed to its attractions and unique sensibilities. He observes that many of the newcomers enthusiastically embrace the city; seen as a "self-selecting" group, these recent residents reveal themselves as "Orleanophilic supernatives" (qtd. in Rivet 17). Rather than diluting the city's culture (and making it more like Portland), they work to secure and perpetuate what is uniquely New Orleans. They often dive into the culture and work to align themselves with tradition, to be a part of it.

And regardless of the attitude one arrives with in New Orleans, the city often brings the newcomer under its sway, as its reputation for seduction is legendary. It is telling that Chinese immigrants in the 1950s were not soon after their arrival celebrating Mardi Gras with their own Krewe of the Golden Dragon (Starr 132). Former teacher and founder of Kickboard software Jen Medberry confirms the assimilative power of New Orleans, suggesting that the city "kind of seeps into your bones" and that people here want to "feel a connection to something bigger than themselves and their jobs" (qtd. in Roig-Franzia, "A 'resilient lab'"). David Rutledge gives personal witness to the city's power: "the culture is resilient, and the outsider who comes to New Orleans is often transformed for the good, I speak from experience" (*Where We Know* xxvii).

Given the assimilationist capacity of the city, and the fact that many who come to New Orleans arrive eager to embrace its culture, one can view Chewbacchus not as a threat to tradition but as a conduit—or mode of transport—into a state of belonging. In a wealth of instances one recognizes how Chewbacchus honors and embraces New Orleans culture, how the parade does not simply showcase sci-fi and fantasy imagery but recontextualizes such content in local terms. The parades demonstrate often clever, imaginative, and affectionate uses of New Orleans symbology. Sub-krewes include Mandolorian Meuniere, Deathbar NOLA, and the Krewe de Who (for Doctor Who). As noted earlier, the official Chewbacchus insignia shows Chewbacca dancing second-line style with umbrella. Recent parades have showcased the following: a replica of the *Star Wars* "AT-AT" all-terrain armored transport vehicle bearing the name "Where Y'at-YAT" (citing the colloquial speech of the city); a large-scale version of the spaceship Borg Cube featuring a *fleur de lis*; Star Troopers marching in purple, green, and gold uniforms (the official colors of Mardi Gras); a model of the Dalek from *Doctor Who* painted purple, green, and gold; a Dead Mau5, from European dub music wearing a jersey of Drew Brees, the Saints' beloved quarterback. And in a humorous homage to another post-Katrina krewe, Carnival's highly popular 610 Stompers, Chewbacchus offers its own version of the men's disco walkers, the 610 Wampas, who wear knee-high tube socks, gym shorts, and white-fur wookiee headdresses.

Such play with melding indicates that Mardi Gras activities are being taken to new and otherworldly realms, though it is also important to note that Chewbacchus provides its members—whether natives, pre- or post-Katrina transplants—a memorable parade event that grounds the participants in the Carnival experience, in effect, bringing them into the fold. This kind of civic absorption may allay some concern over the threat of newcomers. Andy Antippas indeed regards "aliens" with equanimity, assuring that "all of these life forms will be bent to our cultural will" (qtd. in Allman, "The New New Orleans, Part 1").

Carnival and Science-Fiction Utopia

New Orleans may not enjoy a long-standing or fabled position in the genre of science fiction, as the city more commonly in the popular imagination invokes images of jazz musicians, pirates, riverboat gamblers, and downcast, aging southern belles. The rather campy *Abbott and Costello Go to Mars*, however, does show New Orleans as participant in this genre, as this 1953 Universal-International Film production depicts the comedy duo inadvertently launching themselves in a spaceship and inexplicably landing in the city during Mardi Gras, which, due to the zaniness around them, the two immediately assume to be Mars. This low-budget film may stand as an inconsequential B-movie of its time, though the basic premise of the plot—which links science fiction and Carnival—suggests some insightful and provocative convergences, how these two enterprises of fantasy might work in tandem, opening up uncharted potentials, accentuating the ludic effects of Mardi Gras and its capacity for "imagining alternatives to the status quo" (Mauldin 17).

Though one may simply view Chewbacchus as a frivolous event, an opportunity for sci-fi geeks to parade with intoxicated abandon through the city streets, the parade and its krewe may function in a far more purposeful way: opening up Carnival participation and its embedded hierarchies, and modeling progressive outlooks and modes of encounter. In its performance of sci-fi lore and fandom, Chewbacchus's trek to a kind of outer space may open a new space in the city and its social order. The Intergalactic Krewe of Chewbacchus may exhibit what feminist scholar Jill Dolan has described as the "utopian performative," that is, the desire "to reach for something better, for new ideas about how to be and how to be with each other"; she contends that this kind of performance "can articulate a common future, one that's more just and equitable, one in which we can all participate more equally, with more chances to live fully and contribute to the making of culture" (455).

Chewbacchus is forbidden to traffic in outright expressions of political rhetoric; the krewe's 501c3 status as a not-for-profit organization prohibits any partisan endorsements. Though the group cannot promote any particular candidate or party, Chewbacchus does embody views with pointed social implications. The futuristic orientation of the krewe imparts an environmental awareness and support for environmentally friendly practices. Its green policies mandate the construction of non-motorized floats and when possible the use of recycled materials. The krewe models practices that go against consumption and accumulation. Ballard prefers that costumes be homemade rather than bought. The krewe will often hold flea-market events—"space debris sales"—to get rid of accumulated gear and supplies. Emphasis on consumption and sustainability is particularly relevant in New Orleans, where global warming and coastal erosion present existential threats. The ragtag flow of otherworldly creatures on the streets of Mardi Gras—with self-crafted floats and regalia—manifests an anti-corporate, anti-materialist outlook. The effect is almost as much medieval as futuristic, purposefully out of step with a contemporary, consumerist ethos.

In its oppositional stance to traditional Carnival krewes as symbols of affluence and class privilege, Chewbacchus models a powerful egalitarian viewpoint, one that militates against social and economic inequities. The krewe's motto, "saving the galaxy one drunk nerd at a time" ("About IKOC"), is both a joke and an earnest maxim of inclusion. In a city that frequently suffers from glaring divides, Chewbacchus offers its vision of a shoulder-to-shoulder solidarity.

While its members are predominantly white, the krewe welcomes and encourages diversity. The SubKrewe Wonder Women exemplifies a mixed membership under the leadership of Marti Dumas, one of Chewbacchus's first black captains. The Afro-Futurists seek to promote awareness of black contributions to fantasy and science-fiction. Numerous African Americans also march with the Leijorettes and ride with the Rolling Elliots; the Leijorettes feature dancing Princess Leias and is not gender bound. The SubKrewe Gay-braham Lincolns is solely comprised of gay black men. Jose Torres-Tama, local Latino performance artist, marches in his green alien regalia (his Taco Truck Theatre explores civil rights and immigration). The krewe has reached out to youths struggling with autism, creating with them their own SubKrewe, the Stomp Troopers, that marches with musicians from the famed jazz spot Preservation Hall. Mobility-impaired children have received special invitation and roll with the parade, sporting sci-fi decorations and regalia. The krewe is active in a number of outreach ventures, including a summer camp for neighborhood children at the Castillo Blanco. Scott Simmons, head of the Sith Happens, credits Chewbacchus with expanding his social awareness, getting him "out of the box," and for helping his children "appreciate humans for what they are and not for what they have" (interview). Relating that Chewbacchus welcomes all and casts "no judgement," Quincy Castillo, leader of the Redshirts, champions the inclusive aspect of the krewe, building unity from diversity, and how the krewe aspires to ideals expressed in science fiction: "I've always hoped I would see the stages of human beings getting closer to Gene Roddenberry's vision . . . of a level playing field . . . where we're all one" (interview).

This citation of Roddenberry, creator of *Star Trek*, is illuminating, as the enlightened political visions explored in science fiction inspire and instruct Chewbacchus and its egalitarian commitments. A release from the status quo is the primary catalyst of the genre, whose works powerfully explore myriad other worlds, giving shape and life to creatures and civilizations that may bear relation (or little to none) to that of our own, setting forth new rules of cooperation and governance. In this sense, science fiction has admirably worked to explore new possibilities, on the personal and political front. *Star Trek*, for instance, allows for the imagination of a world that

Chewbacchus parade on Mardi Gras 2017. Photo by Brett Duke. Permission of the *Times-Picayune*/NOLA Media Group.

has evolved beyond the capitalist marketplace, where technology provides for all, rendering class distinctions moot. The series was also at the fore in exploring cross-racial and cross-species engagement. In this light, the krewe's embrace of science fiction brings with it the affirmation of forward-thinking values and reimagined social possibilities.

If nothing else, a Chewbacchus parade succeeds in its creation of a public, communal, hallucinatory surrealism. Ballard encourages his krewe to "push boundaries, to make art," much in the manner of Burning Man, with the aim of opening up a kind of collective "psychedelic space" (interview). Taking place in the evening, Chewbacchus enacts a performance of boundary-blurring, as the lights of the streets combine with the colorful, often strobe effects of the floats, contributing to a sometimes dazzling and dizzying experience. The visuals complement a vast, cacophonous array of aural effects—of music, drumming, machinery, laughter, and shouts. Various strange bands of musicians and invented musical devices parade by. One regards what appears as a nonstop flow of fantastic and otherworldly characters: "Gaggles of light sabre-wielding Jedis . . . along with veiled extraterrestrial dancers, tentacle-faced aliens and fedoraed Dr. Whos" (MacCash, "Mardi Gras 2015"). Pulsating with energy, the event generates a kind of sensory overload. At different times large gaps open in the parade procession, which are then followed by a rush of costumed figures. One can lose sense of who is in the parade and who is in the crowd, many of whom themselves are costumed. The event generates a strong sense of flow, of being pulled into the vortex of this upbeat, giddy happening.

Ballard identifies one moment occurring in the 2016 procession as a favorite (interview), an instance that exemplifies the mesmerizing aspect of the parade and its embrace of the random and spontaneous. On this evening, Ballard was walking in accompaniment of a large-scale figure of the wookiee, positioned like a Hindu deity on a tricycle-style vehicle, accompanied by female dancers, or devotees, evocative of Dionysian maenads, who were not only ushering the trike forward but were handing out flower petals and phony money (emblazoned with the image of Chewbacchus). In a sudden, unplanned instant, the power source for the vehicle malfunctioned—causing the wookiee, lights, and music to go still and silent. During the interim, as Ballard worked to correct the problem, the dancers first bowed to the wookiee then began to work the crowd, grabbing onlookers and spinning them with whirling-dervish moves and gestures, encouraging all to dance and to yell. At the peak of this rising intensity, power returned, sending shafts of light into the crowd, suffusing the space with strong, rhythmic music and pulsating drum track. The crowd broke into spontaneous shouts of affirmation, clapping and cheering the wookiee forward. Demonstrating the power of unexpected, unchoreographed performative play, this moment conveys the extraordinary, expansive capacity of Chewbacchus—as Ballard explains, "it's like the whole world opens up, everything's possible" (interview). Such a moment corroborates how communal performance can offer "usefully emotional, expressions of what utopia might feel like" (Dolan 456).

This surreal, evanescent moment demonstrates the potent confluence of Carnival and science-fiction energies. Mikhail Bakhtin writes of the carnivalesque in terms of plasticity, how normal orders and recognized genus and species give over to reimaginings, effecting release from authoritative controls; Bakhtin views such moments in terms of fusion and fertility, carnival "giving birth to new forms and therefore creating the possibility for a new world order" (qtd. in Grams 185). Some scholars question this liberatory potential, holding that carnival only gives the illusion of liberation while disguising social conflict and "mystifying class relations" (Lane 21). Other scholars grant carnival a revolutionary dimension, as a vehicle of "radical oppositional consciousness" (Gilmore 4).

Ryan Ballard forcefully agrees with those who champion the liberating effects of carnival. He argues that the "world is better if loosened up," that bacchanalian revelry can work a sort of "psychological magic," filling one with "joy" and a "sense of oneness" (interview). In opposition to those who see carnival as a temporary pressure valve, only to return celebrants to their prior social positions and hierarchies, Ballard grants it an efficacious, even political dimension: "[It] bleeds over into how people act later, that little span of time can change lives" (interview).

Beyond the embodiment of green environmental practices, beyond its progressive attitudes of egalitarianism and inclusivity, beyond surrealistic communal performances of street theatre, beyond all considerations of utopian potential, Chewbacchus in its deepest of hearts may simply prize *space*—as a sanctuary for the strange. It is a friend of the alien, in solidarity with "the weirdo" (Ballard interview). This affinity significantly places Chewbacchus, despite its novelty and improvisations, squarely within a long-standing New Orleans tradition, that of providing sanctuary for eccentrics.

In calling for a krewe of nerds, Ballard endorses and advances what Robert Tallant once described as New Orleans's "liberal attitude toward human frailties" (xviii). This outlook has given harbor to a long line of New Orleans oddballs and crackpots such as Ruthie the duck lady, or the classicist who regularly consumed a six-pack of Dixie beer in Lafayette Park as he read "Homer's *Iliad* in the original Greek" (Starr 167). Cheryl Wagner confirms the city's reputation as a kind of asylum or holding pen, "the place where Southerners send their laidback people who can't or won't get with the program—their artists, gay relatives, eternal optimists, funny hat wearers, weirdos, and intellectuals" (x). Bartender Morgan Farrington, a proud, self-described "weirdo," remains amazed at the city's stable of bizarre individuals, relating that "she doesn't even register on the scale here" (interview with Wade and Roberts, September 28, 2017).

Chewbacchus in this respect may appear as the conservator of New Orleans tradition, in the face of encroaching pressures for conformity, of American homogenization, of the ridicule aimed at those considered different or out of step—the guardian of an old and forbearing galaxy. Chewbacchus animates New Orleans as a place to be different and to be accepted. It confirms and gives testament to Eve Abrams's wise insight regarding the city: "if you understand the need to eat and parade and congregate and play and listen and sing, space will be made for your particular way of doing these things" (232).

Conclusion

Richard Campanella has given extensive analysis to the shifting landscapes of New Orleans history, noting its recent "unexpected renaissance" and attendant anxieties of change. He writes: "Some see the new New Orleans as a gentrified, self-aware version of its old self, and have come to cast the Katrina catastrophe and the inequities of the recovery in a wistful 'end of history' narrative"; however, he concludes that our present time is not an end but rather a "next chapter" with unknown promise and possibility (Campanella, *Lost* 6).

Campanella's assessment puts into relief the challenges facing New Orleans, whose troubled social conditions sorely need change, but whose vaunted cultural traditions warrant conservation and continuance. The next chapter of New Orleans history will likely be an exercise in negotiation, of how best to unite the old and the new, of how to carry the prized treasures of New Orleans into a future distant time.

Chewbacchus comes as a new player on the Mardi Gras stage, bringing new energy and new possibilities to the Downtown scene. In its outlandish and otherworldly expressions, it validates creativity and makes room for participants with wide-ranging interests and identities. For some, the krewe can seem a threat, alien invaders coming from afar to trample and despoil. A generous reading of Chewbacchus allows a different perspective, recognizing the group in beneficent terms, as an enterprise that contests entrenched interests and seeks to democratize the Carnival landscape, and that stirs utopian imaginings in a way that can translate into purposeful social action. In its embrace of science-fiction universes—and their multifarious inhabitants—Chewbacchus indicates a positive willingness to see complexity in our own world and to regard differences without hostility and fear.

Chewbacchus rather brazenly declares on its website: "Chewbacchus is the Future of Revelry" ("About IKOC"). One recent, fleeting parade moment caused me to reflect on this claim. On this rather cold and damp Carnival evening, I was taking my place along the Chewbacchus parade route when I shared greetings with a smiling mother and her six- or seven-year-old son; he was wearing a *V for Vendetta* Guy Fawkes mask. This encounter humored and heartened me, as I imagined this young boy raised in Carnival culture, always looking forward to the next parade, taught to oppose injustice, inspired by this anti-authoritarian sci-fi hero—a bright harbinger for the future of revelry.

CHAPTER 6

Reclaiming Life and History: The Amazons Benevolent Society and the Black Storyville Baby Dolls

Robin Roberts

The two walking krewes that are the focus of this last chapter share certain significant similarities: both were founded by the same woman, Dianne Honoré. Since many New Orleanians participate in multiple Mardi Gras krewes, and Devin De Wulf, the founder of Red Beans, for example, has also started a second Carnival group, Dead Beans, Honoré's activities with two groups would not alone merit a chapter. However, the Amazons Benevolent Society and the Black Storyville Baby Dolls are remarkable in a number of ways. Unlike the other Downtown marching groups which tend to be white-run and majority-white members, these two organizations are racially integrated. And while both are women's groups, both include men in satellite organizations. The specificity of each group is also distinctive; while other Downtown krewes focus on a theme or a style (such as science fiction for Chewbacchus, or a local food with Red Beans), Honoré's two organizations have very specific distinctive features in the focus on breast cancer and a Mardi Gras tradition started by sex workers in the early twentieth-century.

Exploring the similarities and differences between the Amazons Benevolent Society and the Black Storyville Baby Dolls provides a suitable conclusion for our book on Downtown Mardi Gras. These groups are in one sense more aspirational than the other groups, committing to be racially inclusive in an otherwise racially divided city (and nation). Like the other Downtown krewes in this book, especially the Krewe de Jeanne d'Arc, the Amazons and Black Storyville Baby Dolls present an alternative to traditional, sexist roles for women. Just as important is the group's rein-vention of traditional costuming for women to resist racism and to honor previous generations of women who used Carnival to assert their right to a place in Mardi Gras specifically and, by extension, society at large.

The Amazons Benevolent Society is a social aid society, focused on em-powering women with breast cancer and providing patients with material support and encouragement. That they also parade reveals the importance of Carnival to every aspect of life in New Orleans. Founded in 2012 after Honoré's own diagnosis, the society contains breast cancer survivors and supporters. Using parading as way to demonstrate strength, raise aware-ness of the disease, and to encourage other women, the Amazons have found a way to meld their mission with the city's celebratory style. Wear-ing breastplates and brandishing swords, the group displays a militaristic posture that exudes strength and power. While the group's main focus is social aid and support, the members use Mardi Gras parades as well to make a public statement of women's empowerment. The group draws on the mythological Amazons as figures of female strength. At the same time, the group indirectly evokes the historical use of Amazons by the African American Krewe of Zulu (Vaz 52).

The Black Storyville Baby Dolls trace their creation to the revival of an early twentieth-century Mardi Gras practice. Also founded by Honoré, this krewe draws even more directly on the African American tradition. Baby Dolling is a historical practice where adult women dress as young girls, in beautiful outfits made of satin, and dance in the streets, acting tough and smoking cigars. In *The "Baby Dolls": Breaking the Race and Gender Barriers of the New Orleans Mardi Gras Tradition*, Kim Marie Vaz explains the practice's history from 1912 to 2012. Vaz's work draws on her extensive archival research and interviews "to exemplify the artistic value and clarify the diverse practices . . . as well as to reveal their sociopolitical struggles to realize their own passions, imaginations, historic understandings, and joie de vivre" (10). The Black Storyville Baby Dolls formed just as Vaz's book was in press, confirming her assessment of this practice as an important reemergent tradition.

Women's participation in Mardi Gras is often assumed to be as exploit-ative object, as popularized in the notorious *Girls Gone Wild* videos or *COPS* Mardi Gras specials on television. Yet as Kim Marie Vaz, Carolyn Ware, and this author have documented, women's actual participation in Mardi Gras is often a tactic of resistance to gender stereotypes. Historically, as Lidia D. Sciama and Joanne B. Eicher note, "for women, now and in the past, Mardi Gras has represented an opportunity to rebel against standards of behavior imposed upon them by the patriarchal power structure of society" (204).

Both the Amazons Benevolent Society and the Black Storyville Baby Dolls exemplify the use of Carnival as defiant resistance to restrictive gender norms. These women's Mardi Gras krewes demonstrate the description of "ritual activity . . . in a social context where there is ambiguity or conflict about social relations, and it is performed to resolve or disguise them" (Lane 11). What the krewes share with other new Downtown parades is their emphasis on uplift and/or humor, on the creation of art through costumes and performance, and their commitment to New Orleans culture.

These groups affix themselves to New Orleans through connections to historical Mardi Gras practices and elements of New Orleans culture, but broaden the practices and stress inclusivity. Both the Amazons and the Black Storyville Baby Dolls perform New Orleans's resistance to homogeneity, and the city's insistence on its unique culture heritage. As Jennifer Laing and Warwick Frost describe this practice, "communities strive to preserve and even recreate their traditional events, which may require rituals to be resurrected or reinvented for a new audience" (frontispiece). The women interviewed for this chapter embody Fletcher DuBois et al.'s argument that as rituals are reinvented, the "artists wanted to make sure that their performances are linked to but are differentiated from earlier ritual, a combination that enables them to make statements of desire and community membership" (52). While rituals inevitably change over time, as Christiane Brosius and Karin M. Polit argue, traditions are not "predestined to die out due to this shift of context. The new context is to be understood as an addition to already existing practices and not as a replacement or copy" (7).

The tensions and revisions of Carnival have often focused on the role of women. As with other customs, women's bodies have been used to differentiate between classes. As Frank de Caro and Tom Ireland note, "Carnival symbolically mediates between two social ideals: that of kingship, aristocracy, and class hierarchy on the one hand; that of social equality on the other" (37). If, as Errol Laborde describes it, "the history of Carnival organizations is that of gradual democratization" (121), the fact remains that gender segregation remains legal by law. The City Council desegregation law that made racial discrimination illegal for krewes that publicly paraded initially included sex, but that provision was dropped during negotiations with community leaders, including those from all-female krewes who argued they should not be forced to admit men ("Today in 1991"). Hence, women's public participation has relied on the creation of new krewes like the Uptown parade Orpheus, which was open to men and women, Muses and Nyx, all-women groups, and new Downtown organizations like those discussed in this book. As C. W. Cannon describes Mardi Gras, "it's all a symbolic act of occupation of the public space" (139).

As has been argued by a number of critics (Hemard; King; McKinney; Woods), New Orleans itself is feminized in relation to the rest of the United States, so it is understandable that Mardi Gras krewes, both now and in the past, have always had a space for women's creative expressions (McKinney 56). Between 1910 and 1940, African American women in masks took back the streets of New Orleans in krewes such as Venus and Iris. The Baby Dolls were among the earliest groups of women taking back the streets during Carnival; they first paraded in 1912 (Vaz).

The Need to Rebuild Post-Katrina

Like the other new Mardi Gras groups discussed in this book, the Amazons and the Black Storyville Baby Dolls emerge as a response to life after the catastrophic levee failures that decimated New Orleans. As Mary Fitzpatrick explains, "After Katrina, many of us began digging deeper to find the essence of our beloved New Orleans" (introduction, n.p.). For the Amazons, a personal disaster, that of breast cancer, heightened the need to recover created by the manmade flood after a hurricane. For the Black Storyville Baby Dolls, the need to preserve their cultural histories took on increased urgency after lives and artifacts and records disappeared during the catastrophic flooding.

One Amazon, Lynette Johnson, provides an example of a New Orleanian returning home after the disaster, and finding Carnival a way to cope. In 2006, meeting her mother in a parking lot in Harahan, where she was living until she could find another place to live, Johnson's mother told her, "I told you that you would come home" (Johnson interview with Robin Roberts, August 17, 2017). That was the Sunday before Mardi Gras, and on Mardi Gras Day, Johnson and her husband, Mike Murphy, were on the family float, throwing beads (interview). Of that day, Johnson says, "It was the most beautiful Mardi Gras I had ever experienced . . . [it showed that New Orleanians] were going to be true to our traditions, we're going to get through this" (interview).

Amazon drummers Mike Murphy, Lynette Johnson, and Dawn Webb. Photo by Robin Roberts. Permission of Robin Roberts.

While her family has deep roots in New Orleans, Black Storyville Baby Doll Arsène DeLay and her parents were not living in Louisiana when the levees failed. DeLay herself was in graduate school in California. She returned after Katrina, and now lives in what used to be her grandmother's home. Joell Lee, also a Black Storyville Baby Doll, was living in New Orleans, and evacuated to Bastrop, and then Monroe, in north Louisiana. But as she said, "you wouldn't know that you were in the same state" as New Orleans, "because the culture was so different" (Lee interview with Robin Roberts, August 14, 2017). Watching Mardi Gras on television in exile, Lee said being away made her appreciate her city and culture even more (interview). Honoré, Johnson, DeLay, and Lee were compelled by the threat to their culture to be even more active in that culture, and to create a new organization and parade. In Lee's words, "We are not just women who dance in the community, but empowered women who desire to preserve, educate, and honor our ancestors in the correct way" (gumbomarie.com). To Lee, this means "we aim to keep a sense of professionalism when it comes to maintaining the baby doll tradition" (e-mail, August 30, 2017).

Honoré's experience was similarly cathartic and inspired her to expand her work preserving and performing her cultural heritage. She explains how difficult evacuating was. "I left on a Saturday with the only 2 boxes of stuff I could save from my home. I lost everything else . . . My life as I knew it was gone and the only memories were now in my head" (e-mail, July 11, 2018). Her daughter Hannah was still in high school, and Honoré practiced her skills that have proved valuable in her heritage work and in her two walking clubs; she "volunteered as stage manager and costume designer for Hannah's musicals and plays" (e-mail). Honoré returned to New Orleans after her daughter graduated, and "got back into tour guiding and worked part-time at Destrehan plantation. Within a year I formed a partnership and started writing new tours about the marginalized people in our history" (e-mail, July 11, 2018). Although she had been a tour guide since the 1990s, Honoré found herself doing even more culture work: "Even more than I'd done pre-Katrina . . . I created products like dolls, umbrellas, tshirts, anything to spread the word. They are sold around the world. I am happy knowing that each piece gone out into the world is a piece of our culture, a real tangible TEACHABLE piece of art" (e-mail, July 11, 2018). In addition, she has published two books about her experiences, *Living the Black Storyville Baby Doll Life* and *Amazon Warriors, Crusaders of Hope* (gumbomarie.com). Like the other founders of new krewes, and the other participants in the Amazons and the Black Storyville Baby Dolls, Honoré has found new energy and commitment to New Orleans culture, creating gold from the dross of a terrible disaster.

The Founder and Leadership

New parading opportunities require someone to initiate the paperwork, recruit members, and communicate a vision. When asked to characterize Honoré's leadership, the Amazons and Black Storyville Baby Dolls express appreciation and amazement at her sense of purpose and ability to communicate it to others. Johnson, who has been a member of the Amazons Benevolent Society from the beginning, praises Honoré's "energy, perseverance, and fierceness" (interview). Johnson recalls the first meeting she attended, at a restaurant, describing it as a wonderful gathering where Honoré laid out why she was starting this group. Johnson was pleased to recognize some of the women who are artists and scholars in the community, as well as one woman whom she had not seen since kindergarten. She

Dianne Honoré during the Joan of Arc parade. Photo by Brett Duke. Permission of the *Times-Picayune*/NOLA Media Group.

was also glad that the group was comprised of "a range of ages, background, and races—that was impressive" (interview), she remembers. Johnson herself is not only a musician and a professional graphics editor, but also now works for historypin.org, a social justice group whose current project involves bringing rural Louisianians together through collective public history collection and research. Ann Witucki, a white Amazon who lives in Houston, similarly praises Honoré's leadership and enthusiasm; of the latter, she comments, it is "contagious. I love her sense of fun and I very much enjoy working with her" (e-mail, September 6, 2017). Black Storyville Baby Doll Lee explains, "you can tell who is a leader and who is not. [Honoré] is very organized and professional" (e-mail, August 8, 2017). Dawn Sprague, a white woman from Tyler, Texas, who was a part of the creation of the Amazons, describes Honoré's strength and passion: "She leads by force of personality, untamable exuberance, and experience. I don't know anyone else who could have gotten The Amazons off the ground and running as quickly and soundly as she did" (e-mail, December 11, 2017).

Honoré's pivotal role evokes the analysis of "hot spots," igniting a sense of purpose in a group, where "people flock to it—they want to be a part of it" (Gratton 13). As described by Lynda Gratton, a successful leader communicates a vision and creates friendships (141), a description aptly fitting

Honoré's activities. Admiring her efficiency in running the Black Storyville Baby Dolls, Lee says of Honoré: "she knows how to make things happen but she also listens to our ideas" (e-mail). One lesson of new Mardi Gras is that new traditions require a leader and a visionary, someone who can draw other people to an endeavor that takes time, money, and effort. She has all these qualities, as her fellow krewe members attest. Honoré's multiple Carnival activities occupy her year-round; the work includes planning, meetings, recruiting members, charity and community events, banquets, and creating her costume.

Creole Heritage and Inspiration

Dianne Honoré's knowledge and interest in history are pivotal for her creation of new walking krewes. A native New Orleanian, she draws artistic inspiration from her forbears. She exudes a strong spirit of defiance and artistry, grounded in historical research and perspective. She explains, "This is my life's work ... I have been at this for over 30 years. Not just masking but studying, working, preserving my history/culture. What you see of me on the street dressed in costume is ... a piece of all I do to preserve the things you love so much about this town" (Dianne Honoré Facebook post, August 9, 2017). Believing in "awakening the past by giving voice to history" (gumbomarie.com), Honoré pursues many activities, including writing, producing, and performing numerous historically based food events, classes, panel discussions, tours, and exhibits. Honoré has traced her family roots extensively. She explains that she feels a particular connection with her sixth great-grandmother, Catiché Destrehan. Of her, Honoré says "she's my beacon. In her life she saw French, Spanish, and American rule over New Orleans. She had to wear the tignon—required by an edict for 'good government' meant to oppress and identify women of African ancestry in the 19th century. She also saw the development of Creole culture" (interview with Robin Roberts, August 10, 2017). When she gives tours, Honoré wears a tignon in Catiché Destrehan's memory. Similarly, Honoré creates spectacular millinery for the Black Storyville Baby Dolls, perhaps to honor and express a specific artistic expression that her ancestor was denied due to racist laws. Knowledge and commitment to her ancestors shapes how she creates costumes for her groups.

Catiché was a cook, and there are generations of cooks in Honoré's family, including her parents, Rosemary and Henry Honoré, who owned and ran a Creole restaurant, Hank's Restaurant and Bar, in Treme for fifty years. Among her many other creative endeavors, Honoré presents a history/cooking demonstration at the French Market and the New Orleans School of Cooking, both in the French Quarter. She grew up in both the French Quarter and Treme, attending the French Quarter Catholic School on Dumaine Street. Her interest and expertise in cooking and Creole culture influences not only her costuming for the two parades discussed in this chapter, but explains how she able to quickly whip up a costume for Red Beans in 2014, and to do so well that she was elected queen for that year's parade.

Tracing her love of history to Sister Sheila, who taught her in the seventh grade, Honoré describes her as "an amazing storyteller" who influenced Honoré's decision to become a tour guide. Honoré's mother was also a strong role model for her because she ran a restaurant and bar with her husband. "At the same time," Honoré recalls, "she raised five kids, her own brother, and helped many cousins" (e-mail, August 27, 2017). Her grandmother Eugenia, who suffered domestic violence and who was murdered by her male partner in 1951, is another influence on Honoré's life and activities. She sees the parallels between her grandmother's "abuse, rape, and lack of opportunity" (e-mail, August 27, 2017) also experienced by other black women, including the original Baby Dolls. Determined to honor her grandmother's and mother's strength and struggles has resulted in her commitment to women's parades.

Belief in New Orleans's racial exceptionalism, that it was somehow significantly less racist than other states, has been called into question (Thomas), but there can be no doubt that its unique legal codes and social interactions differentiate it from the rest of the United States. In part because the city's laws were based on the slightly more humane French Code Noir, there emerged more social interaction between whites and blacks, which resulted in a community of well-educated free people of color (Gehman). Honoré comes from this background; among her other notable relatives she counts Lt. General Russel Honoré, who achieved fame in his role as the commander of Joint Task Force Katrina, which ran all military relief efforts in post-levee failure New Orleans.

The Amazons Benevolent Society's full name indicates its connection to the legacy of New Orleans social aid and pleasure clubs. A racist society left African Americans without access to capital and the jobs that allowed white people to accrue a comfortable financial safety net. In New Orleans, as happened elsewhere, African Americans formed cooperative societies, where you could join your money with that of others, insuring funerals and other needs. In New Orleans, however, the burial societies served other functions, stemming in part from the second-line funereal tradition. A brass band would lead a procession of mourners, and participants would wave handkerchiefs and dance toward the end of the march. The Amazons follow this tradition in raising and providing financial support and awareness for breast cancer survivors. Looking at Lynette Johnson's experience with the Amazons reinforces the centrality of African American culture, from social aid groups to music and Mardi Gras Indians to this new organization.

Lynette Johnson, Amazon

That the core of the Amazons is from the predominantly African American Seventh Ward of New Orleans is clear by the associations that Lynette Johnson has with Honoré. Although they didn't know each other then, both attended St. Joseph's Academy in Gentilly (located near Lake Pontchartrain). A mutual friend knew that Johnson had had breast cancer, so the friend told her about the new organization being formed by Honoré. An equally significant similarity between Johnson and Honoré is their interest and knowledge in family history. Like Honoré, Johnson is very interested and knowledgeable about genealogy. Johnson has not only traced her family back to two French brothers who came to New Orleans in 1760, she has also visited the ancestral village of Olliole, France. Like Honoré's ancestors, Johnson's forbears are part European and part African, or Creole. As she notes, her family has deep roots, "over 260 years in New Orleans" (interview). Sharing an interest in history and family history is a quality that informs both women's participation in new Downtown Mardi Gras. Johnson sees the Amazons as fulfilling missions similar to those of the early African American social aid and pleasure clubs, which assisted families with burials and loans. These activities were crucial in a segregated society where African Americans were denied access to credit. Johnson explains, "this group provides succor in the way that those old groups did" (interview). As she notes, the Amazons also "continue the tradition of flashy outfits and cheeky high-stepping on the streets" (interview).

Both her family celebrations and her sense of Mardi Gras history combine to make the Amazons a significant experience for Johnson. At the same time, her experiences as a native New Orleanian makes Johnson an excellent and committed culture bearer. As a child, she had been able to walk to local Mardi Gras parades in the Gentilly neighborhood, and the experience of marching in the French Quarter, in particular, evokes that experience. She describes how the crowd reacts to the Amazons: "When we march in the Joan of Arc parade, we hear people recognize us—'here they are—here are the Amazons'" (interview). Friends and family come out to support the Amazons, and Johnson will stop for a hug or a kiss. She says, "I love the idea of the Joan of Arc Parade. A lot of original parades happened in the French Quarter. It feels good to be back in the original place of Mardi Gras, a sacred space where the city started" (interview). Johnson relishes the closeness of the crowds, explaining, "The French Quarter is very intimate. We are very close to the people watching, and many of them are themselves dressed [costumed]" (interview).

In addition to Johnson's family roots and participation in Carnival, she also comes from a family of drummers. Johnson and her husband, Mike Murphy, who belongs to the Scythians, the auxiliary support group for the Amazons, are the lead drummers for the group. While Johnson remembers enjoying drumming even before she knew of her family history, she recalls as a young girl going to her Uncle Milford Dollio's house. He was a famous drummer who played every year at Jazz Fest and was the drummer for the Onward Brass Band. She was particularly struck by his enormous stacks of drum cases, going up to the ceiling. Her own musical career was primarily guitar and bass, but for the Amazons, she was happy to step into the role of drummer and leader, teaching other women who want to drum how to do so. Johnson also had relatives who were Mardi Gras Indians, and she was impressed as a child by their spectacular suits and by their drumming during parades. While drumming is central to Johnson's role in the Amazons, she supports the group in its mission of social aid as well. Drumming serves to engage, focus, and support the Amazons in bonding and parading.

The Amazons and Female Empowerment

An outpouring of support from friends and community after her diagnosis made Honoré realize the importance of "strength in numbers," which led to her creation of the Amazons ("Amazons Benevolent Society"). Through "volunteer work, fundraising, and service," the group raises awareness of breast cancer, supports patients and survivors, and provides an inspiring narrative of female strength despite the challenge of breast cancer. The website describes their parading as "walking in celebration," explaining: "[we] want to show cancer fighters and those in need and in sickness that they can be a part of the merriment and celebration and we support them. We are strong, fierce, and tireless" ("Amazon Benevolent Society"). The women live up to this description in their splendid outfits. Johnson says, "I feel empowered by that outfit . . . It's strong colors, that burgundy red and gold" (interview). Just as important as their appearance, though, is the feeling of accomplishment that comes from marching in public, and completing a parade route. As Johnson explains, "It's an opportunity for women to do something they never had before, that maybe they didn't know that they had in them" (interview).

In addition to a tenuous connection with the storied Zulu parade, the Amazons' name comes from their reputation as strong, formidable women. The particular legend that the Amazons cut off a breast to improve their skills as archers has particular resonance for breast cancer survivors, many of whom underwent mastectomies as part of the treatment for the disease. In American society, which fetishizes the breast, and during Mardi Gras, where breast-baring and ogling women's bodies is part of Carnival's appeal to some, the Amazons propose an alternative vision of the feminine. It is all the more striking in the sexist carnival context. Johnson praises Joan of Arc and the mythological Amazons of sharing the quality of being "heroic women" (interview). In its vision alone, the Amazons present a defiant and powerful image of feminine strength. As Honoré notes, after a mastectomy especially, "it takes a lot of courage to dance in the streets. It is a resistance to society's view that to be a woman you have to have certain physical attributes and display certain qualities" (interview, August 8, 2017).

The Amazons' costumes accentuate the promotion of powerful femininity, connected to the city of New Orleans. A key feature of the costume is a custom-made breast plate, fitted to each women's form, sporting a large fleur-de-lis, the symbol for New Orleans adopted from the French. Sprague, the krewe's costume designer, explains, "the breastplate and sword are our signature. They evoke the strength we have gained in our struggles and the power that we have to overcome what may come in the future, and to help others do the same" (e-mail). A large plastic sword, plastic breastplate, short leather skirt (made of strips), red leggings, red cape, brown boots, and dramatic individually feathered headdresses complete the outfit. Witucki explains how the costumes make her feel: "I love the magic of dressing up and appreciate the enthusiasm with which it is done in New Orleans . . . our Amazon costumes make me feel powerful" (e-mail, September 6,

Amazons by the Mississippi. Photo by Kim Welsh. Permission of Krewe de Jeanne d'Arc.

2017). The Amazons do not wear masks, part of their defiant statement to the city as to who they are. (Masking is required of all participants in Uptown parades by city code.)

Critical to their marching are the drums and the participants' fierce demeanor. Honoré explains that, initially, she had to rein in some of the participants who, as she describes it, would want to "cut-up" or "dance flirtatiously," actions common to other walking parades. Honoré worried that "somebody is going to get a picture of this [Amazons 'cutting up'] and we're going to be seen as just another female dancing group" (there are several such groups of seductively attired women who perform salacious routines in Mardi Gras parades) (interview, August 8, 2017). In marked contrast to the more customary seductive dancing performed by women in Mardi Gras parades, the troupe of Amazons swings their swords in unison, walk in lines of two across, in time with the drum beats. Looking straight ahead, The Amazons break file only to embrace other survivors in the audience, or to hand out plastic flowers or small swords to children. At regular intervals, the Amazons stand in line, swords overhead, and each Amazon runs through this gauntlet, yelling "All Hail." The Amazons are a dramatic and popular walking krewe, with audience members, especially those who know of its association with breast cancer survivors, shouting encouragement and praise.

While their parading is perhaps the most visible activity of the group, the Amazons fulfill their social aid mission in various ways. One is a major fundraiser each October during Breast Cancer Awareness Month. Selling baked goods and providing information in an event called "Baking for Breast Cancer," the krewe draws on its founder's expertise as a cook, from a family of cooks, as well as women's traditional expertise in baking. The event provides an opportunity for generations of women to work together to raise money for other women. Johnson, a founding Amazon, participates in the bake sale with her mother, Jeanette Dolliole Sylvester, who bakes her famous rum cake, and helps sells the baked goods. In addition to the usual cakes and cookies, the sale also includes clever (and delicious) cupcakes made by Bebe Scarpinato decorated to look like breasts in different skin tones, with candy pieces serving as the nipples. This particular treat exemplifies the whimsy and humor otherwise absent from the Amazons' processions. The bake sale concludes with a walk with music to nearby Bayou St. John, where those who have died are honored with flowers thrown into the bayou; "the flowers drift peacefully away in the water—what better way to memorialize the women gone before us?" (e-mail, August 27, 2017). A somber but emotionally compelling conclusion, this ritual reminds everyone of how precious and short life is. Like tradition second-line funerals, this ritual reminds the participants of the importance of celebrating life even as we face death.

How They Joined; Crossing Racial Divides

In distinction to New Orleans's legacy of racism, Honoré conveys an openness to people of all identities and ethnicities, and a signal feature of her krewes is the range of its participants in terms of class, color, and experience. The Amazons includes natives and non-resident women who live in Texas. Dawn Sprague, key to The Amazons' costume production, lives in Tyler, Texas. Her friendship with Honoré has proven to be one of the cornerstones of the Amazons. She and Honoré had bonded over Facebook over their breast cancer treatment, and when they got together in New Orleans in 2013, they "sat in a park and talked and talked until it was two hours later and we didn't even notice. [Honoré] has a lot of costuming experience ... [but] ultimately, she asked me to design the costumes for The Amazons" (e-mail, December 11, 2017). Sprague's description of the Amazons emphasizes their support and benevolent activity. In the Amazons,

Sprague explains, "I've found a group of women and men who value the strength it takes not just to survive cancer or whatever hardships life gives you, but to thrive and give back what you can. [The Amazons] are not just strength, but compassion and service to others. Our shared background of suffering gives us a perspective on life that pushes us to help alleviate the suffering of others" (e-mail).

Ann Witucki is another current resident of Texas who comes to New Orleans for many of the Amazons' events. Witucki met Honoré in 2013, when they both were part of a service project, assisting with a Christmas party at the John J. Hainkel home. Witucki was drawn to Honoré's vision for the Amazons, both because of its social mission and because it honored breast cancer survivors. In addition, she describes her strong affinity for New Orleans. "I love New Orleans. Although I have no [family] roots there, I do have a history" (e-mail, Sept 6, 2017). For a time in the 1980s, Witucki and her husband rented an apartment on Royal Street in the French Quarter. She helped with evacuees from New Orleans after the levee failures, working at the Astrodome in Houston. In the year following, she made several trips to do volunteer recovery work in the city itself. Without generations of family heritage in New Orleans, Witucki nevertheless evinces a deep passion for the culture. After retirement she plans to move to New Orleans. Until then, the proximity and inexpensive Big Bus fares from Houston means Witucki doesn't miss many Amazons events. Witucki's and Sprague's situations demonstrate a commitment from women who are not only not residents, but who are not even transplants, yet.

Once a year, the Amazons welcome new members. Each member is responsible for ordering her own breastplate, boots, and leggings, but the krewe's very modest dues of $40 include an Amazons T-shirt, a leather skirt, two cloaks, the swords, and shield. Honoré and another member, her second-in-command, Dawn Sprague, make the cloaks, leather skirts, and headdresses. The costume remains constant, with the exception of the headdresses, which, following other carnival customs, are improved and become more elaborate every year. A final item presented to the new members is a gold medal with an "A," hung on a red ribbon and placed over the new member's neck. Also once a year, the group holds a luncheon, in 2017 held at the restaurant in the New Orleans Museum of Art. There, in the beautiful City Park setting, a dozen members congregated in the spring to discuss plans. Honoré presented several members with certificates and plaques, recognizing their service over the past year. Hugs and tears predominated.

Parading

The Amazons attend many city events, but most germane to the focus of this book is their parade participation. As a tour guide and noted culinary expert, Honoré worked with the French Market Corporation, an organization that promotes tourist events in the historical French Market by the river in the Quarter. One event which the FMC co-sponsored was the Joan of Arc Parade, discussed in the first chapter of this book. With its feminist emphasis on a strong female warrior, the parade seemed a natural fit for the also newly formed Amazons. Joan of Arc founder Amy Kirk-Duvoisin invited the group to participate, and asked them to serve a vital role in the ceremonies that conclude the event. The Amazons stand on the Washington Artillery Park steps, and hold up their swords. The king and queen of the parade walk through this arch to receive their crowns. This walking parade emphasizes medieval and ancient attire and walking groups, including friars, nuns, and courtiers, so the Amazons fit in well. The Amazons' image, as exemplified by a spectacular photo of Dianne Honoré, is now regularly used by nola.com and the *Times-Picayune* as the image that typifies the parade.

A combination of an actual historical figure, Joan of Arc with the mythological Amazons recognizes the fundamental similarity of warrior women to each other. A night parade, the Joan of Arc event also allows women to "take back the night," filling the streets and proclaiming their defiance and energy. The participation of a racially integrated krewe (the Amazons) shows how far Mardi Gras rituals have come, from the twentieth-century marginalization of people of color to this twenty-first-century diverse krewe. Sprague explains how this integration has come to pass: "it has been my sister-like friendship with Dianne that has inspired me to be part of The Amazons. We come from vastly different backgrounds and yet we bond on so many levels because we value the same things in life" (e-mail). As a prime tourist destination, the French Quarter provides an important site for the Amazons to march, taking over the space once dominated by white men.

While they are in location and spirit a Downtown walking krewe, in 2014 the Amazons marched the Uptown route with a new all-female, primarily African American krewe. While this book does not focus on Uptown parades, there have been many changes in Uptown Mardi Gras, too, including increased Uptown women's parading krewes with floats and a longer parade route. The Krewe of Muses, founded in 2000 (Roberts), brought all-female parades back with a vengeance. More recent all-women's groups include

The Amazons marching in Femme Fatale parade: Dawn Sprague and Dianne Honoré. Photo by Brett Duke. Permission of the *Times-Picayune*/NOLA Media Group.

Nyx and the Mystic Krewe of Femme Fatale, a primarily African American Uptown parade that rolls on a Sunday morning, two weekends before Fat Tuesday. Like the Amazons, the Femme Fatales are open to "women of all creeds and colors" ("Mission Statement"), but like Rex and other "integrated" krewes, membership skews in this case to African American participants. Another walking krewe founded by Honoré in 2013, the Black Storyville Baby Dolls, marched one float behind the Amazons, with both groups meeting up on the sidewalk as the parade formed. This participation is significant for its mingling of two Downtown krewes with an uptown parade. The Black Storyville Baby Dolls were also invited to parade. Honoré, who leads both the Amazons and the Black Storyville Dolls, had to decide with which group to costume, and she solved this dilemma by dressing out as an Amazon, but rendezvousing with the Black Storyville Baby Dolls, and ensuring that they marched a float behind the Amazons.

In 2018, due to a change to the enforcement of city codes concerning the number of walking groups in Uptown parades, the Amazons lost their spot in the Femme Fatale parade. Intrepid as ever, Honoré arranged permits, bands, and invited the Ritmeaux Krewe to march in the first-ever Amazons Lundi Gras parade. The event included the first Amazons queen, Janice Smith, riding in a horse carriage, along with Cherise Harrison-Nelson,

The Amazons dove release, Lundi Gras 2018. Photo by Geoff Clayton. Permission of Geoff Clayton.

Amazons drummers, the Scythians. Lundi Gras 2018. Photo by Geoff Clayton. Permission of Geoff Clayton.

the parade's honorary muse. Part of the proceedings include the release of doves in Washington Square Park, and honoring ancestors. The Downtown route included a march from the Park to Backstreet Cultural Museum, where the drum corps played for an additional half hour. The Amazons first solo Lundi Gras Parade marked their status as a significant Downtown Carnival group.

The Black Storyville Baby Dolls

A group with a different but related attitude toward female strength and empowerment is the Black Storyville Baby Dolls, founded by Dianne Honoré in 2013. While the Amazons Benevolent Society draws on mythical women with extraordinary powers, the Black Storyville Baby Dolls revives the tradition of real, everyday women who worked the sex trade at the beginning of the twentieth century. Storyville was a red-light district where prostitution was legal from 1897 to 1917. Like every other aspect of American and New Orleans life, the activity was a site of racial contestation, with a legal struggle to create a "Black Storyville." Kim Marie Vaz makes a compelling case for understanding the women who came from this district as defiant and proud, women who challenged their subordinate structural position in a racist hierarchy. Vaz traces their history to women named Beatrice Hill and Leona Tate, who in 1912 gathered fellow sex workers, deciding that they too deserved a presence in Mardi Gras (22).

In the early twentieth century, African American participation in Mardi Gras took place outside of the legally sanctioned Uptown parades. The Zulu Social Aid and Pleasure Club began parading in 1909, but their irreverent procession had no defined route, and it consisted primarily of men. Women were eventually included in the 1930s as the Amazons, but the krewe's focus was and remains the image of the male Zulu warrior. The men who founded Zulu were laborers and men with trades, a financial rung above the sex workers, whose jobs were only marginally legal, and who were subject to harassment by others, black and white, who considered themselves superior to Black Storyville's prostitutes. The gender bias can be seen in an acknowledgement by the Zulu president, Mr. Glapion, who admitted that "We were integrated even when [racial] integration was illegal." But Zulu, "and some members of the Autocrat Club and the Original Illinois Club, also all-male African American organizations, say privately that they opposed [the 1992 Mardi Gras krewe de-segregation ordinance] because they will have to open their doors to women" (Rohter).

What is known about the Baby Dolls, of whom there were several different groups between 1912 and 1950, with revivals beginning in the 1970s, relies heavily on the research done by Robert Joseph McKinney, a graduate of the renowned historically black New Orleans college Xavier. McKinney's work for the Works Project Administration focused on African American life. The interviews that McKinney did on black Carnival were the primary source material for the section on this subject in Robert Tallant's famous book, *Mardi Gras . . . As It Was* (1948). A few famous photographs of Baby Dolls exist, showing the aptness of their costume to their name—but with an edge. These women, as Vaz persuasively argues, reclaimed the idea of a woman as a doll, as a sexual object, and played with it. Their costuming and parading insisted on their right to exist and on their strengths and courage. Vaz explains, "the women from the Perdido and Gravier area who decided to mask one Mardi Gras, imitating little girls with short skirts and bonnets, were playing with conventional, paradoxical notions of gender" (2).

A few decades after the first Baby Dolls appeared, Baby Doll costuming was adopted by "the mixed-race Creole families in the Seventh Ward and Treme" (2). The Baby Dolls' use of satin and their custom of carrying large sums of cash demonstrated their worth to a society that would ignore, belittle, and subordinate them. The customary call, "Hey, Baby Doll," was inverted as the women dressed beautifully, but also smoked large cigars and carried knives and flasks. Occasionally, men would also dress as Baby Dolls, adding an element of gender transgression to the practice. Like the Mardi Gras Indians, the Baby Dolls were seen as a group of paraders who were not respectable (Vaz 20). The Black Storyville Baby Dolls illustrate Vaz's description of contemporary Baby Doll groups: "The common denominator of all Baby Doll groups is the celebration and promotion of the fierce independence of New Orleans's Creole women and their cultural traditions, emphasizing not only dance, but costuming, pageantry, beauty, independence, and, above all, spirituality" (6).

The Black Storyville Baby Dolls embrace and honor the earthy sexual nature of the first Baby Dolls, not only in their outfits, but also in their dancing and raucous music. Another revival of the Baby Dolls, Ernie K'Doe Baby Dolls, began in the early 2000s, named after the famous musician by his wife, Antoinette. Antoinette K-Doe emphasized her group's composition of business leaders and professional women to distinguish them from the original Baby Dolls (Vaz 112–13). The Black Storyville Dolls are also composed of professional artists and businesswomen, but they are at pains not to dismiss the legacy of the first Baby Dolls. As BSBD Arsène DeLay and Honoré stress, the first Baby Dolls had few options for employment, due to race discrimination. While African American men also faced horrible discrimination, they had more possible career paths than the women. If, as Zora Neale Hurston has a character claim, in her 1935 novel *Their Eyes Were Watching God*, "black women are the mule of the world," women who worked as prostitutes were at the bottom of a racist and sexist social hierarchy. That is one reason the main character's grandmother is so insistent on arranging marriage for her at a young age. But Hurston exposed racism and colorism in her novel, as well as the traps for women of assuming that respectability provides protection. Books like Victoria W. Wolcott's *Remaking Respectability: African American Women in Interwar Detroit* (2001), and Kate Dossett's *Bridging the Race Divides: Black Nationalism, Feminism, and Integration in the United States, 1896–1935*, detail the importance of black women's networks and the issues they faced in dealing with ideas of respectability. But, as always, the situation in New Orleans was more complicated and unique. New Orleans was alone in having both legalized prostitution and a large community of people of color who had some limited rights unavailable elsewhere in the United States.

Carnival and Celebrating Family

The Black Storyville Baby Dolls thus represent the case of tradition and change: in reviving this Carnival tradition, the participants honor its past and the women who created such a defiant and feminist ritual, while at the same time altering the custom to suit their contemporary needs and visions of themselves and of New Orleans. To Honoré, DeLay, and Lee, history and family are paramount aspects of Carnival, and the specific aspects of the Black Storyville Baby Dolls highlight their world view. By presenting the Black Storyville Baby Dolls in a variety of contexts, from community celebrations such as Mardi Gras, St. Joseph's Day, and Downtown Super Sunday, these women ensure that the creativity and power of African American women is visible and engaging. Through their parading and other activities, the Black Storyville Baby Dolls are working to ensure that the original women receive their due recognition. As Honoré explains, "When people think of the black Mardi Gras heritage, they think of Mardi Gras Indians, they think of Skulls and Bones, the last thing people

The Black Storyville Baby Dolls: Arsène DeLay, Dianne
Honoré, Joell Lee. Photo by Ryan Hodgson-Rigsbee.
Permission of Ryan Hodgson-Rigsbee.

think of is the Baby Dolls. We're trying to change that. We're trying to give
them a name and their proper place in history and educate people as to
who they were" (Perkins). One way that the Baby Dolls honor their place
and history is through an awards banquet, the first of which was held in
September 2017.

The migration of the Baby Doll tradition from the darker-skinned African American prostitutes to the Creole women of the Treme and 7th Ward
was a significant expansion of the practice. While the original Baby Dolls
were from Downtown, there was also a rival Baby Dolls from Uptown, also

sex workers. In some ways, the Baby Dolls' appearance in more respectable black neighborhoods made the costuming even more radical. Conventional women dressing up and acting like aggressive, autonomous women presented a strong challenge to conventional ideas of black womanhood. Vaz describes the original Baby Dolls as having "a reputation as agile dancers, sharp entrepreneurs in the sex industry, and as tough women" (14). A well-known local restaurant owner (on whom the television show *Frank's Place* was based), Chef Austin Leslie describes the Baby Dolls by emphasizing their fierceness: "all those women dressed like little babies, in hot pink and sky blue. You fool with them, they'd cut you too" (Mick Burns, qtd. in Vaz 14–15). By "Baby-Dolling," the Black Storyville Baby Dolls not only pay homage to their foremothers, but also acknowledge the obstacles they faced, and the courage of contemporary African American women. Explaining why she carries a knife as part of her costume, Black Storyville Baby Doll DeLay reminds me, "you have to remember that the human condition has not changed that much—we have not evolved that much" (interview).

The Black Storyville Baby Dolls represent a much more historically and racially specific group than do the Amazons, with the result that the connection to the city and the city's culture is more concrete and direct. The connection is very personal for both the krewe's founder, Honoré, and to DeLay and Lee, both of whom joined in 2015 after being recruited by Honoré. The women are from well-respected Creole families, and both are justifiably proud and knowledgeable about several generations of their families. Honoré traces her family back seven generations, and DeLay is the thirteenth generation of her family to live in New Orleans. Honoré has researched her own family history in New Orleans archives, and DeLay's mother and other relatives have extensive photographic and letter collections tracing their family's history. Honoré's parents owned a restaurant in Treme, and DeLay comes from the famous family of musicians, the Boutté clan. The women are steeped in the core of New Orleans cultural products, food and music. Joell Lee attended the prestigious Xavier Preparatory High School, and paraded with the marching parade because she was a cheerleader. She also has a cousin who is a Mardi Gras Indian. Her mother is a minister who is now active in Mardi Gras herself, but she supports Lee's participation in the Black Storyville Baby Dolls, even commenting that Lee now smiles more, after joining the group. Lee's grandmother lived in the 7th Ward, in the 1700 block of N. Dorgenois, and Lee's family lived next door when she was a child. Fond memories for

Lee include black-owned stores, Aubrey's and Sander's, "playing cool can on the sidewalk, eating huck-a-bucks, and skating on the porch" (e-mail, August 30, 2017). Lee moved back to the house when she was pregnant with her son, and stayed there until the Katrina disaster. Like Honoré and DeLay, Lee has strong roots in the community, and her family "has always lived in New Orleans" (e-mail). Lee's family participation in Mardi Gras continues with her daughter participating in the first Black Storyville Baby Dolls parade, and subsequently being chosen as princess for her school's Carnival court.

The Art of Costuming

Their professional accomplishments help explain their skill and interest in costuming and parading. Honoré has done years of historical research for her position as a tour guide (her professional name is Gumbo Marie), for her numerous interviews and cooking/historical lectures at the New Orleans School of Cooking and the French Market. An accomplished costumer, Honoré attributes part of her ability to making numerous costumes for her daughter, who attended NOCCA (the New Orleans art high school) and is now a professional actress. Her skill at designing and creating costumes can be seen not only in the Amazons' spectacular outfits, but also in the Baby Dolls' numerous sophisticated and extravagant designs. While the Amazons wear the same costume, with improvements in cloaks and masks, the Baby Dolls have several new outfits every year. One tribute to Honoré's skill was her construction, in only hours, of a beautiful design for the Red Beans Parade (discussed in chapter 4). A professional musician and actress, DeLay also has considerable skill in creating designs. She holds an undergraduate degree in costume design from Marquette, and this professional training has proved very helpful. With a bit of a dismissive gesture, she explains that some of the other Baby Dolls have to employ a seamstress, while DeLay is able to custom-fit her dresses and hats herself. Lee, who works at the Tulane University Graduate Medical Education School, takes great pride in decorating her parasols and creating her hats, while admitting "thank God for fabric glue" (interview). Her co-workers know and admire her work as a Black Storyville Baby Doll, and she has been featured in the local newspaper and Tulane University publications.

This seamstress, Miss Ruth Jones, also known as "Pee-Wee" due to her diminutive stature, recently appeared on a radio interview with Honoré and Joell Lee, another Black Storyville Baby Doll. Lee confessed that failure to learn how to sew had kept her from participating in Mardi Gras. She expressed gratitude to Miss Ruth, whose beautiful work enables her to be a Baby Doll. Lee creates her own parasols and hats, but on occasion she has had a crisis, when a costume has been too big. "She's like a Godsend," Lee explains. Lee said that she has contacted Miss Ruth on a Monday for a costume she needs for Wednesday. "Don't kill me," Lee tells Miss Ruth, and the costume is done, fitting perfectly. Lee attributes Miss Ruth's commitment to the Black Storyville Baby Dolls in part to the fact that she "loves interesting material" (interview). Miss Ruth has created costumes for many Baby Doll groups, and she particularly praised the Black Storyville Baby Dolls for their designs. Honoré explained that had tried to get Miss Ruth to parade, but that she was more comfortable creating their gorgeous costumes. As Lee describes it, "I am a queen on Mardi Gras Day—I have on a new satin dress" (Perkins). Miss Ruth echoes this vision, saying "I like to see them shine . . . I love putting them together and . . . I love to help create whatever they pick" (Perkins). When asked how the Black Storyville Baby Dolls compare to other groups from the past, Miss Ruth says, "The Black Storyville Baby Dolls brought a whole new fashion" (Perkins). For Miss Ruth, the reward is the acknowledgment of her craft and skill. "I love it when people say, 'Oh, Miss Ruth made that'" (Perkins).

As photographs of the Black Storyville Baby Dolls show, the results are perfectly fitted and jaw-droppingly beautiful costumes. While the handwork is not as complicated as the beading done by Mardi Gras Indians, the Baby Dolls' costumes do get more elaborate each time, with enormous hats, and for their 2018 costume Swarovski crystals were ordered from New York. As Honoré characterizes it, they have to "up their game" (interview). The Black Storyville Baby Dolls, she says, set a high standard that the other Baby Doll groups try to emulate. They create at least five, and one year eight, completely different costumes. That puts pressure on Honoré to make the next outfit even more spectacular and eye-grabbing. While the dress is central to the Baby Dolls' performance, their accessories are equally significant in terms of defying gender roles and creating a commanding physical presence in a parade or on the street. The hats are towering works of art unto themselves, and as DeLay explains, part of the challenge with the millinery (they are really too enormous to be called bonnets) is creating a work of art that is also wearable. Their parasols are beautifully decorated, providing a useful and engaging prop for dancing and twirling. Other accoutrements can be bought, such as the cigars Honoré brandishes (unlit), the flask and knife that DeLay carries, and the flask that Lee tucks into her dress neckline. Appropriating symbols of masculine indulgence and revelry, the Black Storyville Baby Dolls challenge gender stereotypes and assert a strong and happy female presence. In the context of Storyville and New Orleans, these outfits belie the stereotype of New Orleans and Mardi Gras of *Girls Gone Wild*, as in stupid, drunk, self-exposing victims, and substitute another image of female autonomy and pleasure. In addition, the Black Storyville Baby Dolls have not only a brass band, but also the Basin Street Characters, historically costumed men and women, including white people, who accompany the Baby Dolls.

Naming and Creating Personae

The Black Storyville Baby Dolls create a self-conscious, historically based performance. Not coincidentally, the Basin Street Auxiliary includes people who perform as part of New Orleans Living History troupe. Nina Hansen Quinn dresses as "Hammie the Can Can dancer"; Antoinette Bebe Scarpinato is "Bebe the Gilmore Girl"; Angela Caril is "Angela, the Woman about Town"; Abigail Thayer parades as "Madam Rebecca." In addition, the young Black Storyville Baby Dolls Evangeline Marsalis appears as "Baby Doll Fancy." Each Black Storyville Baby Doll chooses a name to represent her character. In this regard the group creates and encourages individual identities and theatrical performances. (In contrast, the Amazons use their own names.) Honoré is familiar with and easily speaks of the women in Vaz's book, *The "Baby Dolls."* To the Black Storyville Baby Dolls, these women are culture bearers who are to be respected. While Honoré, DeLay, and Lee acknowledge and object to current racism and obstacles placed particularly in front of black women, they both express admiration at the courage of women who, without the opportunities for education and jobs available now, still insisted on their identities and rights to a place in carnival.

Since their literal female ancestors also faced obstacles, Honoré and DeLay dedicate their performances to these women. For Honoré, as already mentioned, she looks to Catiché Destrehan, a woman who was enslaved and who saw many changes in the city, from Spanish, to French, to American rule. By parading, Honoré sees herself as honoring Destrehan's life and work. Honoré's Baby Doll name, the Sugar Baroness, is a nod to another part of family history. One of her seventh-generation uncles was purportedly a sugar baron, and Honoré chose the name not to honor him, but "as a slap across the face of the institution of slavery"; and at the same time, the name holds reference to the original Baby Dolls through "sexual innuendo" (interview). Similarly, DeLay speaks of her maternal grandmother, Gloria Boutté, in whose home she lives, a home built by her grandfather George Boutté and other members of the family. A dedicated gardener, DeLay explains that part of her inspiration was her great-great-grandfather, Arsène Duvigneaud, who also was known for extensive gardening. DeLay's grandmother's favorite color was scarlet—she would never leave her home without her lipstick and nails brightly painted so. DeLay belongs to Project Monarch, in which gardeners raise plants to attract the monarch butterfly to help the species survive. Her Baby Doll name, Scarlett Monarch, brings together her family and a symbol of beauty and survival, as well as evoking the regality of royalty.

The selection of a name affects the creation of character, in the street performance that emerges every time the Black Storyville Baby Dolls parade. Each Baby Doll chooses a name that has personal significance, but Honoré insists that the names be serious, "no silliness," she said. She cited a name from another Baby Doll group, "Candy Bar," as an example of a name that was not connected to African American family or culture. Lee's Baby Doll name, "Jo Baby," shows how intertwined the activity is to her everyday identity. She uses an abbreviation of her own name, a combination that people have actually used in addressing her. Her commitment to New Orleans culture can also be seen in her family nickname, "Miss New Orleans." This seriousness about naming and the historical aspects of "Baby Dolling" are features that distinguish the Black Storyville Baby Dolls from other Baby Doll groups. As Honoré describes it, "We are the most serious, with the most messaging and most educational and community support events. We spend thousands of dollars annually. Before us, Baby Dolls were 'tea-partying'" (interview). Honoré's words, as well as those of DeLay and Lee, show how seriously they take their cultural practice, and to what high standards they hold themselves.

Evolution from Another Group

As do other Downtown walking clubs, the Black Storyville Baby Dolls evolved from another Carnival group. In this regard, the group reflects the ways that Carnival grows. Members group and regroup as they search for the precise vision of performance that suits their needs. The Black Storyville Baby Dolls are perhaps the most recent development in this tradition, having evolved from the Treme Baby Dolls. While there is no animosity between these two groups—both marched in the 2017 Femme Fatale parade, for example—there are some differences of style and emphasis. Organizational issues were one reason the three women decided to form a new krewe. Working for a medical school, Lee has been accustomed to an efficient and tightly organized work space. She was looking for that efficiency in the Baby Doll world, and found it in Honoré. The dizzying number of parades in which the Black Storyville Baby Dolls appear makes this efficiency and commitment on the women's parts clear: Decadence Festival, Satchmo Festival, Tomato Festival, Mardi Gras Day, Downtown Super Sunday, Red Beans, and even private tours. One recent Jazz Tour featured Black Storyville, with participants ending up in the Basin Street Lounge. There they were treated to a one-act play, *Millie's Bag*, written by Honoré and performed by Lee and Honoré, that focuses on the original Baby Dolls. The performance focuses on the limited options that black women faced in the early nineteenth century, but also emphasizes their sisterhood and support for each other. Through their public appearance as Baby Dolls, these women create what in Diana Taylor's words are "'Acts of transfer' [that] transmit information, cultural memory, and collective identity from one generation or group to another through reiterated behaviors" ("Performance and intangible" 92). Taylor emphasizes the importance and impact of such performances, explaining that "while these acts are living practices, they nonetheless have a staying power that belies notions of ephemerality" ("Performance and intangible" 92).

Focus on Improvisational Performance and History

Unlike for example, the New Orleans Baby Doll Ladies, who mask and emphasize dance, the Black Storyville Baby Dolls evince an improvisational performance style grounded in music and dance. The level of their artistic preparation includes knowledge and promulgation of history, but also connections to New Orleans's signal cultural products, music and dance. In *The "Baby Dolls,"* Vaz stresses the importance of the Baby Dolls to the creation of jazz. Jazz is above all, a music that was created for dancing, and the Baby Dolls' dancing helped shape jazz. Part of the process of jazz involves musicians and dancers striving to outdo each other. Vaz explains that "The Baby Dolls were part of a culture in which competition among artistic groups was common" (65), and this aspect continues today with contemporary Baby Doll groups. In traditional Uptown parades, the competition is for the biggest and best decorated floats and the largest, most unusual throws, while for the Baby Dolls the competition involves having the most beautiful and arresting costumes. And also the greatest number of costumes: as Honoré wryly notes, "most groups did 1–3 costumes" (interview) before the Black Storyville Baby Dolls raised the ante. Lee also points to the beautiful fabrics that these Baby Dolls use, such as in 2017, when they sported a beautiful brocade material. In addition, each woman personalizes her costume, with Lee having her dress cut in a sweetheart style and eschewing, as the others did, the bonnet for a more rakish top hat. The other Baby Doll groups, as Lee notes, "all look the same" (interview), while the Black Storyville Baby Dolls stand out due to their more extravagant and spectacular costumes.

Investment in a Performance Vision

The Black Storyville Baby Dolls are accompanied by a brass band, which for Mardi Gras Day or St. Joseph's Day can be a large expense. For Mardi Gras 2017, for example, the group paid the Free Spirit Brass Band $1,600 for two hours of playing. This is a considerable sum of money, but exemplifying her efficiency, Honoré organized a raffle to cover most of the cost. In other parades, such as Femme Fatale or the Satchmo or Tomato Festival, or a second-line funeral, the band and the Baby Dolls are paid for by the sponsoring organization or family. Given the number of entirely new costumes, usually at least five per year, and performances, at least that many, the cost and time of participation are considerable. Yet to the Baby Dolls, the resulting live art form is well worth the investment of time and money. As Lee explains, she considers herself "a culture bearer," so her costumes are "a good investment" for her and for the city (interview). As she also points out, people come from all over the world to partake in New Orleans culture, and to keep the traditions alive takes effort and funds. She wishes that the city would do more to support the African American culture bearers, and plans to apply for grants to support the Black Storyville Baby Dolls. As a professional at a university, Lee knows well that grants are vital for funding education and culture.

Black Storyville Baby Dolls at Funerals

Each parading event takes place in front of a different audience. DeLay, a member of the group, first connected with the Black Storyville Baby Dolls as a way to honor her grandmother, Gloria Boutté. A well-respected matron of an influential musical family, Gloria Boutté had always wanted to parade as a Baby Doll. In a brief excerpt from a film by James Demaria (available on YouTube), Boutté explains "I wanted to dance." As a young woman, her respectable family forbade her to dress as a Baby Doll, but she had seen and admired their flair and beauty. She had planned to dress out as a Baby Doll when she turned eighteen, but World War II intervened; it was one of the rare occasions when Mardi Gras was officially cancelled. Then, as Boutté explains, "but then I had children and I couldn't turn out" (video). The enthusiasm and delight with which Boutté describes this lost ritual is captivating. When she died, her daughters and her granddaughter wanted to honor their heritage and Boutté's love for the Baby Doll tradition by having them parade in her funeral second-line.

There were two Baby Doll troupes at Boutté's funeral, but only the Black Storyville Baby Dolls went into the church, at the family's request. Honoré explains: "We would never show up dressed out at a funeral without a request from the deceased family. Some dolls do that but we are strictly professional and very respectful of our dead" (e-mail, August 22, 2017). "We escorted the body out to the street. Then, we along with her son, the Grand Marshall, we secondlined until the body was taken to the cemetery. It was one of the most absolutely beautiful secondlines I have been in" (e-mail). The Black Storyville Baby Dolls do not do a lot of funerals, but as Honoré notes, "Today secondlines are not what they used to be. They used to be very respectful with a lot less hoopla" (e-mail). Yet in 2018, when an honored member of the African American community like Tee Eva passes, the Black Storyville Baby Dolls are there to honor her.

After seeing the Black Storyville Baby Dolls dance at her grandmother's funeral, it was an easy decision for DeLay to join the troupe. She sees it as another way to honor her grandmother's memory, as well as that of the black women who began the tradition. Lee moved the tradition into the next generation, parading with her then nine-year-old daughter Jayden also dressed as a Black Storyville Baby Doll for Mardi Gras 2016. That year, the Black Storyville Baby Dolls jumped in and out of the Zulu parade, a prestigious and high-visibility event on Mardi Gras morning.

Achieving Their Own Parade

While she was proud to march in Zulu, Lee prefers the 2017 Mardi Gras experience, where the Baby Dolls created their own parade and had their own band. After meeting up at 5:00 a.m. with the North Side Skulls and Bones krewe at Backstreet Museum in Treme, the Black Storyville Baby Dolls sashayed around the 7th Ward, accompanied by the aforementioned brass band. The Backstreet Museum houses artifacts from black culture, including Mardi Gras Indian costumes, and as Honoré notes, artifacts "born out of segregated Mardi Gras" (e-mail, August 22, 2017). Located across from the oldest continuously operating African American Catholic church, St. Augustine, the museum starting point allows the group to pray and contemplate history at the exterior monument to the Unknown Slave. Honoré explains, "Usually that spot comes with tears. It is very spiritual for us" (e-mail). The Black Storyville Baby Dolls process first with the Northside Skulls and Bones Gang, then return to the Backstreet Museum with them to begin their own parade. This is the neighborhood in which Honoré grew up, and where her parents' restaurant still stands, though they sold it years ago. The neighborhood has significance for the other Black Storyville Baby Dolls, because, as Honoré explains, "many of us are connected to this area whether born, reared, or had relatives, so we are all comfortable to dance through those streets in the 6th and 7th Wards" (e-mail). Their dance moves are traditional second-lining three-step patterns.

Educating Visitors to New Orleans

Another aspect of the Black Storyville Baby Dolls' promulgation of the tradition occurs in more tourist-oriented events. Because she has worked with the French Market Corporation that sponsors, among other events, the Satchmo Festival and the Tomato Festival, Honoré had a connection and was also well positioned to observe what was missing from these festivals. The second-line funeral procession with a brass band and dancers is an African American tradition, yet the parades put on by the French Market Corporation had only parody or fun, ahistorical women's dancing troupes, like the Muff-a-lottas, a krewe named after a famous New Orleans sandwich. Honoré felt that these "second lines" were "losing the message—losing the history" (interview), so she approached Amy Kirk-Duvoisin, then the marketing director of the organization, who immediately agreed that the

Dianne Honoré, Dawn Sprague, and a young admirer. Photo by Robin Roberts. Permission of Robin Roberts.

parades needed more historical depth and respect for African American krewes. The association with the Satchmo Festival is particularly significant, for Louis Armstrong lived in the neighborhood where Baby Dolls originated (Vaz 20). Armstrong is credited with popularizing jazz, which drew on their dancing; he specifically wrote about Baby Dolls' impression on him as a young man. The connection to the Tomato Festival may seem more tenuous, but in their bright red costumes the Black Storyville Baby Dolls remind the audience of black women's presence in the French Market and their significance to New Orleans cuisine through their positions as cooks. In a beautifully illustrated book available on her website, Honoré has published an account of her experiences, entitled *Living the Black Storyville Baby Doll Life*. The Amazons Benevolent Society and the Black Storyville Baby Dolls provide representative examples of how new Downtown Mardi Gras draws on New Orleans culture to revise, revitalize, and expand its traditions.

The women involved in these parades love New Orleans, value performances of strength and femininity, and are determined to acknowledge the part played by race and gender in Mardi Gras. Their walking parades emphasize common themes of struggle, social justice, an insistence on being recognized, and a celebration of life and spirit. and shows the importance of demonstrating that breast cancer survivors are strong and beautiful. The Black Storyville Baby Dolls have an equally specific, historically based message of social justice. The Baby Dolls did not receive full recognition for their Carnival rituals at the time, but now through the Black Storyville Baby Dolls' and other Baby Doll groups' revitalization of the practice, the original Baby Dolls are being recognized by scholarly books, media, and museums.

Appropriation of Their Performance for Profit

Yet along with this recognition comes the danger of appropriation. Honoré has been frustrated by blatant instances of copying or using her image without her consent. American culture has a long, terrible practice of stealing African American culture without attribution, and by performing in the streets in her own costumes, Honoré has experienced this many times. While she is phlegmatic about the occurrence, it is nevertheless upsetting to her to find a large portrait of herself in her Black Storyville Baby Doll Costume for sale in an art gallery, or to see her designs copied by others. For example, she was distressed to get a call from a friend who saw a portrait of her in Black Storyville Baby Doll costume at the New Orleans Art Center on St. Claude. A few days after an emotional second-line honoring the recently deceased Fats Domino, a photo of Honoré in her custom creation, a blueberry print dress, was shown for sale for $300. In general, Honoré is concerned that, as she explains, "There's also NO etiquette at second lines. People seem to have forgotten that second line means behind the band and any club or family members and friends. They just jump in. They stop you. They ride bikes through the thing. They want to take selfies with you

Dawn Sprague and Joell Lee, the two traditions together. Photo by
Robin Roberts. Permission of Robin Roberts.

IN THE MIDDLE OF THE second line for goodness sakes!" (e-mail, December 5, 2017). The Amazons Benevolent Society also has been affected by
disturbing imitations. As she explains, "There's a group called the Wonder
Women and they all dress in those Wonder Woman party city costumes
which would be fine but their cartoon drawing they use as a picture mimics
our Amazon photos. There is a cartoon of a Wonder Woman in a wheel
chair. If you see our Amazon photos Nelita is prominently in most of our
pictures in her wheelchair" (e-mail). Yet despite these dispiriting instances,
Honoré continues to promote New Orleans culture heritage in a historically specific fashion.

Conclusion

Keeping the Baby Doll tradition alive is critical to its participants, who see that their ancestors persisted despite tremendous obstacles of racism and sexism. Educating the crowds about the significance of the Black Storyville Baby Dolls as defiant, living art is one goal of their existence. By parading as Baby Dolls, the group also reminds viewers that, while racism and sexism still exist, Creole women of New Orleans aren't accepting the stereotypes and limitations that others would like to put upon them. In their defiant, uplifting response to negative situations, these women are responding as New Orleanians did after the catastrophic levee failures that decimated the city. Determined to keep their city and culture alive, these New Orleans women draw on female role models from the past to create a present that must acknowledge women's, especially black women's, significant place in the world.

In a related fashion, the Amazons Benevolent Society also performs the importance of women supporting each other, in this case across racial lines, to combat and to encourage each other in the instance of breast cancer. Using costuming and marching to empower participants and the audiences for their parades, the Amazons demonstrate Carnival's commitment to life. Adopting Lundi Gras as a day to celebrate life, the Amazons also used a dove release ceremony to remind all of transformation and liberation.

In her ability to reclaim African American history and identity, Honoré faces many challenges, of logistics, economics, that are not faced by women who step into demanding but already structured roles (such as that of Zulu royalty, or Mardi Gras queens). Her success at creating racially diverse groups, and of including men in allied walking groups, presents a challenge to the other krewes discussed in this book, which are primarily run by white people. A recent event at the French Quarter's Old Mint exemplified the straddling that Honoré does. She was part of a panel of culture bearers, of whom three were members of established Mardi Gras Indian tribes, their queens. In explaining the similarities and differences between her two groups and the Indians, she was enthusiastic about the latter's traditions, while claiming space for her new, contemporary, socially activist groups. And just the week before, she had marched as a Black Storyville Baby Doll with the Ritmeaux Krewe, as their banner declares, "Louisiana's First Ever Latin Dance Mardi Gras Marching Group," after previously inviting them to march in the inaugural Lundi Gras Amazons parade. Months before, the Black Storyville Baby dolls walked in the Decadence Parade, New Orleans' preeminent gay parade, held Labor Day weekend—in costumes that were Day of the Dead–inspired. For new Downtown Mardi Gras to continue to thrive, these interactions are essential in preventing conflict and hostilities, such as erupted when a group of white women called themselves "Glambeaux" and were soundly and widely criticized for appropriating black men's history of carrying lit torches in parades. In contrast to that debacle, Dianne Honoré recently received a Capturing the Spirit Award from the Mardi Gras Indian Hall of Fame. With this recognition (among others) of her important work as a culture bearer from what could be seen as a competitor Carnival tradition, Honoré shows the possibility and importance of cultural preservation and innovation.

Exceptional Performance, Exceptional Place

Leslie A. Wade

Regardless if one is a New Orleanian by birth or by choice, the question of whether to leave the city for other prospects is one that almost inevitably rises at one time or another. New Orleans has the perennial problems of termites, hurricanes, bureaucratic incompetence, racial and economic inequity, etc. The widening sinkhole—stretching more than twenty feet, with a projected repair cost of over three million dollars (Adelson)—that opened on Canal Street in May 2016 seemed to signify the continual struggle of the city to keep up, to manage, to stay on top of all of the forces that continually assail it and its future. For some the sinkhole warranted hand-wringing; for others it provided, in typical New Orleans dark humor, the occasion for dance and a Cinco de Mayo street party.

An article in the local weekly the *Gambit* in August 2017, "Is New Orleans Worth It?," brought considerable attention and discussion. In this piece Kat Stromquist gave voice to the issues of young professionals who had moved to New Orleans for its many allures but had found limits to upward mobility, including "rising housing costs, stagnant wages and dim job prospects" (15). Backlash to the article characterized these discontents as those "with a relatively short investment in the city" (Mock) and emphasized their privilege in the face of so many minimum-wage workers for whom career mobility is not an option. Nevertheless, the issues raised found resonance—including the city's nepotism, underfunded public education, and failing infrastructure (typified by the Canal Street sinkhole); stories of individuals leaving the city and finding better situations elsewhere have continued to multiply, as that of Jeremy Labadie, who left in 2017 after over twenty years in New Orleans. Labadie reported: "My salary is double . . . I was able to afford to buy a house, the public schools where I am are all rated highly and I live 8 miles from the beach" (7).

The attrition highlighted by the *Gambit* article has proven a concern to city leaders, but it has also factored as a new element in the post-Katrina narrative. Stories of out-migration have challenged the motif of continuous renewal. In short, one hears concerns that the post-Katrina renaissance has reach its zenith and is in danger of losing momentum. Though she does not declare it a trend (admitting the possibility of "estimation errors"), Allison Plyer, chief demographer at the Data Center, a New Orleans–based non-profit, has observed: ""For the first time there's a very small estimated negative net domestic migration" for the New Orleans populace (qtd. in Brasted, "Why do people"). Such data suggests that the city may be coming to a new kind of population plateau, which invites questions regarding the trajectory of New Orleans, and by extension the future of Mardi Gras. What will be the next chapter of the city's history, the next phase of Downtown Carnival practice?

The 2015 Fodor travel guide curiously observes that present-day New Orleans is "on the verge of . . ." (11). The reluctance to complete the sentence indicates the many possible directions of the city's future, which, as the guidebook author notes, is something perhaps not even a Jackson Square fortune-teller can foresee. Positive and negative dynamics continue to be in play that seemingly place the city in a sort of holding pattern.

Certainly New Orleans continues to struggle in often glaring and unconscionable ways. The city's poverty rate is twice as high as the national average ("Is the New Orleans economy"). Crime remains an intractable problem. The city struggles with a shortage of affordable housing, an economy too dependent on low-wage service-industry jobs. Its judiciary and educational systems are often woeful in practice and outcomes. The surprise flooding of August 5, 2017, which inundated neighborhoods not normally susceptible, led to outrage—when word emerged that city pumping stations were not properly engaged, or even operable—and the firing of numerous Sewer and Water Board officials ("For the Sewage and Water Board"). This incident alarmed citizens and prompted national media attention—the *Washington Post* presented the flood in nearly despairing terms, as "another sign that neither money nor leadership will be enough to keep New Orleans above water forever" (Craig).

In hand with such downcast evidence of the city's social, economic, and environmental ills, significant upbeat evidence incites hope and gives testament to an improving New Orleans. Test scores indicate improvement in the city's school system. As a culinary capital, New Orleans has seen the number of new restaurants accelerate, outpacing its pre-Katrina number. Tourism has rebounded; the *New York Times*, in fact, identified New Orleans as its number one recommended destination for 2018 ("52 Places"). The city's economy is experiencing welcome diversification. The landing of DXC Technology, a global IT services firm, was hailed as a great win, bringing new jobs and "a 12 percent increase in tech employment in the metro area" (Tim Morris). The city recently elected African American mayor LaToya Cantrell, who represents a new kind of politician in that office; the city's first female mayor, she is a non-native who arose through the not-for-profit ranks. In face of the city's housing shortage, HousingNOLA has launched a community-inspired, ten-year plan that seeks to add 33,000 affordable units (Evans). A new city council has shown signs of taking on Airbnb, the Water and Sewage Board, and the Entergy Corporation. Racial justice has moreover seen progress. Then-Mayor Mitch Landrieu led the controversial effort to remove Confederate monuments around the city in the spring of 2017. In a speech in defense of the action, that was praised around the country, Landrieu described the removal effort as choosing "a better future for ourselves, making straight what has been crooked and making right what was wrong" ("Mitch Landrieu's Speech"). The following August thousands marched in solidarity in the French Quarter protesting the white supremacists in Charlottesville. And after several lethargic seasons, the Saints returned to the NFL elite and won the conference championship of the NFC South.

Rather than viewing New Orleans in terms of rising or falling, it may be more appropriate to regard the city in a new mode of stasis. Richard Campanella, author of *Bienville's Dilemma*, recently opined that New Orleans has experienced a kind of leveling: "Frankly, after all the turmoil of the past 12 years, after all the tragedy and triumph, all the lows and highs, I think stabilization will be the tone for the next few years . . . The 'new normal' is no longer new; now it's just normal" (qtd. in Woodward). Interestingly, Campanella made this observation on the occasion of being named the honorary king of Krewe du Vieux, the long-established walking parade that served as the progenitor of Downtown Mardi Gras. He enjoyed his reign in 2018, proceeding through the Downtown streets amid satirical signage and lewd revelers, waving to crowds on the curbside, at the helm of the parade themed "Bienville's Wet Dream."

Just as the city has emerged in the post-Katrina era to a new status quo, Downtown Mardi Gras has come now to exist as a regular and accepted feature of the Carnival season. Beginning as an upsurge of creative energy in dark and challenging times, an example of the post-Katrina hope that rose "through the gaping cracks in the sidewalks" (Colton 61), these krewes took to the streets in motley form, testing new routes, practices, and presentations. Marked by wit and innovation, the krewes gained an increasing visibility, to the degree that by 2014 they were publicized as an "alternative" Mardi Gras (Hartman). Their stock on the Carnival scene continued to rise. A pamphlet distributed at the 2016 'tit Rəx parade, "A Diminutive Guide to an Alternative Mardi Gras," gave dates and parade times of various krewes, corroborating further the emergence of the Downtown phenomenon ("A Diminutive Guide"). Krewes such as Red Beans, 'tit Rəx, and Chewbacchus are now regarded almost reverentially, and residents look forward to their parades with keen anticipation. While still alternative in disposition, these krewes have gained entreé in the Carnival calendar, and in some respect have become mainstreamed. In fact, an installation highlighting the city's walking krewes (with Downtown krewes chief amongst the number) is featured in the new Mardi Gras Museum of Carnival and Culture, which opened in 2017 in the French Quarter; the exhibit lists over forty-nine such walking krewes.

Further evidence of the rising profile and importance of Downtown Mardi came in January 2017, which saw the first "meeting of the downtown courts" at the New Orleans Art Center on St. Claude (MacCash, "The first downtown"), an event that brought together representatives of older Downtown enterprises, including Krewe du Vieux and the Golddigger Baby Dolls, with those of the newer enterprises, such as Chewbacchus and 'tit Rəx. Under the direction of master of ceremonies Chuck Perkins, the leaders stood together in an arc; to the left were members of the older krewes, members of the newer krewes on the right. Amidst the proceedings, despite some "incoherence," "a spirit of happy unanimity swiftly arose" (MacCash, "The first downtown"). Perkins credited "the new cats" for adding "their own flair" (qtd. in MacCash, "The first downtown"). The meeting brought visibility and confirmation to this new Mardi Gras constellation, giving homage to the younger krewes and their newly gained status on the Carnival scene.

With some Downtown krewes now entering their second decade of existence, one notes evidence of maturity and regularization, a new normalcy and sense of prestige. Significantly, the krewes have gained visibility beyond the city. Chewbacchus parades have been featured on CBS News and have drawn international press coverage (in the UK's *Guardian* and *Independent*). Nationwide television audiences have watched the 610 Stompers marching in the Macy's Thanksgiving Day Parade. Krewes have appeared in many local TV and movie shoots, as signifiers of Carnival and New Orleans itself. In some respect these practices are becoming archival, recalling Diana Taylor's terms—widely accepted, regularized, and somewhat institutionalized. The krewes and their practices now enjoy the trappings of legitimacy, with widespread press and publicity, citations in scholarly histories of Mardi Gras, and recent museum enshrinement. Downtown Mardi Gras is now part of traditional Carnival.

As Downtown Mardi Gras has entered a kind of archival status, it is curious to note how energies of stasis and change continue to inform the phenomenon. As is common with organizations under the leadership of strong inspirational figures, the passing of years can incite fatigue on the leaders' part and open opportunities for new individuals to rise up, in effect bringing a changing of the guard. Chewbacchus has recently experienced the ending of an era, with the resignation of Ryan Ballard, who has decided to forgo his Overlord status and look toward other pursuits. Mardi Claw of Skinz n Bonez has also voiced a desire to step back and reduce her responsibilities; while retaining status as Big Queen, she is delegating authority to Queen 1, Dhani Adomaitis, and Queen 2, Katie Harvey.

While the krewes discussed in this book have attained an almost canonical status in the Carnival canopy, their stature and practices have inspired other groups and have witnessed dispersive, even contestatory energies. The precedents established by Downtown Mardi Gras have helped inspire new Carnival ventures, such as Ritmeaux Krewe, a dance troupe celebrating Hispanic/Latin heritage. 2018 saw the first installment of Krewe du Kanavale, a new enterprise founded by members of the Montreal-based rock group Arcade Fire (Win Butler and Regine Chassagne, now New Orleans residents) and Ben Jaffe of Preservation Hall. Exhibiting a Caribbean flair, the krewe on the Tuesday before Fat Tuesday proceeded through the French Quarter to Treme's Congo Square (raising funds for Haitian relief efforts). A more volatile kind of energy infuses Ryan Ballard's recently formed, heavy-metal group Krewecifer, an alliance of metal-heads who "bang for truth, freedom, and the removal of censorship" ("Krewecifer"). Ballard's group shares in the more unchecked energies expressed by the anarchic Krewe of Eris, founded in 2005, named after the goddess of discord, whose 2011 procession led to confrontations with the police (Bentley). The efforts of Eris have engendered an offshoot, the Krewe of Heiress; in 2015 this group exulted in the setting of an unauthorized bonfire "on the tourist-ridden Frenchman Street" ("With New Orleans' Carnival"). Darker Downtown energies have also given rise to a new walking krewe that operates outside of Carnival, the Krewe of Krampus. Founded in 2015 by Mike and Diana Esordi, the group parades through Bywater during the Christmas season, masking as hairy horned Alpine creatures that threaten to carry away naughty children.

One notes the success of Downtown Mardi Gras by the continued proliferation of Downtown groups, by the spaces and identities that are set in play between these enterprises. Downtown Mardi Gras can also take some credit for the general, wider proliferation of the Carnival walking krewes that now operate across the city, the ascent and cachet of which can be certified by the recent pushback they have received from city government and the older krewes. Carnival 2018 saw the enactment of a new policy aimed at regulating the participation of walking krewes in parades along the traditional Uptown St. Charles route. Desiring to cut down on the duration of the parades, and to lessen the cleanup demands of workers, the city—in league with parade captains—enacted limits on parade size and procession order; regulations "required parades to be capped at 12 krewes marching ahead of a parade's first float, and only one krewe between floats" (Brasted, "Mardi Gras parades"). As a result, the NOLA Showgirls, who had worked all year on their dance routines, were scrubbed from participation. The Amazons were displaced from the Femme Fatale parade after being included the prior two years. In recent Carnivals, the walking krewes— Skinz n Bonez as an example—have enjoyed rank among the most popular elements of the Uptown parades; this measure, in sum, had the effect of prioritizing the floats and presence of the established organizations, while diminishing the involvement of walking krewes (suggesting a tacit contest between old-line groups and the upstarts). Doug MacCash, a fan of the walking krewes, wrote a rebuttal to this measure in his *Times-Picayune* column; he suggested that rather than displacing the pedestrian krewes the city should limit the number of title and royalty floats—in effect, less of the old, more of the new. MacCash implored: "City Hall: Please don't mess with my nutty marching groups" ("City Hall").

It is the argument of this book that Downtown Mardi Gras has emerged as a highly important and influential component of Carnival, and a notable, positive force in the wider post-Katrina landscape. Downtown Carnival highlights the difference between local practices of Mardi Gras and the clichéd, national representations catering to the tourist market, that trade in excess and titillation—Mardi Gras as a citywide orgiastic debauch of nudity and inebriation. Downtown Mardi Gras also draws distinction in its contrast to the larger, more expensive, and tradition-bound Carnival of Uptown, as it showcases no elevated royalty, no dukes on horseback, operating in effect as an egalitarian counterspace. In contrast to the scale embraced by the long-standing krewes—the Krewe of Endymion recently "created a record-breaking float that measured 330 feet long, held 230 people, and cost \$1.2 million to build" (Matisse)—the Downtown groups operate with a different sense of scope and dimension, embodying a different aesthetic and performance ethos. Instigating a handcrafted, do-it-yourself celebration, these krewes provide a vibrant, often stunning display of ingenious costume design and imaginative mixed-media forms, passing through the Downtown streets shoulder to shoulder with appreciative onlookers, generating an exuberant, communal sense of celebration.

In documenting and giving analysis to the Downtown Mardi Gras krewes, this book has identified basic similarities between the groups but also notable differences. These krewes are all marked by strong, imaginative artistic sensibilities and exhibit striking creative expressions, largely evidenced in handcrafted costumes, floats, and throws. That noted, the specific krewes vary widely in their aesthetics, with Joan of Arc drawing on medieval iconography, Red Beans utilizing the local food staple for its intricate designs, and Chewbacchus giving vent to all range of sci-fi imaginings. The groups also highlight different performative practices. Drumming is an element for both Skinz n Bonez and the Amazons. Red Beans and 'tit Rəx incorporate walking brass bands. Chewbacchus showcases dancing and widespread cosplay. Members of Skinz n Bonez pass out champagne corks as throws; the Amazons distribute hand-sewn red aprons with golden "A" insignias.

Most of the krewes have strong ties to local neighborhoods and demonstrate an active sense of community participation. They may draw membership from across the city but retain connection to specific areas—Skinz n Bonez manifests a strong lineage from the St. Roch neighborhood, Chewbacchus represents Marigny and the Bywater, Red Beans parades Downtown but draws heavily from Mid-City. The Amazons connect to Treme (their route terminates at the Backstreet Cultural Museum). The parade routes themselves vary, often shifting from year to year, testing one street and then another, though they remain geographically focused, traversing and celebrating the territories of Downtown.

In addition to representing various neighborhoods, these krewes demonstrate a range of demographic affiliations. The krewes are for the most part open and welcoming (Chewbacchus has no membership limit; 'tit Rɔx, however, does cap its numbers). Participation cuts across class lines as educators, young professionals, artists, and service-industry workers parade alongside one another. Membership costs are affordable; many krewes charge less than fifty dollars to join. While these krewes are largely white in membership, the ranks do exhibit racial and ethnic diversity. It should be noted that women play a major driving force. Figures such as Mardi Claw Gehrke (of Skinz n Bonez) and Dianne Honoré (of the Amazons and the Black Storyville Baby Dolls) demonstrate effective leadership and bring strong inspiration to their krewes. Many women also serve in administrative fashion, proving crucial to the group's operation, such as Brooke Ethridge, an Overlord of Chewbacchus, who serves as representative for the krewe's female (perhaps majority) membership; as Functional Force Mistress, she oversees essential logistical responsibilities, securing the route and city permits for the parade (e-mail to Wade, June 14, 2018).

And it should be noted—perhaps underscored as a defining attribute—that a jester-like quality infuses Downtown Mardi Gras. Its krewes exhibit a distinctive esprit de corps, a pronounced sense of playfulness and whimsy (and edgy critique). In contrast to the stately, tradition-bound ostentation seen in Uptown Carnival practice—Rex in his satin breeches, with golden goblet and scepter—Downtown displays a vitality that frequently borders on the insouciant, evident in the Red Beans queen of 2018, a rouge-cheeked male in a Marie Antoinette wig with a bean-encrusted bustier. Given to parody, to pop-culture imagery, these krewes are often rascal-like in attitude, exhibiting a resistive aspect, opening new space, challenging expectations and straining norms. Eccentricity is prized—it is quirky Carnival, a kind of people's Carnival that has endeared itself to Mardi Gras revelers for more than a decade. One witnesses a potent iconoclastic blend of civic affection and boundary-testing—Downtown Mardi Gras leans the city forward. It is in these walking krewes that one finds "the 21st century Mardi Gras trailblazers, the democratic dancers, the phalanxes of feminists, the promenading performance artists, and wandering weirdos that make the city what it is. They're what's happenin'" (MacCash, "City Hall").

Concluding on such a celebratory note is an intended outcome of this book, as the authors seek to highlight the achievements of these krewes and the civic optimism they embody. Certainly, not all readers will come to the same conclusions. Any assessment of the city, as Brian Boyles reminds us, "depends on whose porch you sit" (9), and New Orleanians are famous for their contentiousness, for seeing many different cities within the city. The wrangling dispersion of voices and viewpoints, what at times can seem Babel-like, points to the intensity of feeling so many experience regarding the New Orleans (and its characterizations). Different stakeholders may advance different views, some appeasing, some acrimonious; by and large they share the belief that New Orleans dearly matters.

The profiles and practices of Downtown Mardi Gras can invite skeptical (if not cynical) readings. One could highlight an adversarial nexus, where the various krewes play out divisions and differences, and could argue that these groups reinforce lines of demarcation, separating populations and outlooks—creative types, often transplants, descending upon the city, taking to the streets in narcissistic display. And certainly the emergence of the krewes has not been a purely utopian exercise. Within and between the krewes one can note bickering and squabbles, battles over turf, individual-istic status-seeking, debates over lineage and authenticity, cultural-capital envy: Whose costumes are the wildest? Who has the best dance moves, the cleverest theme? Who gets to parade where and at what time? Who is more New Orleanian?

The contestatory dynamics of these krewes should be acknowledged, and we hope that in the course of analysis this book has done so. Yet, as in many performative expressions of culture, different energies can operate simultaneously, with impulses that both corroborate and contradict. This book highlights the beneficent and efficacious aspects of Downtown Mardi Gras, as an organic, community-driven enterprise that has served as an important kind of crucible, a meeting place in the streets, where citizens have come to express, funnel, embody, and work through their exhilarations and anxieties of living in a post-Katrina world. This Carnival provides in-stances of encounter and engagement, where, both within the memberships of the krewes and in front of spectators on the streets, citizens come before other citizens, in ways that might not otherwise occur. Rather than closing in and sheltering the self, participation can counteract insularity, bringing moments of dialogue and exchange—new relationships, new conversations, new commitments to material change. Jan Cohen-Cruz has written that the radical element of street performance inheres in its capacity to "transport everyday reality to something more ideal" (1). In this light, one can see Downtown Mardi Gras as a vast piece of egalitarian street theatre, whose process may witness ego rivalries and identity contestations but whose final performance achieves something greater than the sum of its parts: the physical manifestation of an aspirant desire, for a reanimated city of tolerance, equity, and mutual respect. Downtown Mardi Gras may portend a new future for Carnival practices, the opening of the door to further, yet-to-be-realized ludic expressions and energies; it may also point to new civic constellations, themselves yet unmaterialized, that could help elevate actual lives, spreading more widely the benefits of post-Katrina recovery.

In the face of the question, is it worth it to stay? many New Orleanians express a deep sense of faithfulness, though committing to the city comes with open eyes (global warming is real), a recognition of trade-offs, how strong affection is often measured against indignation and disappointment. Dichotomies and contradictions abound; Jason Berry identifies New Orleans as a "city, teeming with cultural wealth, saddled by Third World sorrow" (299), and one can view evidence of both within the space of a city block, within the blink of an eye.

Ian McNulty challenges the city's appellation as the Big Easy and writes: "people don't live in New Orleans because it is easy. They live here because they are incapable of living anywhere else in just the same way" (163). McNulty's contention underscores the challenges of residing in the city but also the rich, singular living experience that New Orleans provides, through its rituals, its neighborhoods, its exchanges between people on the sidewalk, its sounds, its tastes—a habitus that can be found nowhere else. One commonly hears that New Orleans is out of step with the rest of America, due to its European and African heritages, the number of flags that have flown over the city, its often easy dismissal of the Protestant work ethic, its capacity for communal enterprise and celebration. In the recent study *American Nations: The Eleven Rival Regional Cultures of North America*, Collin Woodard divides the continental map into eleven separate "nations." In this map New Orleans sits contiguous to the "Deep South," an Anglo-influenced region noted for its "very rigid social structure," but the city itself occupies a position in "New France," a "pocket of liberalism" that is "consensus-driven," "tolerant," sharing the New France designation with the Canadian region of Quebec (Speiser).

The distinctive lifestyle, culture, and people of New Orleans can create an enthralling, potent magnetism. Natives are defiantly proud of their home. Stories of visitors coming to the city and planting roots are legion.

The city is famous for its enchantment, an allure corroborated by Rebecca Solnit in *Unfathomable City*: "Like a lot of the volunteers I met, who came for a week or month and never left, I fell in love with New Orleans" (7). Longtime residents often feel that life in the city envelops them to such a degree that relocation holds no appeal. The city compels with such an "irrefutable sense of place" that living elsewhere can seem unthinkable—"We can't leave. Where would we go?" (Mimi Read, qtd. in Fitzpatrick). On the death of music icon Fats Domino, Jarvis DeBerry wrote: "We can all be sure that the Lord called Fats Domino home Tuesday: otherwise, he'd still be around New Orleans" ("Fats Domino").

Actor John Goodman has spoken of the city's distinctive qualities in almost therapeutic fashion, figuratively suggesting that for many "an incomplete part" of their "chromosomes . . . gets repaired or found" in New Orleans (qtd. in Dawn). The city regularly incites hyperbole, and rhapsodic tributes to the city are plentiful, furthering the theme of New Orleans exceptionalism. Such a tendency warrants vigilance, a wariness regarding images manufactured for tourist consumption and the kind of romantic reverie that obscures material realities and needs. Richard Campanella's *Geographies of New Orleans: Urban Fabrics Before the Storm* serves as something of a corrective, illustrating how much New Orleans in fact follows patterns in line with the rest of the country. However, elsewhere his writing discloses instances that reinforce the uniqueness of New Orleans, underscoring "the wonder and curiosity evoked by this splendid, tragic, festive, and distinguished American city," citing residents as "those fortunate enough to live within its limits" (*Time and Place in New Orleans* 9). The city's sense of its own exceptionalism is indeed a part of its cultural fabric, an element that spurs mythic imaginings, which inform and inspire material practices, beautiful expressions of body and sound, that in turn engender further rhapsodizing (in a sort of self-nurturing, circuitous dynamic).

In its emergence, Downtown Mardi Gras has contributed to the claims of New Orleans exceptionalism, as a kind of self-aware embrace of the city's distinction, conveyed in astonishing visual and kinetic forms, flesh-and-blood expressions of arresting brilliance. In the shadow of the city's recent tricentennial celebration, Downtown Mardi Gras reveals itself as one among many reasons to stay, to remain within the life of the city—to share in a street theatre rivalled by no other in the country. These walking performances contribute to a localized, saturated experience, what Eve Abrams calls life that "is thick with living" (236), that seizes the eye, the ear, and the mind—the Sacred Wookiee in drunken frolic; drumming skeletons in flowers and bones; white-clad, candlelit angels at the heels of St. Joan, streaming the centuries-old streets of the Quarter. As is often the experience in New Orleans, other places recede and "cease to occupy much territory in your mind" (Solnit and Snedeker 7). Krewedelusion exults in this sort of thrall, announcing the city as the "center" of the universe ("About"). Downtown Mardi Gras has emerged from Carnivals past to promote the here and now, to defend New Orleans as a remarkable place, an exceptional place, a city where, as Andrei Codrescu reminds us, "there are doors older than most American trees" (131).

It is often a call, a few blocks removed—the trombone blast, a shout, laughter, the beat of a drum. Come to the street. Feathers, beads, day-glo wigs, rhythm and riot—enter in. It's Carnival time.

WORKS CITED

"31 marvelous Mardi Gras dance groups . . . and counting." *Mardigras.com*, February 15, 2017. Accessed July 9, 2017. https://www.mardigras.com/news/2017/02/post_23.html.

"52 Places to Go in 2018." *New York Times*, January 10, 2018. Accessed July 4, 2018. https://www.nytimes.com/interactive/2018/travel/places-to-visit.html.

"About." *Krewedelusion*. Accessed July 7, 2018. http://krewedelusion.org/about/.

"About IKOC." *Intergalactic Krewe of Chewbacchus*. Accessed December 16, 2017. https://chewbacchus.org/about-ikoc/.

Abrahams, Roger D., Nick Spitzer, John F. Szwed, and Robert Farris Thompson. *Blues for New Orleans: Mardi Gras and America's Creole Soul*. Philadelphia: University of Pennsylvania Press, 2006.

Abrams, Eve. "Borrowed Time." In *Where We Know: New Orleans as Home*, edited by David Rutledge. Seattle: Chin Music Press, 2010.

Adelson, Jeff. "'This is nothing short of incredible': Massive hole appears on Canal Street, could cost $3–5 M to repair." *New Orleans Advocate*, May 3, 2016. Accessed July 2, 2018. https://www.theadvocate.com/new_orleans/news/article_ae8d31b5-2845-5a33a584-70582458ccb8.html.

Allman, Kevin, ed. "The New New Orleans, Part 1." *Gambit*, December 31, 2013. Accessed December 15, 2017. https://www.bestofneworleans.com/gambit/the-new-new-orleans-part-2/Content?oid=246662.

Allman, Kevin, ed. "The New New Orleans, Part 2." *Gambit*, July 7, 2014. Accessed December 15, 2017. https://www.bestofneworleans.com/gambit/kevin-allman/Profile?oid=1234374.

"Amazons Benevolent Society." *Gumbo Marie New Orleans Culture Queen*. Accessed December 17, 2017. https://gumbomarie.com/amazon-benevolent-society.

Asher, Sally. *Hope and New Orleans: A History of Crescent City Street Names*. Charleston: The History Press, 2014.

Atkinson, Rowland, and Gary Bridge, eds. *Gentrification in a Global Context: The New Urban Colonialism*. London: Routledge, 2005.

Ball, Millie. "There's a Post-Katrina Joie de Vivre in New Orleans." *Los Angeles Times*, August 22, 2014. Accessed December 15, 2017. http://www.latimes.com/travel/la-tr-d-new-orleans-20140824-story.html.

Ballard, Ryan. "Artist Guest: Ryan Ballard." *CONtraflow V*. Accessed December 16, 2017. http://contraflowscifi.org/speakers/ryan-ballard/.

Baum, Daniel. *Nine Lives: Death and Life in New Orleans*. New York: Spiegel & Grau, 2009.

Beeton, Sue. "Mardi Gras Indians: Rituals of resistance and resilience in changing times." In *Ritual and Traditional Events in the Modern World*, edited by Jennifer Laing and Warwick Frost. London: Routledge, 2014.

Bendix, Regina. *In Search of Authenticity: The Formation of Folklore Studies*. Madison: University of Wisconsin Press, 1997.

Bentley, Jules. "Interview with the Krewe of Eris Founders." *Raging Pelican: Journal of Gulf Coast Resistance*. Accessed July 5, 2018. http://ragingpelican.com/interview-krewe-of -eris-founders/.

Beriss, David. "Red Beans and Rebuilding: An Iconic Dish, Memory, and Culture in New Orleans." In *Rice and Beans: A Unique Dish in a Hundred Places*, edited by Richard Wilk and Livia Barbosa. New York: Berg, 2012.

Berry, Jason. "Mardi Gras in New Orleans, USA: Annals of a Queen." In *Carnaval!*, edited by Barbara Mauldin. Seattle: University of Washington Press, 2004.

Bickford, Chris. "Death, Rebirth, and Celebration in New Orleans." *Burn Magazine*, March 8, 2011. Accessed December 14, 2017. http://www.burnmagazine.org/essays/2011/03 /chris-bickford-new-orleans/.

"The birth of the Mardi Gras superkrewe marked a new era of Carnival inclusiveness and extravagance." *Advocate*, June 30, 2017.

"Black Storyville Baby Dolls." *Gumbo Marie New Orleans Culture Queen*. Accessed December 17, 2017. https://gumbomarie.com/storyville-baby-dolls.

Blum, Alan. "The Imaginary of Self-Satisfaction: Reflections on the Platitude of the 'Creative City.'" In *Circulation and the City*, edited by Alexandra Boutros and Will Straw. Montreal: McGill–Queen's University Press, 2010.

Boyles, Brian W. *New Orleans Boom and Blackout: One Hundred Days in America's Coolest Hot Spot*. Charleston: History Press, 2015.

Brasted, Chelsea. "Mardi Gras parades facing marching krewe cap in 2018; report." *New Orleans Times-Picayune*, January 2, 2018. Accessed July 8, 2018. https://www.nola.com /mardi_gras_nola/2017/12/mardi_gras_shorter_2018_walkin.html.

Brasted, Chelsea. "Why do people leave New Orleans?" *New Orleans Times-Picayune*, September 28, 2017. Accessed July 8, 2018. https://www.nola.com/business/index .ssf/2017/09/why_do_people_leave_new_orlean.html.

Brenner, Neil, Peter Marcuse, and Margit Mayer. *Cities for People, Not for Profit: Critical Urban Theory and the Right to the City*. London: Routledge, 2012.

Bronston, Barri. *Walking New Orleans*. Birmingham: Wilderness Press, 2015.

Brosius, Christiane, and Karin M Polit, eds. *Ritual, Heritage and Identity*. London: Routledge, 2011.

"Bruce 'Sunpie' Barnes." WWOZ.org. Accessed April 4, 2016. https://www.wwoz.org/acts /bruce-sunpie-barnes.

Burdeau, Cain. "New Orleans' post-Katrina gentrification is touchy." *Washington Times*, August 28, 2012. Accessed December 14, 2018. https://www.washingtontimes.com /news/2012/aug/28/new-orleans-post-katrina-gentrification-touchy/.

Burns, Peter F., and Matthew O. Thomas. *Reforming New Orleans: The Contentious Politics of Change in the Big Easy*. Ithaca: Cornell University Press, 2015.

Burns, Mick. *Keeping the Beat on the Street: The New Orleans Brass Band Renaissance*. Baton Rouge: Louisiana State University Press, 2008.

Bynum, Chris. "In its own small way, tiny parade 'tit Rəx changes Mardi Gras." *New Orleans Advocate*, February 15, 2017. Accessed December 14, 2017. www.theadvocate.com/new_orleans/entertainment_life/mardi_gras/article_6d717af0-efd3-11e6-aaa3-03e16643d156.html.

"Bywater." Witrycollective.com. Accessed January 28, 2016. http://www.witrycollective.com/neighborhoods/detail/71/Bywater.

Campanella, Richard. *Bourbon Street: A History*. Baton Rouge: Louisiana State University Press, 2014.

Campanella, Richard. "Gentrification and its Discontents: Notes from New Orleans." Newgeography, March 1, 2013. http://www.newgeography.com/content/003526-gentrification-and-its-discontents-notes-new-orleans.

Campanella, Richard. *Geographies of New Orleans: Urban Fabrics Before the Storm*. Lafayette: Center for Louisiana Studies, 2006.

Campanella, Richard. *Lost New Orleans*. London: Pavilion, 2015.

Campanella, Richard. *Time and Place in New Orleans: Past Geographies in the Present Day*. Gretna, LA: Pelican, 2002.

Cannon, C. W. "The New Orleans Manifesto." In *Do You Know What It Means to Miss New Orleans?*, edited by David Rutledge and Bruce Rutledge. Seattle: Chin Music Press, 2006.

Capper, Andy. "Appetite for destruction." *Guardian*, March 19, 2006. Accessed December 14, 2017. https://www.theguardian.com/music/2006/mar/19/jazz.

Carlson, Marvin. *Places of Performance: The Semiotics of Theatre Architecture*. Ithaca: Cornell University Press, 1989.

Carrico, Rachel. "On Thieves, Spiritless Bodies, and Creole Soul: Dancing through the Streets of New Orleans." *Drama Review* 57 (2013): 70–87.

Chachere, Gianna. "Glambeaux: Taking Cultural Appropriation Too Far." Louisiana justiceinstitute.blogspot.com. February 24, 2014. Accessed December 16, 2017. http://louisianajusticeinstitute.blogspot.com/2014/02/glambeaux-taking-cultural-appropriation.html.

Chapman, R. W., ed. *Jane Austen's Letters to Her Sister Cassandra and Others*. London: Oxford University Press, 1959.

Codrescu, Andrei. *New Orleans, Mon Amour*. Chapel Hill, NC: Algonquin, 2006.

Cohen-Cruz, Jan, ed. *Radical Street Performance: An International Anthology*. London: Routledge, 1998.

Colton, Craig E. "Conclusions." In *City of Memory: New Orleans Before and After Katrina*, by John Woodin. Chicago: Center for American Places at Columbia College, 2010.

Costello, Brian J. *Carnival in Louisiana: Celebrating Mardi Gras from the French Quarter to the Red River*. Baton Rouge: Louisiana State University Press, 2017.

Coviello, Will. "Walking krewes of New Orleans Carnival: Chewbacchus, Barkus, 'tit Rəx, and Krewe of Cork step off." *Gambit*, January 25, 2016. Accessed December 14, 2017. https://www.bestofneworleans.com/gambit/walking-krewes-of-new-orleans-carnival/Content?oid=2860599.

Cox, John Bailey. "North Side Skull and Bone Gang." *Media Nola*. Accessed December 13, 2015. http://medianola.org/discover/place/948/North Side-Skull-and-Bone-Gang.

Craig, Tim. "It wasn't even a hurricane, but heavy rains flooded New Orleans as pumps faltered." *Washington Post*, August 9, 2017. Accessed July 3, 2018. https://www.wash ingtonpost.com/national/it-wasnt-even-a-hurricane-but-heavy-rains-flooded-new -orleans-as-pumps-faltered/2017/08/09/b3b7506a-7d37-11e7-9d08-b79f191668ed_story .html?utm_term=.6133e033791c.

Crutcher, Michael E., Jr. *Treme: Race and Place in a New Orleans Neighborhood*. Athens: University of Georgia Press, 2010.

Danahay, Martin. *Gender at Work in Victorian Culture*. 2005. Rpt. New York: Routledge, 2016.

Dart, Tom. "What Katrina left behind: New Orleans' uneven recovery and unending divisions." *Guardian*, August 22, 2015. Accessed December 14, 2017. https://www.theguard ian.com/us-news/2015/aug/22/hurricane-katrina-recovery-lower-ninth-ward.

Dawn, Randee. "Contender Q&A: John Goodman." *Los Angeles Times*, June 16, 2010. Accessed July 3, 2018. http://articles.latimes.com/2010/jun/16/news/la-en-goodmanqa-20100616.

DeBerry, Jarvis. "Fats Domino never forgot (or left) where he came from." *New Orleans Times-Picayune*, October 25, 2017. Accessed July 6, 2018. https://www.nola.com/opin ions/index.ssf/2017/10/fats_domino_dies_at_89.html.

DeBerry, Jarvis. "Parades for celebrities aren't the most questionable second-lines." *New Orleans Times-Picayune*, January 4, 2017. Accessed December 14, 2017. http://www.nola .com/opinions/index.ssf/2017/01/carrie_fisher_second_line.html.

de Caro, Frank. "Emerging New Orleans Mardi Gras Traditions: The St. Joan of Arc Parade and the Red Beans Krewe, 2010." *Louisiana Folklore Miscellany* 20 (2010): 1–29.

de Caro, Frank. *Folklore Recycled: Old Traditions in New Contexts*. Jackson: University Press of Mississippi, 2013.

de Caro, Frank. "Legends, Local Identity, and a New Orleans Cookbook." *Louisiana Folklore Miscellany* 19 (2009): 23–31.

de Caro, Frank, and Tom Ireland. "Every Man a King: Worldview, Social Tension, and Carnival in New Orleans." In *Mardi Gras, Gumbo, and Zydeco: Readings in Louisiana Culture*, edited by Marcia Gaudet and James C. McDonald. Jackson: University Press of Mississippi, 2003.

Demaria, James. "Gloria Boutté: I Wanted to Dance." YouTube. August 29, 2015. Accessed December 17, 2017. https://www.youtube.com/watch?v=pRQtz0NEAIc.

Deren, Maya. *Divine Horsemen*. Documentary film. USA: 1947–51/1977.

"A Diminutive Guide to an Alternative Mardi Gras." Pamphlet distributed by the 'tit Rəx parade, January 30, 2016.

Dolan, Jill. "Performance, Utopia, and the 'Utopian Performative.'" *Theatre Journal* 53.3 (2001): 455–79. Accessed December 14, 2017. https://muse.jhu.edu/article/34872.

Dossett, Kate. *Bridging the Race Divides: Black Nationalism, Feminism, and Integration in the United States, 1896–1935*. Gainesville: University of Florida Press, 2008.

DuBois, Fletcher, Erik de Maaker, Karin Polit, and Marianne Riphagen. "From Ritual Ground to Stage." In *Ritual, Media, and Conflict*, edited by Ronald Grimes, Ute Husken, Udo Simon, and Eric Venbrux. Oxford: Oxford University Press, 2011.

Dikec, Mustafa. *Space, Politics and Aesthetics*. Edinburgh: Edinburgh University Press, 2015.

Elder, David. *An Insider's Guide to Mardi Gras 1982*. New Orleans: David Elder, 1982.

Etheridge, Frank. "Soundcheck: Five Questions with Ryan Ballard." *Offbeat*, September 29, 2015. Accessed October 30, 2017. http://www.offbeat.com/articles/soundcheck-five -questions-ryan-ballard/.

Evans, Beau. "New Orleans affordable housing not keeping pace with goals, report says." *New Orleans Times-Picayune*, June 14, 2018. Accessed July 1, 2018. https://www.nola .com/politics/index.ssf/2018/06/affordable_housing_more_units.html.

Ewy, Christine Allen. *Why People Live in New Orleans*. Metairie, LA: Calereka, 2009.

Fink, Shawn. "Krewed Art: Four Mardi Gras Must Sees." February 5, 2015. Accessed December 17, 2017. http://www.wheretraveller.com/new/Orleans/krewed-art-four-mardi -gras-must-sees#ixzz3Q481Nb11.

Fitzpatrick, Mary. *New Orleans: Life in an Epic City*. New Orleans: Preservation Resource Center, 2006.

Flaherty, Jordon. "Seven Years After Katrina, a Divided City." Louisianajusticeinstitute .blogspot.com. August 30, 2012. Accessed November 7, 2014. http://roars41.rssing.com /browser.php?indx=7410499&item=1.

Flake, Carol. *Behind the Masks of America's Most Exotic City*. New York: Grove Press, 1994.

Fodor's Travel: New Orleans 2015. New York: Random House, 2015.

"For the Sewage & Water Board, 2017 has been a year of boil and trouble." *New Orleans Times-Picayune*, September 22, 2017. Accessed July 1, 2018. https://www.nola.com/pol itics/index.ssf/2017/09/for_sewerage_water_board_2017.html.

Franklin, Sara B. "Tradition, *Treme*, and the New Orleans Renaissance: Lolis Eric Elie." *Southern Cultures* 18: 2 (2012): 32–44.

Gehman, Mary. *The Free People of Color of New Orleans: An Introduction*. New Orleans: Margaret Media, 1994.

Gehrke, Claudia. "Envision the Vision." *Skinz n Bonez*. February 26, 2014. Accessed December 15, 2017. http://skinznbonez.com/?p=398.

Gill, James. *Lords of Misrule: Mardi Gras and the Politics of Race*. Jackson: University Press of Mississippi, 1997.

Gilmore, David D. *Carnival and Culture: Sex, Symbol, and Status in Spain*. New Haven: Yale University Press, 1998.

Giordano, Tony. *The Ladders of Mardi Gras*. New Orleans: self-published, 2010.

Godet, Aurélie. "'Meet de Boys on the Battlefront': Festive Parades and the Struggle to Reclaim Public Spaces in Post-Katrina New Orleans." *European Journal of American Studies* 10:3 (2015). https://journals.openedition.org/ejas/11228. Accessed September14, 2018.

Gotham, Kevin. *Authentic New Orleans: Tourism, Culture, and Race in the Big Easy*. New York: New York University Press, 2007.

Gotham, Kevin Fox, and Miriam Greenburg. *Crisis Cities: Disaster and Redevelopment in New York and New Orleans*. New York: Oxford University Press, 2014.

Grams, Diane. "Hybridity in Street Performance of Zulu and Mardi Gras Indians in New Orleans." In *Taking the Square: Mediated Dissent and Occupations of Public Space*, Edited by Maria Rovisco and Jonathan Corpus Ong. London: Rowman & Littlefield, 2016.

Gratton, Lynda. *Hot Spots: Why Some Teams, Workplaces, and Organizations Buzz with Energy—And Others Don't.* San Francisco: Berrett-Koehler, 2007.

Grimes, Ronald, Ute Husken, Udo Simon, Eric Venbrux, eds. *Ritual, Media, and Conflict.* Oxford: Oxford University Press, 2011.

Hales, Stephen W. *Rex: An Illustrated History of the School of Design.* Mandeville: Arthur Hardy Enterprises, 2010.

Hardy, Arthur. "The 1970s a defining decade for New Orleans Mardi Gras." *New Orleans Advocate,* February 21, 2015. Accessed December 14, 2017. http://www.theadvocate.com /new_orleans/news/article_f5f1e259-76f2-5842-9969-e09ceb464d5b.html.

Hartman, Shelby. "Alternative Mardi Gras Krewes to watch." *Gambit,* February 18, 2014. Accessed July 1, 2018. https://www.theadvocate.com/gambit/new_orleans/events/article _96b6c50a-4f8c-5180-932e-71f3c7af7965.html.

Harvey, Daina Cheyenne. "'Gimme a Pigfoot and a Bottle of Beer': Food as Cultural Performance in the Aftermath of Hurricane Katrina." *Symbolic Interaction* 40:4 (2017): 498–522.

"hello, mardi gras!" *Mardi Claw / The Big Easel.* December 12, 2012. Accessed January 24, 2014. http://mardiclaw.com/?tag=nola.

Hemard, Ned. "New Orleans Nostalgia: Is New Orleans Feminine?" *New Orleans Bar Association.* 2011. Accessed December 17, 2017. http://www.neworleansbar.org/uploads /files/IsNewOrleansFeminineArticle.3-23.pdf.

Hirsch, Jordon. "End of the Line." *Slate,* August 25, 2015. Accessed December 14, 2017. http:// www.slate.com/articles/news_and_politics/history/2015/08/katrina_anniversary_the _second_line_has_become_a_symbol_of_new_orleans_resilience.html.

Honoré, Dianne. *Amazon Warriors, Crusaders of Hope.* gumbomarie.com, 2018.

Honoré, Dianne. *Living the Black Storyville Baby Doll Life.* gumbomarie.com, 2017.

Howard, Kate. "The Evolving Traditions of the Jefferson City Buzzards Carnival Club." *Louisiana Folklore Miscellany* 11 (1996): 1–15.

Huber, Leonard. *Mardi Gras: A Pictorial History of Carnival in New Orleans.* Gretna: Pelican, 1977.

Irrera, Joseph. "Celebrating the City's 300th in Song." *Gambit,* January 2018.

"Is the New Orleans economy at a tipping point?" *New Orleans Times-Picayune,* September 21, 2017. Accessed July 3, 2018. https://www.nola.com/business/index.ssf/2017/09/new _orleans_economy_jobs_futur.html.

Johnson, Dani. "A Response from the Glambeaux." Louisianajusticeinstitute.blogspot.com. February 25, 2014. Accessed December 16, 2017. http://louisianajusticeinstitute.blogspot .com/2014/02/a-response-from-glambeaux.html.

Kane, Harnett T. *Queen New Orleans: City by the River.* New York: William Morrow, 1949.

Karlin, Adam. "All hail Chewbacchus: The nerds have supplanted the kings." *New Orleans. Me.* February 24, 2014. Accessed December 16, 2017. http://www.neworleans.me /journal/detail/435/All-hail-Chewbaccus-The-nerds-have-supplanted-the-kings.

King, Grace. *New Orleans: The Place and the People.* New York: Macmillan, 1915.

Kinser, Samuel. *Carnival American Style: Mardi Gras at New Orleans and Mobile.* Chicago: University of Chicago Press, 1990.

Kirshenblatt-Gimblett, Barbara. *Destination Culture: Tourism, Museums, and Heritage.* Berkeley: University of California Press, 1998.

Klinedinst, Mark, ed. *Katrina: Ten Years After: The Rebuilding of New Orleans and the Mississippi Coast.* Hattiesburg, MS: Katrina Ten Years Later LLC, 2015.

Kolb, Carolyn. *New Orleans Memories: One Writer's City.* Jackson: University Press of Mississippi, 2013.

Kotkin, Joel. "America's New Brainpower Cities." Forbes.com. April 3, 2014. Accessed April 28, 2016. https://www.forbes.com/sites/joelkotkin/2014/04/03/americas-new-brain power-cities/#6cbb82cd613b.

"Krewecifer—Heavy Metal Mardi Gras Parade." *Facebook.* Accessed July 7, 2018. https://www.facebook.com/events/229147604160708/.

Labadie, Jeremy. "N.O. Comment." *Gambit,* September 2017.

Laborde, Errol. *Mardi Gras: Chronicles of the New Orleans Carnival.* Gretna: Pelican, 2013.

Laing, Jennifer, and Warwick Frost, eds. *Ritual and Traditional Events in the Modern World.* London: Routledge, 2014.

Leathem, Karen Trahan. *"A carnival according to their own desires": Gender and Mardi Gras in New Orleans, 1870–1941.* Diss., University of North Carolina. Ann Arbor: UMI, 1994.

Leathem, Karen, and Sharon Stallworth Nossiter. "Red Beans and Rice." In *New Orleans Cuisine: Fourteen Signature Dishes and Their Histories,* edited by Susan Tucker and S. Frederick Starr. Jackson: University Press of Mississippi, 2009.

LaMancusa, Phil. "Po-Boy Views: Neck Deep or Ten Years On." *Where Y'at,* September 2015.

Landrieu, Mitch, and Judith Rodin. "How We Built a Better New Orleans." *Politico.* August 28, 2015. Accessed December 28, 2015. https://www.politico.com/magazine/story/2015/08/how-we-rebuilt-a-better-new-orleans-213085.

Lane, Christel. *Ritual in Industrial Society: The Soviet Case.* Cambridge: Cambridge University Press, 1981.

Lind, Angus. "Half-Fast at 50." *New Orleans* 44.5 (2010): 68–71.

Litwin, Sharon. "Skull and Bones Gang channels spirit of Mardi Gras." *New Orleans Times-Picayune,* February 16, 2012. Accessed May 1, 2016. http://www.nola.com/nolavie/index.ssf/2012/02/skull_and_bones_gang_channels.html.

Lott, Eric. *Blackface Minstrelsy and the American Working Class.* New York: Oxford University Press, 2013. http://o-ite.ebrary.com.library.uark.edu/lib/uark/docDetail.action?docID=10734592.

MacCash, Doug. "Chewbacchus 2013 Mardi Gras parade was a cosmic triumph." *New Orleans Times-Picayune,* January 26, 2013. Accessed October 30, 2017. http://www.mardigras.com/news/2013/01/chewbacchus_2013_mardi_gras_pa.html.

MacCash, Doug. "Chewbacchus is conceptual artist Ryan S. Ballard's masterpiece." *New Orleans Times-Picayune,* August 9, 2012. Accessed October 30, 2017. https://www.nola.com/arts/index.ssf/2012/08/chewbacchus_is_conceptual_arti.html.

MacCash, Doug. "City Hall: Please don't mess with my nutty marching groups." *New Orleans Times-Picayune,* January 2, 2018. Accessed July 6, 2017. https://www.nola.com/mardi_gras_nola/2018/01/mardi_gras_2018_shorter_parade.html.

MacCash, Doug. "Controversial graffiti artist won't ride in Chewbacchus shoe box parade." *New Orleans Times-Picayune*, June 13, 2017. Accessed December 14, 2017. http://www .mardigras.com/news/2017/04/chewbacchus_muck_rock_graffiti.html.

MacCash, Doug. "The first downtown Mardi Gras marching group meet-up: What does it mean?" *New Orleans Times-Picayune*, January 19, 2017. Accessed October 30, 2017. http://www.mardigras.com/news/2017/01/mardi_gras_orleans_2017_chewba.html.

MacCash, Doug. "The former 'tit Rəx and Chewbacchus arty Mardi Gras parades, Sat. in New Orleans." *New Orleans Times-Picayune*, January 21, 2013. Accessed October 24, 2017. http://www.mardigras.com/news/2013/01/tit_rex_and_chewbacchus_arty_m.html.

MacCash, Doug. "Mardi Gras 2015: Chewbacchus parade took the party to the streets." *New Orleans Times-Picayune*, February 8, 2015. Accessed December 14, 2017. http://www .nola.com/arts/index.ssf/2015/02/mardi_gras_2015_chewbacchus_pa.html.

MacCash, Doug. "The New Mardi Gras: Is there really such a thing?" *New Orleans Times -Picayune*, February 22, 2017. Accessed December 14, 2017. http://www.mardigras.com /news/2017/02/mardi_gras_2017_new_red_beans.html.

MacCash, Doug. "New Orleans' most annoying people: Are you on the list?" *New Orleans Times-Picayune*, July 28, 2017. Accessed October 30, 2017.

"Mardi Gras Bourbon Street Awards." Nola.com. Accessed July 8, 2017. https://www.newor leans.com/event/mardi-gras-bourbon-street-awards/3333/.

Martinez, L. C., and Margaret Le Corgne. *Uptown/Downtown: Growing Up in New Orleans.* Lafayette: Center for Louisiana Studies, University of Southwestern Louisiana, 1986.

Matisse, Nathan. "An Arduino-controlled, fire-breathing Godzilla at Mardi Gras?! Blame Chewbacchus." *Arstechnica*. February 22, 2014. Accessed December 15, 2017. https:// arstechnica.com/gaming/2014/02/an-arduino-controlled-firebreathing-godzilla-at -mardi-gras-blame-chewbacchus/.

Mauldin, Barbara. "Introduction: Carnival in Europe and the Americas." In *Carnaval!*, edited by Barbara Mauldin. Seattle: University of Washington Press, 2004.

Mayer, Vicki. "Letting It All Hang Out: Mardi Gras Performances Live and on Video." *TDR: The Drama Review* 51 (2007): 76–93.

McKinney, Louise. *New Orleans: A Cultural History.* Oxford: Oxford University Press, 2006.

McNulty, Ian. "Keeper of Carnival." *New Orleans City Business*, February 8, 2000.

McNulty, Ian. *A Season of Night: New Orleans Life after Katrina.* Jackson: University Press of Mississippi, 2008.

Michna, Catherine. "Performance and Cross-Racial Storytelling in Post-Katrina New Orleans: Interviews with John O'Neal, Carol Bebelle, and Nicholas Slie." *TDR: The Drama Review* 57 (2013): 48–69. Accessed May 1, 2016. http://0-ww.mitpressjournals .org.library.uark.edu/doi/abs/10.1162/DRAM_a_00234.

"Mission Statement." Krewe of Femme Fatale. mkfemmefatale.org. Accessed December 17, 2017.

"Mitch Landrieu's Speech on the Removal of Confederate Statues in New Orleans." *New York Times*, May 23, 2017. Accessed July 1, 2017. https://www.nytimes.com/2017/05/23 /opinion/mitch-landrieus-speech-transcript.html.

Mitchell, Reid. *All on a Mardi Gras Day: Episodes in the History of New Orleans Carnival.* Cambridge: Harvard University Press, 1995.

Mock, Brentin. "How New Orleans Has Failed Its Workers Since Katrina." *Citylab,* August 29, 2017. Accessed July 3, 2018. https://www.citylab.com/equity/2017/08/evacuation -to-new-orleans-not-an-option-for-houston/538164/?utm_source=SFFB.

Morris, Leon. *Homage: New Orleans.* Melbourne, AU: Leon Morris, 2015.

Morris, Robert. "Freret's Changing Again." *Gambit,* July 8, 2014.

Morris, Robert. "Size Matters." *Critical Inquiry* 26.3 (2000): 474–87.

Morris, Tim. "Big tech payoff for New Orleans: Jobs are coming." *New Orleans Times -Picayune,* January 7, 2018. Accessed July 6, 2018. https://www.nola.com/opinions/index .ssf/2018/01/technology_jobs_dxc_new_orlean.html.

"New Orleans Original Skull and Bones Gang—the North Side Skeletons." Nolaskull andbones.blogspot.com. March 11, 2012. Accessed December 17, 2015. http://nolaskul landbones.blogspot.com/.

O'Neill, Rosary. *New Orleans Carnival Krewes: The History, Spirit and Secrets of Mardi Gras.* Charleston: History Press, 2014.

Oring, Elliott. *Just Folklore: Analysis, Interpretations, Critique.* Los Angeles: Cantilever Press, 2012.

Osborn, Royce. *All on a Mardi Gras Day.* Documentary film. PBS, 2003.

Osborne, Mitchel, and Errol Laborde. *Mardi Gras! A Celebration.* New Orleans: Picayune Press, 1981.

Perkins, Chuck. "The Baby Dolls" (radio interview). *The Conscious Hour with Chuck Perkins.* WBOK 1230 AM. New Orleans, August 15, 2017. .

"Phunny Phorty Phellows." *The Phunny Phorty Phellows.* Accessed December 17, 2017. http://www.phunnyphortyphellows.com/history.

Piersen, William D. *Black Legacy: America's Hidden Heritage.* Amherst: University of Massachusetts Press, 1993.

Pope, John. "The Springsteen session: When the Boss helped New Orleans heal." *New Orleans Times-Picayune,* August 22, 2017.

"Presenters and Performers: Dhani." Drums in the Swamp 2018. Accessed December 16, 2017. http://www.drumsintheswamp.com/presenters-performers.html.

Plyer, Allison. "Facts for Features: Katrina Impact." Data Center. August 26, 2016. Accessed July 8, 2018. https://www.datacenterresearch.org/data-resources/katrina/facts -for-impact/.

Ramsey, David. "The life and times of Bruce 'Sunpie' Barnes." *Arkansas Times,* June 19, 2014. Accessed December 28, 2015. https://www.arktimes.com/arkansas/the-life-and-times -of-bruce-sunpie-barnes-andmdash-zydeco-superstar-naturalist-full-time-park-rang er-former-nfl-player/Content?oid=3351562.

Ramsey, Jan. "We're All in This Together." *Offbeat,* September 2014.

"Red Beans Parade." Accessed December 17, 2017. http://www.redbeansparade.com.

Redshirt Rebellion. Closed Facebook group. 498 members.

Regis, Helen A. "Second Lines, Minstrelsy, and the Contested Landscapes of New Orleans Afro-Creole Festivals." *Cultural Anthropology* 14 (1999): 472–505.

Regis, Helen A. "Skeletons." In *The House of Dance and Feathers*, edited by Richard Breunlin and Ronald W. Lewis. New Orleans: University of New Orleans Press, 2007.

Regis, Helen A., and Shana Walton. "Producing the Folk at the New Orleans Jazz and Heritage Festival." *Journal of American Folklore* 121 (2008): 400–440.

Reid, Mitchell. *All on a Mardi Gras Day: Episodes in the History of New Orleans*. Cambridge: Harvard University Press, 1997.

Reid, Molly. "Grand Delusion." *New Orleans Times-Picayune*, January 30, 2010.

Ricks, Laura. "*Gambit*'s 40 Under 40 (2015)." *Gambit*, November 2, 2015. Accessed October 24, 2017. https://www.bestofneworleans.com/gambit/gambits-40-under-40/Content?oid=2802146.

Rivet, Ryan. "Gentry, Transplants and Newbies." *Tulane* (December 2013).

Rivlin, Gary. *Katrina: After the Flood*. New York: Simon and Schuster, 2015.

Roach, Joseph. *Cities of the Dead: Circum-Atlantic Performance*. New York: Columbia University Press, 1996.

Roberts, Robin. "New Orleans Mardi Gras and Gender in Three Krewes: Rex, the Truck Parades and Muses." *Western Folklore* 65 (2006): 303–28.

Robertson, Campbell. "36 Hours: New Orleans." *New York Times*, February 16, 2012. Accessed November 7, 2017. http://www.nytimes.com/2012/02/19/travel/36-hours-new-orleans.html.

Rohter, Larry. "Bias Casts a Pall Over New Orleans Mardi Gras." *New York Times*, January 29, 1992. Accessed May 1, 2015. http//:nytimes.com/1992/02/02/us/bias-law-casts-pall-over-new-orleans-mardi-gras.html.

Roig-Franzia, Manuel. "Rebirth and resentment in New Orleans." *The Week*, September 4, 2015.

Roig-Franzia, Manuel. "A 'resilient lab.'" *Washington Post*, August 22, 2015. Accessed December 14, 2017. http://www.washingtonpost.com/sf/national/2015/08/22/a-resilience-lab/?utm_term=.710c0d8ad4e7.

Roques, Greg. "Marching Groups of Mardi Gras." *Where Y'at*. January 26, 2016. Accessed December 14, 2017. https://whereyat.com/marching-groups-of-mardi-gras.

Rose, Chris. *1 Dead in Attic*. New Orleans: Chris Rose Books, 2005.

Rose, Chris. "After Hurricane Katrina, Neighborhoods Get Hit with a Rush of Wealth and Gentrification." Takepart.com. August 2015. Accessed December 16, 2017. http://www.takepart.com/article/2015/08/17/katrina-new-orleans-bywater/.

Rose, Chris. "Before and After." *My Rouses Everyday* (July/August 2015).

Rovisco, Maria, and Jonathan Corpus Ong. "Introduction." In *Taking the Square: Mediated Dissent and Occupations of Public Space*, edited by Maria Rovisco and Jonathan Corpus Ong. London: Rowman & Littlefield, 2016.

Rutledge, David. "Preface." In *Do You Know What It Means to Miss New Orleans?*, edited by David Rutledge. Seattle: Chin Music Press, 2006.

Rutledge, David, ed. *Where We Know: New Orleans as Home*. Seattle: Chin Music Press, 2010.

Saxon, Lyle. Fabulous New Orleans. Gretna: Pelican Publishing Company, Inc., 2004.

Schechner, Richard. "Performers and Spectators Transported and Transformed." *Kenyon Review* 3 (1981): 81–113. Accessed May 1, 2016. http://o-eb.ebscohost.com .library.uark.edu/ehost/pdfviewer/pdfviewer?vid=4&sid=b6c1135c-d694-4994-a2b9 -dee38394d79e%40sessionmgr113&hid=118.

Scheld, Suzanne. "Complementary Angles and Inclusive Perspectives: Rounding Out Integrative Views of Material Culture." *American Anthropologist* 108.1 (2006): 221–24.

Sciama, Lidia D., and Joanne B. Eicher. *Beads and Beadmakers: Gender, Material Culture, and Meaning.* Oxford: Berg, 1988.

Shrum, Wesley, and John Kilburn. "Ritual Disrobement at Mardi Gras: Ceremonial Exchange and Moral Order." *Social Forces* 75 (1996): 423–58.

"Skinz n Bones." July 2, 2013. Last accessed January 24, 2014. http://skinznbonez.com /?author=1.

Smith, Neil. *The New Urban Frontier: Gentrification and the Revanchist City.* London: Routledge, 1996.

Somosot, Maki. "Life expectancy is low in some parts of New Orleans." *New Orleans Times -Picayune*, June 20, 2012. Accessed May 1, 2016. http://www.nola.com/health/index .ssf/2012/06/life_expectancy_is_low_in_some.html.

Solnit, Rebecca. "Rebecca Solnit: if I were a man." *Guardian*, August 26, 2017. Accessed December 14, 2017. https://www.theguardian.com/lifeandstyle/2017/aug/26/rebecca -solnit-if-i-were-a-man.

Solnit, Rebecca, and Rebecca Snedeker. *Unfathomable City: A New Orleans Atlas.* Berkeley: University of California Press, 2013.

Souther, J. Mark. *New Orleans on Parade: Tourism and the Transformation of the Crescent City.* Baton Rouge: Louisiana State University Press, 2006.

Spera, Keith. *Groove Interrupted: Loss, Renewal, and the Music of New Orleans.* New York: St. Martin's Press, 2011.

Speiser, Matthew. "This map shows the US really has 11 separate 'nations' with entirely different cultures." *Business Insider*, July 27, 2015. Accessed July 9, 2018. http://www.busines sinsider.com/the-11-nations-of-the-united-states-2015-7.

Starr, S. Frederick. *New Orleans Unmasqued: Being a Wagwit's Affectionate Sketches of a Singular American City.* New Orleans: Dedeaux Publishing, 1985.

Stokes, Niall. "Edge, this song doesn't have a chorus . . ." *Hot Press.* November 23, 2006. Accessed December 17, 2017. http://www.hotpress.com/U2/music/Edge-this-song -doesnt-have-a-chorus/2895579.html?new_layout=1.

Stromquist, Kat. "Is New Orleans Worth It?" *Gambit*, August 22, 2017.

Sullivan, Jack. *New Orleans Remix.* Jackson: University Press of Mississippi, 2017.

Swenson, John, and Frank Etheridge. "All on a Mardi Gras Day: New Orleans' unique carnival traditions," *Offbeat* (February 2016).

Tallant, Robert. *New Orleans City Guide.* Revised. American Guide series. W.P.A. Boston: Houghton Mifflin, 1952.

Tama, Mario. *Coming Back: New Orleans Resurgent.* Brooklyn: Umbrage Books 2010.

Tansley, Laura. *Two inches of ivory: short-short forms and feminine expression.* Ph.D. thesis University of Glasgow, 2011.

Tassin, Myron, and Gaspar "Buddy" Stall. *Mardi Gras and Bacchus: Something Old, Something New*. Gretna: Pelican Publishing Company, 1984.

Taylor, Diana. *The Archive and the Repertoire: Performing Cultural Memory in the Americas*. Durham: Duke University Press, 2003.

Taylor, Diana. "Performance and intangible cultural heritage." In *The Cambridge Companion to Performance Studies*, edited by Tracy C. Davis. Cambridge: Cambridge University Press, 2008.

"The Ten Best Places to Live Now." *Men's Journal*, March 12, 2015.

Thier, David. "As Mardi Gras Nears, Watch out for Wookiees." *New York Times*, February 18, 2012. Accessed October 24, 2017. http://www.nytimes.com/2012/02/18/us/wookiee -invasion-at-new-orleans-mardi-gras-parade.html.

Thomas, Lynnell L. *Desire and Disaster in New Orleans: Tourism, Race, and Historical Memory*. Durham, NC: Duke University Press, 2014.

Thompson, Derek. "The Big Comeback: Is New Orleans America's Next Great Innovation Hub?" *Atlantic*, April 8, 2013. Accessed January 22, 2014. http://www.theatlantic.com /business/archive/2013/04/the-big-comeback-is-new-orleans-americas-next-great -innovation-hub/274591/.

Throw Me Somethin', Mister! Mardi Gras Madness. Gretna, LA: Her Publishing Co., 1982.

Tiggs, Leith. "8 Tips for 'New' New Orleanians." *Where Y'at*. September 2015.

"'tit Rəx Parade." Accessed December 14, 2017. http://www.yelp.com/biz/tit-Rex-parade -new-orleans.

titrexparade.com. Accessed December 17, 2017. http://www.titrex.com.

"Today in 1991: Mardi Gras Krewes Desegregated." lunolaw.blogspot.com. Accessed December 17, 2017. /2011/12/today-in-mardi-gras-krewes.html.

Vaz, Kim Marie. *The "Baby Dolls": Breaking the Race and Gender Barriers of the New Orleans Mardi Gras Tradition*. Baton Rouge: Louisiana State University Press, 2013.

Wagner, Cheryl. *Plenty Enough Suck to Go Around: A Memoir of Floods, Fires, Parades, and Plywood*. New York: Citadel Press, 2009.

Walker, Rob. *Letters from New Orleans*. New Orleans: Garrett County Press, 2005.

Ware, Carolyn E. *Cajun Women and Mardi Gras: Reading the Rules Backward*. Urbana: University of Illinois Press, 2007.

Wattercutter, Angela. "Meet the Man Bringing DIY Star Wars to Mardi Gras." *Wired*. January 25, 2013. Accessed December 16, 2017. https://www.wired.com/2013/01/worlds -most-wired-float-builder-ryan-ballard/.

Wehmeyer, Stephen C. "Playing Dead: The North Side Skull and Bone Gang." In *In Extremis: Death and Life in 21st-Century Haitian Art*, edited by Donald Cosentino. Los Angeles: Fowler Museum at UCLA, 2012.

Welch, Michael Patrick (with Brian Boyles). *New Orleans: The Underground Guide*. 3rd ed. Baton Rouge: Louisiana State University Press, 2014.

White, Millisia. "Prelude: On Being an Example of Hope." In *The "Baby Dolls": Breaking the Race and Gender Barriers of the New Orleans Mardi Gras Tradition*, by Kim Vaz. Baton Rouge: Louisiana State University Press, 2013.

"With New Orleans' Carnival forthcoming, a look back at last year's chaos." *It's Going Down*. December 23, 2015. Accessed July 2, 2017. https://itsgoingdown.org/new-orleans -carnival-forthcoming-look-back-last-years-chaos/.

Wolcott, Victoria W. *Remaking Respectability: African American Women in Interwar Detroit*. Chapel Hill: University of North Carolina Press, 2001.

Woodard, Collin. *American Nations: The Eleven Rival Regional Cultures of North America*. New York: Penguin Books, 2011.

Woods, William S. "L'Abbe Prevost and the Gender of New Orleans." *Modern Language Notes* 66 (1951): 259–61.

Woodward, Alex. "Krewe du Vieux celebrates New Orleans' birthday, with 'Bienville's Wet Dream.'" *Gambit*, January 22, 2018. Accessed July 2, 2018. https://www.theadvocate.com /gambit/new_orleans/events/stage_previews_reviews/article_e5f5f051-3fc3-5e03-90af -58dce85f7810.html.

"Wrapping up a good year." *New Orleans Times-Picayune*, December 29, 2013.

INDEX

References to illustrations appear in **bold**.